ASTROLOGICAL
MANAGER

ASTROLOGICAL MANAGER

a new approach to: business, success and destiny

john alexander

southwater

Millionaires don't hire astrologers; billionaires do. J P Morgan

Thus does your destiny lie within yourself, and the destiny of the world. Edgar Cayce

This edition is published by Southwater

Southwater is an imprint of Anness Publishing Ltd
Hermes House, 88–89 Blackfriars Road, London SE1 8HA
tel. 020 7401 2077; fax 020 7633 9499
www.southwaterbooks.com; info@anness.com

© Anness Publishing Ltd 1992, 2004

UK agent: The Manning Partnership Ltd, 6 The Old Dairy, Melcombe Road,
Bath BA2 3LR; tel. 01225 478 444; fax 01225 478 440; sales@manning-partnership.co.uk

UK distributor: Grantham Book Services Ltd, Isaac Newton Way,
Alma Park Industrial Estate, Grantham, Lincs NG31 9SD; tel. 01476 541080;
fax 01476 541061; orders@gbs.tbs-ltd.co.uk

North American agent/distributor: National Book Network, 4501 Forbes Boulevard,
Suite 200, Lanham, MD 20706; tel. 301 459 3366; fax 301 429 5746; www.nbnbooks.com

Australian agent/distributor: Pan Macmillan Australia, Level 18, St Martins Tower,
31 Market St, Sydney, NSW 2000; tel. 1300 135 113; fax 1300 135 103;
customer.service@macmillan.com.au

A CIP catalogue record for this book is available from the British Library.

Publisher: Joanna Lorenz
Managing Editor: Judith Simons
Editor: Molly Perham
Designer: Mike Morey
Jacket Design: Balley Associates
Editorial Reader: Penelope Goodare
Production Controller: Lee Sargent

1 3 5 7 9 10 8 6 4 2

The publishers and author thank the Pictorial Press for providing the pictures.

CONTENTS

INTRODUCTION:
Why Astrology?

Management and leadership now require different skills from the traditions we are used to. In a complex and global business world, leadership skills go beyond corporate visions and mission statements. It is about understanding human behaviour. It is about what motivates people. It is about accepting the differences of personality and creating relationships that work. Is astrology a viable approach to improving management skills? Absolutely. The claim of astrological management is a simple one: a balanced use of psychological astrology provides an invaluable guide to the rich diversity of individual personalities, leadership styles, motivations and human behaviour.

Astrology in Business

Why should anyone consider using astrology in business and management? How can astrology actually be used as an aid to running a company? Most business people can provide clear reasons for dismissing astrology altogether. Reasons such as: astrology is newspaper horoscopes; astrology is about predicting the future; astrology is about Sun-signs. And as we know, newspaper horoscopes are nonsense, predicting the future is scientifically unsound, and Sun-signs are so general as to be meaningless.

The curious thing is that most serious astrologers would agree with all the above. In fact most discussions about astrology and business are never about astrology at all, but about attitudes to astrology – attitudes that have been based on newspaper horoscopes, astrological fortune-telling and Sun-signs. And these are easy to dismiss.

Newspaper horoscopes were a flight of fancy devised by a UK astrologer, encouraged by the editor of *The Express* newspaper. The year was 1930. The astrologer was R H Naylor. He had cast a chart for the newborn Princess Margaret. Readers wanted more, so *The Express* commissioned the weekly newspaper horoscope. They proved so popular that other newspapers quickly followed, emulating the spread of comic strips and crossword puzzles some decades earlier.

What about predictive astrology? There are serious practitioners of predictive astrology, especially in the field of financial astrology – just as there are serious meteorologists who make a career in weather forecasting. As a comparison, with all the financial and official support for weather bureaus throughout the world, the fact remains that a weather prediction is valid for two days. According to meteorologists, the variables are such that forecasting is quickly reduced to speculation beyond two days. The movements of the planets can be accurately predicted for centuries ahead, but they can only indicate general trends and influences – astrologers cannot produce detailed predictions of events.

Sun-sign astrology is a subject that arouses scepticism and derision, even amongst astrologers, with some justification. After all, there are 12 Sun-signs, each one attempting to describe the attributes of a twelfth of the entire population.

Personality descriptions are firmly planted in the realm of broad generalities. You can say anything about anyone and it just about always fits. We enjoy reading them though, they confirm our prejudices. We all know a talkative Gemini. We've all met a hard-working Capricorn. Sun-sign descriptions are not necessarily wrong – just imprecise. A month of the year can be described with a few generalities. If you live in the northern hemisphere, August is hot and sunny, and January is cold and dark. But there are wet days in August and sunny days in January. The 30 or so days to a month broaden the possibilities of generalization and imprecise descriptions of the months. There are 30 degrees to each Sun-sign, each with its own quality.

Furthermore, a Sun-sign is only part of the complex picture of the human personality. Astrologers emphasize the importance of the Ascendant (the point in the zodiac that is on the eastern horizon at the moment of birth), which, when included in the analysis of the horoscope, provides 12 times the types described by Sun-signs – 144 personality types. The addition of the Moon-sign creates 144 x 12 possible combinations: 1728 different personality descriptions.

When we further consider there are at least nine more planetary positions in the natal chart to assess, together with the aspects they form with each other – oppositions, conjunctions, trines, squares, sextiles and others – in addition to the planets' significance within 12 houses, it becomes apparent that the possible combinations in any given natal chart amount to variations numbering millions. Each chart is as individual as the personality it represents.

Yet, increasingly, Sun-sign astrology is finding a place in the world of business and commerce. In 2001 the Australian newspaper *The Courier-Mail* reported that Geminis are the 'most accident-prone drivers'. Suncorp Metway compiled a survey based on 160,000 Australian car accident insurance claims over a three-year period. Geminis are the most likely to have a crash. Taurean and Piscean drivers come in second and third place. Capricorns are least likely to have accidents. Warren Duke, Suncorp's national manager of personal insurance, commented: 'Geminis are typically described as restless, easily bored and frustrated by things moving slowly… Taureans are thought to be stubborn and inflexible, while Capricorns are generally thought of as patient. The full list, starting with the most accident-prone star sign, is as follows: Gemini, Taurus, Pisces, Virgo, Cancer, Aquarius, Aries, Leo, Libra, Sagittarius, Scorpio, Capricorn.

Tesco, the UK supermarket chain, commissioned a report in the mid 1990s on customer shopping habits and Sun-signs, to help make their marketing and mail shots more effective – to target marketing to customer profiles, in other words. An overview of their findings revealed:

ARIES	quick, effective, aggressive use of trolley
TAURUS	traditional, basic commodities buyers
GEMINI	trend motivated – high awareness of new products
CANCER	brand loyal
LEO	spends more time browsing and buying at delicatessen counters than any other sign
VIRGO	shop according to a list and stick to it
LIBRA	warm to attractive displays, serene music, tasteful packaging
SCORPIO	discerning taste and an eye for quality
SAGITTARIUS	big buyers; well-filled trolleys
CAPRICORN	spend most time searching for perfect ingredients
AQUARIUS	ecologically and environmentally aware purchases
PISCES	buy instinctively, not practically; more subject to impulse purchases than other signs

If Sun-signs can be criticized for being too general, the justification is that we have to begin somewhere. In this study of astrology and management, our beginnings are going to be even more general. Rather than 12 signs, let us first consider four basic personality types.

Personality Types

There are many approaches to business and management, and we shall begin with four basic approaches – four different styles – in companies, in leadership and in individuals: four styles we can identify and apply in our own work situations.

This system is based on models and stereotypes: the model of astrological elements, and the stereotypes characterized by natal astrology. A model is a simplification, a way to describe a strategy. It is a not a representation of reality. In reality there are many different management styles, leadership styles and individual styles. We should understand the limitations of a model's simplified version of a frequently complicated reality. We should also appreciate the possibilities such models can provide.

The same can be said of stereotypes. A stereotype is a label, an identifiable tag defining specific characteristics. A stereotype does not have to imply a value judgement. You can describe a stereotype with good qualities or bad qualities – it is a question of interpretation. A management style, an individual style, or a company culture, is made up of many different qualities. A pragmatist might be a problem solver for one manager, or a pessimist for another.

Stereotypes have their shortcomings – they can lead to a failure to see people as individuals. When stereotypes are ingrained with prejudice they can work against us. Natal astrology sets out to make stereotypes work for us. In creating a typology, we can identify differences in business and management styles, in approaches to leadership, in individual personalities. Provided we do not go down that road of ill-conceived assumptions, misguided preconceptions and intolerance, the kind of typecasting outlined in the following pages can help us become more tolerant and more adaptable in our daily business routines.

The idea of four stereotypes has been around a long time. In 500BC the Greek philosopher Empedocles said that all matter was made up of four elements: fire, earth, air and water. A century later Hippocrates designated these four elements to the human body, which Claudius Galen, a Greek physician of the second century AD, redefined as four humours or temperaments. Galen's typology was based on body fluids: choleric, melancholic, sanguine and phlegmatic, describing irritable, depressed, optimistic and stolid character types.

Closer to our present day, psychologist Carl Jung devised a typology of personalities functioning mainly through intuition, sensation, thinking and feeling. Jung's typology, which astrologers have equated to the four elements, continues to have far-reaching influence in contemporary management and recruiting. Today's management books describe four leadership styles, four management styles, four team roles, four company styles, and so on, as we shall explore further in Part Two. Stereotypes are as popular today as ever.

Classifying and categorizing is a basic function of the human brain – it is our way of making sense of the world around us. Stereotypes have their limitation, yet providing we understand how stereotypes work, our study of them can help us better understand strengths and weaknesses in the people we work with, and in ourselves.

Astrological Management

There are three main areas in which companies are finding astrology a useful aid to corporate decision-making: financial (or predictive) astrology, corporate (or mundane) astrology, and natal astrology, which looks at the birth chart of the individual.

Financial astrology is used to predict market trends and changes. The financial astrologer looks at correlations between planetary cycles and stock market fluctuations to make analyses and forecasts. No predictive system can boast 100 per cent accuracy, but financial astrologers in New York and London are showing above average success rates in forecasting market trends. Financial papers and journals are beginning to take astrology seriously. The New York based International Society of Business Astrologers is increasingly attracting media attention – chance alone cannot account for the accuracy of their forecasts. (See www.afund.com)

Corporate astrology (a branch of mundane astrology) provides insights into the workings and potentials of an organization. Just as mundane astrology analyzes a political state based on a chart relating to treaties, or a declaration of independence, company astrology makes a 'first trade' chart of when an organization comes into being.

More and more companies seek advice from astrologers when to initiate a new enterprise or brand, or even start up a company. A UK television documentary commissioned an astrologer to analyze marketing and future trends for Body Shop. Founder Anita Roddick (see Libra) opened the first Body Shop in Brighton in 1976; today Body Shop is a multinational empire with around 800 shops in over 40 countries. The analysis was 'spot on', said Anita Roddick and in tune with her own view of company development.

And then there is natal astrology, where birth chart readings can be incorporated into recruiting, team building and leadership. Natal astrology is the focus of this book. It looks at astrology as an approach to the kind of psychological insights that are essential for successful management in today's competitive business world.

So financial astrology for yield, corporate astrology for strategy and natal astrology for making the most of relationships between people. Astrology alone is not the easy answer to the complexities of management. Recruiting on the basis of astrology and nothing else is a recipe for disaster and a sad indication of severe managerial limitations. However, astrology combined with common sense and an understanding of company needs is an invaluable asset both to building the right team and managing creatively.

Astrology can help you:
- recruit the best team
- understand the decision-making processes at all levels
- motivate people
- understand and deal with 'management crises'

Astrology cannot tell you the best partner, the best sales person, nor the best employee or employer. It can tell you something of the quality of the relationship upon which you are about to embark, whether you are a manager, an employee, or running your own company. Nor can astrological signs indicate success or failure. Astrology will not tell you who is lazy and who works hard. Some astrology books will tell you that certain signs are associated with people who are better at certain jobs. Scorpios make good surgeons and detectives, Libras are diplomats, and Cancers are good cooks! Which sign makes the best manager? Any sign! There are Taurean managers and Gemini managers, managers born under Aquarius and Leo, and every other sign. Their Sun-sign will not indicate how capable they are in managing people. A natal chart, however, will indicate certain qualities in the way in which they exercise responsibility. An Aquarian manager may emphasize the latest developments in management theory – or may just have a knack for putting the right people together. The Taurean manager may be blunt and conservative, but may have an innate ability to get to the heart of the matter. The Gemini might adapt quickly to a changing situation, and gain a person's trust through talking and listening.

The study of astrology helps us appreciate the differences in people. We often fail to see an issue from another point of view. We think our own perspective must be the right one. If we are optimistic, expansive, and hungry for sales, the accountant who talks about budgets and bottom line reality is a pessimist. If we are the accountant, the over-enthusiastic sales manager is a reckless irresponsible type who does not understand the reality of finances. In astrological terms this describes a conflict between a Fire type and an Earth type. A psychologist might refer to the dynamic between an Intuitive type and a Sensation type. One type is no more nor no less favourable than another type – we are simply recognizing the many ways in which the human personality can be expressed.

A good starting point in astrological management is the four types. This is where we shall begin. Then we shall consider the characteristics and qualities of signs. They may be generalities, but, as we have said, we have to start somewhere. Then follows a closer look at natal charts of prominent people, from risk-takers and financial fiasco-makers to monarchs and political leaders, to help provide some insight into astrology's deeper possibilities.

MANAGING PEOPLE:
The Signs

The twelve signs of the zodiac represent twelve different personality types, which in turn provide us with twelve different approaches to business, management and leadership. However, Sun-signs are only part of the story. The position of the Moon and planets, and the position of the Sun at sunrise, are calculated into each individual's horoscope based on the exact time and place of their birth. Before we consider the complexities of the horoscope we will take an in-depth look at what Sun-signs can tell us about our different styles in business and management.

The Elements

We begin by looking at the signs, grouped according to element: fire, earth, air and water. The reasons are twofold: first, each element represents certain psychological qualities, as outlined in the introduction. Fiery personalities are enthusiastic, Earth signs are practical, Air signs are analytical and Water signs are imaginative, feeling types. Second, these divisions by element correspond to types not only familiar in the typology of psychology, but also in the breadth of business and management literature, recruiting tests and leadership styles. We will explore these more fully in Part Two.

These sections also include natal charts, which provide a more detailed reading of personality and leadership qualities than Sun-sign readings alone can provide. If you are not familiar with chart interpretation, looking at the elements is a good starting-point. If you feel you are not typical of your sign, perhaps you are more typical of your dominating element.

A detailed approach to chart interpretation is outlined in Part Three. When analyzing charts, it is useful to remember that a horoscope is made up of signs and houses. Planets in signs describe personality traits ('who you are'); planets in houses describe the actions you take ('what you do'). The fiery signs and houses (Aries, Leo, Sagittarius; First, Fifth and Ninth Houses) tell us 'anything is possible'. Earth signs and houses (Taurus, Virgo, Capricorn; Second, Sixth and Tenth Houses) indicate a more practical, realistic approach; these are the 'get real' signs and houses. Air corresponds to 'analyze this!' (Gemini, Libra, Aquarius; Third, Seventh and Eleventh Houses); and Water to 'feel but don't show' (Cancer, Scorpio, Pisces; Fourth, Eighth and Twelfth Houses).

A full natal chart, or birth chart, requires the date, time and place of birth. If the time is not known, a 'solar chart' (or sunrise chart) can be produced, which gives the positions of the Sun and planets in the signs (though the Moon is only accurate within about 15 degrees), but not the ascendant or house position.

The Sun-sign descriptions in the following pages include sections on leadership styles, approach to work, the company car, the office and the business lunch. OK, Sun-sign descriptions can be general and vague. Can they really tell us what company car we drive? Or what our office looks like? Well, perhaps not the car itself, or the actual office, but even a Sun-sign can tell us about why we might prefer a particular kind of car, or office, business lunch – or even suitcase. Virgo, for example, wants security rather than style, statement or sentiment, and would probably choose a suitcase that is reliable and has least chance getting lost.

It is possible that four managers of four different signs will choose the same car, but their motivations will be quite different. Fire signs opt for style, elegance and 'personal statement'; Earth signs choose a model for sound practical reasons; Air signs are in tune with trends, peer group pressure (with or against) or team allegiance; Water signs, given the choice, are swayed by sentimental reasons, brand loyalty or simply because this is the model that 'feels right.'

Fire Signs

Aries

F W Woolworth
J P Morgan
Ingvar Kamprad
Gloria Swanson
Charles Chaplin
Hugh Hefner
John Major
Alan M Sugar

Leo

Bill Clinton
Monica Lewinsky
Norman Schwarzkopf
Sir Clive Sinclair
Henry Ford
Mae West
Madonna Ciccione

Sagittarius

Jeff Bezos
J P Getty
Sir Stanley Unwin
Walt Disney
Steven Spielberg

Aries

21 March–20 April
Ruling planet: Mars
Element: Fire
Quality: Cardinal
Symbol: The Ram

For Aries, business is a contest. Making a sale is a gladiatorial battle of wills which the Arian enters with the conviction of imminent victory. Aries is competitive, loves risks, hates to lose – and lives for the rush of adrenalin when the gamble pays off. When an Aries loses the sale it's from selling too hard, or being ill-prepared. Like the ram, Aries lowers the head and charges.

Arians are restless souls constantly seeking stimulation. A low threshold of boredom endears Aries to travelling, seeking new conquests, new territories, new faces. A tendency to hard living and hard drinking suits a life on the road. Aries is quick to make friends and quick to ruffle the fur of rivals.

If business runs smoothly Aries is unlikely to stay at the same job for great lengths of time. The Aries who 'sticks around' is the Aries who has their own business (something to leave for the offspring), or the Aries who constantly faces adversity. The trouble-free, easy-going and have-a-relaxed-time-at-the-company's-expense scenario does not wear well with Aries. Arians are not ambitious for power or wealth for its own sake, but see themselves as natural leaders, so positions of sales managers, directors, or setting up a company are in line with a natural course of events, rather than a deliberate career minded course of action. The love of risk and an innate trust in life, in spite of all the setbacks, pays off. Better to have loved and lost, thinks Aries; better to have risked all and lost all than to have kept their hoard safely stashed under the mattress, with nothing to show for it.

Aries loves quick success and instant results. Aries is 'me first', and 'I want it and I want it now!' Aries, always anxious to enter the arena of contest, either enters with dignity, showmanship and panache, or, over-anxiously, with clumsiness and arrogance.

Arians have an inbuilt self-destruct button, so that when on the verge of success at the age of 23, they engage in conflict with a member of the board or a company director, resign in a fit of pique, and set up on their own. If they look older than their years, it's due to working hard and playing hard, and extracting the most from every moment. Better to burn out than never to burn at all.

Aries is a sucker for a hard luck story and lost causes. Aries gives lifts to tramps, picks up stray dogs and plunges headlong into companies bound for ruin. What Aries lacks in good judgement is made up for in enthusiasm.

Aries is the first sign of the zodiac, and is bursting with life-force. Consequently Arians are constantly striving for ways of achieving eternal life, either through offspring, great works or great deeds. For Aries, a company emblazoned with their name is a means of cheating death – a chance at immortality.

Arians have a strong sense of ego, which means successes and failures are taken personally. However, there's a big difference between a strong ego, which is essential in the gladiatorial arena of big business, and a large ego – which can be destructive. Strong-ego Arians know their own strengths, are confident, and have a realistic idea of what can be achieved. The well-balanced Aries strides purposefully towards a chosen task and accomplishes it even if it means bumping a few heads on the way, especially their own.

Aesop told a fable about an oak tree and a reed that contains an invaluable lesson for Aries. Sometimes you have to bend with the wind in order not to get blown over.

Aries as Leader

Arian leaders function well in smaller organizations or companies, especially ones they've created themselves. The larger the organization, the more toes there are to be trodden upon, and Arians invariably, though unintentionally, tread on a good many toes. Arians adapt readily to the task of running a business on the brink of ruin, battling against the odds, or leading the small company against the 'dinosaur' conglomerate.

The role of leader comes naturally to Fire signs – they generally like to be noticed. This does not mean they make the best leaders, only that they would rather be leaders. Arians are quick on the initiative, enjoy the role of taking command, and are adept at delegating. The words 'tyrant', 'dictator' and 'slave-driver' flow freely in the Aries-administered enterprise. Arians who give everything of themselves expects nothing less from everyone else, whom they refer to as the 'team' and treat as subordinates.

Arians may have an innate trust in life, but their faith in people can be naive – they tend to take people at face value. They are not always good judges of character, which makes them vulnerable to acts of disloyalty.

Given a choice Aries invariably favours the direct approach. If something needs doing they do it. This is referred to as the 'bulldozer effect' and Arians are expert in its execution. Aries is the terror of administration and bureaucracy – they prefer to make up their own rules as they go along rather than adhere to the prescribed rules and regulations of the establishment.

But it works both ways. Administration and bureaucracy terrorize the Aries 'lone wolf' with expense forms, budgets, accounts reports, and filing in triplicate. At the two o'clock budget meeting, the Aries leader is usually still out to lunch. When surrounded by entanglements and complications Aries will suddenly be incapable of coping, develop a migraine, and call in the subordinates to sort everything out.

For all their bravado, self-styled image of ebullient leadership and facade of strident self-confidence, Aries leaders actually need a good deal of looking after. And the well-balanced Aries leader inspires the kind of devoted loyalty that will happily give it.

Aries as Manager

Arians are not especially diplomatic, and mediating is not their forte. However, as head of a team Aries inspires enthusiasm, and has an uncanny knack of bringing out latent talents in others. Arians may not always be good at understanding others, but they have an instinctive drive to succeed and help those close to them succeed. This allows Aries to shine in the role of teacher and mentor. The Arian manager finds fulfilment in the role of building up a team and 'educating' team members into complying with the 'vision'.

Aries often works best under adverse circumstances. Whereas many managers would avoid walking into a company on the verge of ruin, crisis or even a new and untried company, Aries rises to the challenge. Only when business is running smoothly, and the future seems trouble-free, is Aries tempted to jump ship, preferably in favour of a leaky one bound for uncharted seas.

The Aries manager has an uncanny knack of bringing out the best in underlings and inspiring loyalty and hard work, which they demand when the occasion arises. Excellent judges of talent, but not necessarily character, they are often victims of betrayal by those they most trust. The Aries manager will find and encourage talent in the least expected quarters. It is the Aries manager who will employ the underdog, someone too young, too old, too inexperienced, handicapped, or down on their luck, against the advice of all colleagues, and prove them all wrong.

The Aries manager revels in the 'shaping' process – from restructuring staff duties, rearranging a filing system or rescheduling timetables, to chastising subordinates for messy hair or sloppy dressing. Image is paramount to Aries.

It is the Aries manager who will insist on some grand new marketing scheme, and choose the smallest and most unproven company. It may go broke in six months and end in disaster, or deliver all they promised and more, outperforming all the competitors.

Arians relish the role of 'captain of the team', and nothing is more gratifying for the Aries manager than leading 'the team' into new ventures, new enterprises. This has disadvantages. An Aries manager taking over a new and well-functioning team will make changes in order to inject the feeling of 'my team' and 'me-leader'.

An Aries manager working within a 'dinosaur' company is a restless spirit. The large conglomerate or multinational is big enough not to have to be concerned with innovation and new ideas. If Arians cannot see changes forthcoming, they either make changes themselves or get a job somewhere else. Job security, which many managers regard as a plus, is anathema to the Aries manager. Too much harmony and too much security, and they are off seeking challenges elsewhere. Looking for trouble and proud of it!

The Aries manager abhors stagnation and instigating changes will arouse cries of indignation from colleagues and subordinates averse to having their boats rocked. Aries is suddenly the focal point of a dispute – loyalties are divided. Aries inspires fierce allegiance or equally fierce opposition, but never apathy.

Aries as Employee

Here is the 'troubleshooter'. Outside the office, Aries thrives on the role of company troubleshooter – clinching the impossible sale from the impossible client, opening the account no one could open, making the deal Head Office could only dream about.

Inside the office Aries likes variety, change and the sense of things happening. If necessary, Aries will inject a sense of dynamics into the proceedings. Re-filing, refurnishing, rearranging – Arian employees take the initiative, they don't need to be asked to do things, and they do not appreciate being told how to execute their given tasks. Aries likes to learn from their own mistakes rather than those of someone else.

From troubleshooter to troublemaker? When Aries is on the road to success, the hunt, the conquest, the fight, the 'career' is all-embracing. Aries is the warrior who will go forth and do battle at the Stock Exchange, at the board room, with bank managers, with business rivals.

Self-confident, brash and aware of their identity, Aries regards the sale as the ritual of conqueror and conquered. The Aries competitive spirit and keen sense of the challenge, the 'game', means that Arians succeed in achieving their goal, or die trying. Aries will not only go in 'where angels fear to tread', but thrives on the challenge of 'difficult' customers, 'impossible' customers and the 'small' customer no one considered worthwhile. Aries will make sure such customers become 'worthwhile.' On the negative side, 'fools rush in...' as the saying goes, and Aries prefers the customers who put up a good fight and provide a challenge over those who just make a profit.

So how does this image of the Aries warrior, the dynamic go-getting and strident achiever of great deeds, comply with the overweight, bespectacled, slightly balding and quietly spoken colleague who has a sandwich in his office at lunchtime, filling in the newspaper crossword, who just happens to be born in the middle of April? Don't be fooled by appearances. When the time is right he will put down his sandwich and crossword puzzle, don his armour, and charge forth to do battle with executive rivals.

A Profile of the Aries Manager

The Office

Chaos rules in the Aries office, OK? For Aries it's quite OK because Aries is in the office as little as possible. Aries likes to be out doing things, even if it's only in someone else's office. Papers, files, coffee cups and brief cases lie indiscriminately in unexpected places, and when that important file that must be presented at the board meeting in two minutes time is 'missing', the Aries manager transforms into a terrifying, if entertaining, spectacle of someone going to pieces very loudly. This is an occasion when the Aries manager needs 'looking after'.

The decor is likely to be sparse, with a 'just moved in' look, as Arians never know when they're just about to move out. The Aries domicile is invariably transitory – on the way to something bigger and better. The desk is large, though – it needs to accommodate a maximum of enterprise with a minimum of order – and the chair is very large. It is likely to be a modern, high-backed, black leather swivel model with armrests, and must be seen to be larger than that of any colleague on the same floor with the possible exception of Leo. For Aries the office chair embodies prestige and strength – it is a seat of power from where important decisions are made.

Arians dread confinement of any kind and favour large open windows and space – if they don't get it, they have an uncanny knack of creating space at the expense of less dominant individuals. Arians are the terror of the open plan office. Wall decorations are minimal, but the Aries office is likely to be filled with objects and illustrations that highlight individuality – photograph of self with leading Korean businessman, a sports trophy, the garter of a young lady in the case of a male Arian, or a token pair of men's underpants in the case of an up-and-coming young woman Aries executive. If you are visiting the Aries office, be prepared to take your own chair.

The Company Car

A red Lamborghini? OK, there are few red Lamborghinis cruising the roads, and there are many, many Aries managers. Most Aries managers are compelled to yield to the practicalities of family and business considerations, but given free rein to appease the virulent Aries ego, an aggressively coloured sporty vehicle capable of leaving everyone else standing at the traffic lights is choice number one.

Financial stability, if it comes to Aries at all, occurs later in life rather than sooner, and come the mid-life crisis at approximately age 42 (the age at which Uranus is in opposition to its position at a person's birth – which tends to stir up trouble), successful Arian managers, grasping for the youth they claim they never had, are likely to throw the practical considerations out the window. Ever wondered about those temple-grey or balding gentlemen cruising the city streets in red Porsches with personalized number plates? Tearing along the highways like there's no tomorrow?

The car may be bought, it may be rented, it may be on hire purchase. The Aries manager is en route to one more challenge, one more contest, one more gladiatorial encounter in the arena of life. And win or lose, best to have transport the competition is going to stare at, and ignore the unkind comments alluding to masculinity complexes.

The Business Lunch

The Taj Mahal Tandoori? The Sawadee Extra Spiced Thai? No curry is too hot, no spice too strident for the pitiless Arian palate. Do not be lured into a contest of hot curry endurance with your Aries host. Nor the consumption of high-alcohol content imported lagers to cool the burning gums. Arians are often unaware of how they transform the rich and varied avenues of human pleasure and endeavour into arenas of contest, and eating is no exception. The Aries manager will out-curry, out-lager, and out-whisky any contender, or die trying. In the right frame of mind this can make for memorable and spectacular business lunches. Should the client have provided good competition during the meal, but tactfully 'lost' ('No, really. Fifteen lagers is my limit. But you have another!'), the possibilities for success when it comes to 'the deal' are boundless. Having won one battle (the most lagers, the hottest curries) the Aries defences are down, and the time to strike with the contract and pricing of your choice is now.

The Aries Business Venture

Arians delight in starting projects but find it difficult to see them through. The Aries venture can be anything and everything – what matters is initiating something. It could be starting a publishing company, a school of any kind, (Arians like to 'teach' no matter what line of business they are involved with), a department store, a hairdressing salon, a multinational business corporation, a mail-order company for replica weapons. Arians are zealous regardless, providing it's their idea and they can persuade other people to believe in it too. Because, for all their bravado and high-spirited enthusiasm in the face of overwhelming opposition, Arians need reassurance. A team leader without a team is a sorrowful sight, but even one solitary subordinate can be sufficient to fulfil the Aries requirements for 'being in charge'. The husband or wife Aries in charge of the devoted and hardworking spouse (preferably capable of untangling complications and taking care of practicalities and paperwork) is a time-proven well-functioning combination.

Aries needs to feel that the venture has inbuilt continuity – something that can be passed on to 'offspring', and an ongoing line of descendants way into an indeterminate future. The '& Sons' appendage to the family company must surely be the inspiration of the Arian entrepreneur?

Aries Natal Charts

F W Woolworth

Frank Woolworth worked as a farm labourer until the age of 21, when he got a job as a shop assistant. He persuaded his employers to finance his scheme to open a store for five-cent merchandise in Utica in 1879. The store went broke. He was 28 years old and was devastated by a transit known as the Saturn return. Saturn takes 28 to 29 years to complete one cycle, and most people experience 'coming down to earth' at this age, in the form of marriage, children, or a change in career – a major step experienced by many as a form of restriction or discipline. Earth signs generally cope well with a Saturn return, Fire signs such as Aries less well.

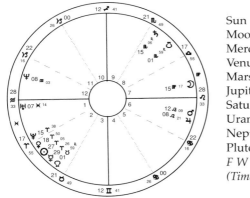

Sun	23 37 Ari
Moon	17 18 Aqr
Mercury	12 22 Tau
Venus	06 51 Gem
Mars	02 29 Leo
Jupiter	21 19 Scor
Saturn	05 39 Tau
Uranus	03 43 Tau
Neptune	10 31 Psc
Pluto	00 08 Tau

F W Woolworth 13 April 1852 Rodman NY
(Time unknown)

Undaunted, Woolworth opened a second store within a year, in Lancaster, Pennsylvania, this time selling both five- and ten-cent goods. It was the success that became the Woolworth hallmark. In partnership with his employers, a brother and a cousin, Woolworth began building a large chain of stores, and at the time of his death in 1919 the F W Woolworth company had over 1000 stores across the United States, with a head office in New York. In line with the Arian quest for prominence, Woolworth's skyscraper was for a time the tallest building in the world (792 ft/241 m), its rocket-like shape leaving little doubt as to the anatomical source of inspiration for the building's design (Arians place great value on potency and virility). The first British Woolworth's store opened in 1910, and the world expansion of the Woolworth company continued after the founder's death.

Arians enjoy attention, and most Aries or First-house types attempt to ensure their immortality through having their name displayed. Where possible Arians will incorporate their own name into an enterprise, unlike, say, Water signs, who favour symbolic names, and Earth signs, who favour practical and descriptive names. Similarly, erecting the tallest building satisfies the Aries conscious drive for prominence, as well as their frequent need to prove their virility. Ironically, Woolworth's Arian drive to create a dynasty to ensure the continuance of the family name through the ages was doomed to fail. Barbara Hutton (Scorpio, b.14 November, 1912), the single heir to the Woolworth millions, lived in relative poverty in 1978 after seven marriages and a lifetime of extravagance, drink and drugs. Her lifestyle was the antithesis of her grandfather's life of struggle and success. Rags to riches, riches to rags.

Success against all odds, championing the less well-to-do, initiating an original and challenging enterprise – these are key Arian issues exemplified in the life of F W Woolworth.

J P Morgan

The chart of millionaire philanthropist J P Morgan has six Fire planets – Sun, Venus, Mercury and Pluto in Aries, Mars and Jupiter in Leo. These are the 'anything's possible' positions. Yet all these planets are placed in the Earth 'get real' Second and Sixth Houses respectively. A strong Fire personality combined with dominating earthy attitudes is a powerful one. This is especially true with such a strong Second House (money, property, possessions).

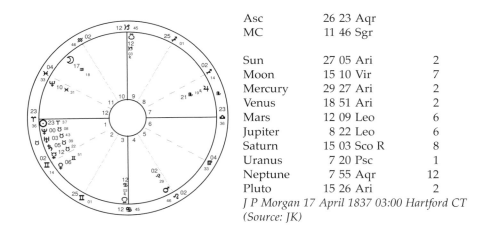

Asc	26 23 Aqr	
MC	11 46 Sgr	
Sun	27 05 Ari	2
Moon	15 10 Vir	7
Mercury	29 27 Ari	2
Venus	18 51 Ari	2
Mars	12 09 Leo	6
Jupiter	8 22 Leo	6
Saturn	15 03 Sco R	8
Uranus	7 20 Psc	1
Neptune	7 55 Aqr	12
Pluto	15 26 Ari	2

J P Morgan 17 April 1837 03:00 Hartford CT (Source: JK)

In business Morgan was a risk-taker, a strong Aries quality, but also a consolidator, thanks to the Earth element. Under his jurisdiction J P Morgan and Company organized the Steel Trust, formed an Atlantic shipping combine, controlled railways and transport, and was involved in many aspects of the public sector. Under his leadership the company expanded in every area, and on his death in 1913 he left a large fortune to charities and aid organizations. His capacity for making money was balanced by his capacity for good works and a passion for art – he left a formidable collection and had financed a number of organizations involved in philanthropic works. Firmly convinced of his own sense of destiny, he coined the phrase: 'Millionaires don't hire astrologers. Billionaires do.'

Ingvar Kamprad

A more contemporary story of an Aries personality struggling against all odds – and winning – is the story of IKEA's founder, Ingvar Kamprad. Remember how Arian entrepreneurs must have their name incorporated into the company? IKEA stands for Ingvar Kamprad of Elmtaryd in Agunnaryd. This is the name of the community in Småland where Kamprad grew up, a region of Sweden known for a down-to-earth and penny-pinching approach to business.

He has incorporated these values into the IKEA concept – today an international chain of about 200 outlets in more than 30 countries. The outlets maintain a Swedish profile, keeping difficult-to-pronounce names for the furniture and other products, and serving Swedish meatballs in the restaurants.

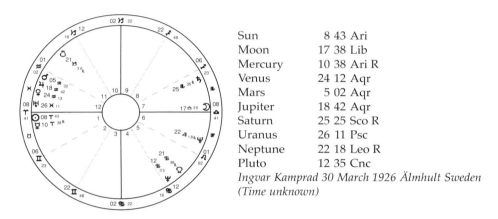

Sun	8 43 Ari
Moon	17 38 Lib
Mercury	10 38 Ari R
Venus	24 12 Aqr
Mars	5 02 Aqr
Jupiter	18 42 Aqr
Saturn	25 25 Sco R
Uranus	26 11 Psc
Neptune	22 18 Leo R
Pluto	12 35 Cnc

Ingvar Kamprad 30 March 1926 Älmhult Sweden (Time unknown)

Unlike the typical Arian, Kamprad shows modesty in his business and leadership style. In the late 1980s he sent a letter to then Soviet Premier Gorbachev, proposing opening a branch of IKEA in Moscow. 'Dear Premier,' he wrote, 'I am a humble businessman from a small country called Sweden, with a proposal to open a furniture retail outlet in your country...' 'Humble businessman... small country... who needs it?' was Gorbachev's quoted response, and he threw the letter away. An economic adviser pointed out that IKEA was one of the world's largest furniture retailers, and perhaps the proposal was worth consideration. 'World's largest? Why doesn't he tell us?' replied Gorbachev.

Ingvar Kamprad's modest approach and low profile extends throughout the company. For all his wealth he maintains a low-key lifestyle, flies economy on his business trips – and expects IKEA employees to do likewise. If Kamprad does not fit the general expectations of a typical Aries, we can note that his Moon sign is Libra and all the 'personal planets' (Mercury, Venus, Mars, Jupiter) are in Aquarius. And what is the Aquarian business style? It is indeed the 'modest' approach of personalities such as Sven Göran Eriksson, Percy Barnevik, and a long line of inventors and original thinkers.

Gloria Swanson

Another Swedish entrepreneur (by descent at least) who made good in the United States was Gloria Swanson (born Svenson). When her career as an actress declined she directed her entrepreneurial talents to the cosmetic, fashion and health food industries. If these activities seem Libra-orientated, it is no surprise to note a Libra mid-heaven, and Moon in Libra conjunct to the midheaven. She was always a self-publicist, from her early days as screen siren to later life as a business woman. At age 77 she married for the sixth time to a man 20 years younger. Even as an actress she quickly took control of the business side of film making. In 1926 (Saturn return year) she left the Paramount studios to set up her own company, financed initially by Joseph Kennedy (see Virgo).

Her most ambitious project was *Queen Kelly* (1928), directed by Erich von Stroheim, whom she fired for his financial excesses. The film had censorship problems in the US, and encountered competition from the now established sound cinema. Scenes that outraged censors included Gloria Swanson as a convent girl, Mary, who loses her underwear before a group of cavalrymen. In the 1950 film *Sunset Boulevard*, Swanson made a comeback in what many consider her best film. She plays Norma Desmond, a retired silent film star who enlists the aid of screenwriter Joe Gillis to re-write her script of Salome. 'What sign are you?' she asks Gillis (William Holden). Sagittarius, she discovers. 'That's good,' she says 'you can trust Sagittarius.' Sagittarius is the Rising Sign of Gloria Swanson, but her Norma Desmond character is a Scorpio. Too bad for Gillis, who narrates the story as a dead character – shot in the back by an insanely jealous Norma Desmond.

Asc	20 13 Sag	
MC	12 30 Lib	
Sun	6 22 Ari	3
Moon	6 23 Lib	9
Mercury	24 12 Ari	4
Venus	23 28 Aqr	2
Mars	23 35 Cnc	8
Jupiter	08 44 Sco R	11
Saturn	23 38 Sag	1
Uranus	07 58 Sag R	12
Neptune	22 08 Gem	7
Pluto	13 51 Gem	8

Gloria Swanson 27 March 1899 00:20 Chicago IL (Source: MP)

Charles Chaplin

The career and natal chart of Gloria Swanson bear comparison to those of Charles Chaplin, also Aries, with a Scorpio Ascendant and Leo Midheaven. Both screen stars began their film careers with Mack Sennet, both started their own film companies, and both came unstuck with self-produced films centred around fictionalized monarchs. For Gloria Swanson it was *Queen Kelly*, for Charlie Chaplin *A King in New York*. The Leo Midheaven is significant – the Midheaven indicates aspirations and goals, and Leo is 'king of the beasts.'

Asc	08 34 Sco	
MC	22 37 Leo	
Sun	27 00 Ari	6
Moon	09 24 Sco	1
Mercury	17 48 Ari	5
Venus	18 07 Tau R	7
Mars	13 34 Tau	7
Jupiter	08 10 Cap	2
Saturn	13 26 Leo	9
Uranus	19 39 Lib R	12
Neptune	00 44 Gem	7
Pluto	04 35 Gem	8

Charlie Chaplin 16 April 1889 20:00 London
(Source: JK)

Chaplin has Jupiter in the Second House, indicating an easy acquisition of money, and a flamboyant demeanour with regard to wealth, in contrast to the burden of responsibility that Saturn in the Second House suggests. The Second House is the House of Taurus, the sign in which both Mars and Venus are placed in Chaplin's chart, suggesting a sensuous nature, with the sexual element intensified by Moon in Scorpio, and a Scorpio Ascendant.

Chaplin was 30 when he founded the United Artists Corporation in partnership with Mary Pickford, Douglas Fairbanks and D W Griffith. From a London street urchin he became the highest-paid entertainer in Hollywood: an Aries tale of rags to riches. His life was a series of struggles against adversity: after overcoming poverty, his later successes as film actor, writer, director and producer were followed by recriminations and accusations. After his anti-Establishment films *Modern Times* (1936) and *Monsieur Verdoux* (1947) he was branded a communist and subpoenaed to testify before the House of Un-American Activities

Committee. In the early 1950s Chaplin settled in Switzerland with his family, vowing never to return to the United States, but in 1972 he did return to receive a special Academy Award for the 'incalculable effect he has had on making motion pictures the art form of this century.' In 1975 he was knighted and he died two years later, aged 88.

Hugh Hefner

Like Chaplin, Hugh Hefner is a self-made man who takes his image seriously. As with Chaplin, the Second House is emphasized (Moon, Venus, Jupiter, Uranus), indicating a preoccupation with the sensual, and an easy acquisition of wealth and possessions. Many Arians tend towards a spartan lifestyle, but four planets in the Second House suggest otherwise.

Hefner founded *Playboy* magazine and the Playboy clubs in the 1950s, and although the magazine still flourishes, the Playboy club concept, with tailor-made Bunny girls well versed in the teasing smile and bouncing bobtail, is so deeply rooted in the mores of the 1950s that by the 1980s, with society less inclined to see women as submissive sex toys, virtually all the clubs had closed down. In the 1970s Hefner became involved with film production, and in the 1980s Playboy Productions invested in video and cable television.

Hugh Hefner epitomizes the Arian preoccupation with sexual conquest, but with Capricorn Ascendant and a loaded Second House he succeeded in making a career out of what most Arians would consider a hobby.

Asc	06 20 Cap	
MC	01 45 Sco	
Sun	19 38 Ari	3
Moon	18 42 Psc	2
Mercury	03 08 Ari R	3
Venus	03 39 Psc	2
Mars	13 03 Aqr	1
Jupiter	20 44 Aqr	2
Saturn	25 05 Sco R	11
Uranus	26 47 Psc	2
Neptune	22 08 Leo R	8
Pluto	12 37 Cnc	7

Hugh Hefner 10 March 1926 22:38 Chicago IL (Source: MP)

John Major

A vocation in politics appeals to many Aries types, as politics is concerned with ideals more than tangibles; with the projection of an image and winning over a public. When John Major was elected as leader of the British Conservative Party to become the Prime Minister in 1991, he joined forces with a fraternity of contemporary British political party leaders born under the sign of Aries, including Labour Party leader Neil Kinnock, David Steel, the former Liberal Party leader, and Anthony Wedgwood Benn, self-appointed leader of Labour's extreme left.

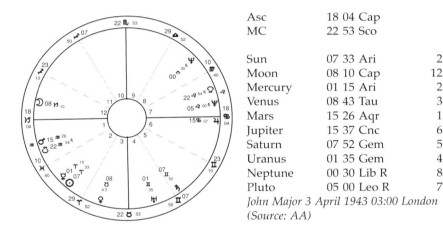

Asc	18 04 Cap	
MC	22 53 Sco	
Sun	07 33 Ari	2
Moon	08 10 Cap	12
Mercury	01 15 Ari	2
Venus	08 43 Tau	3
Mars	15 26 Aqr	1
Jupiter	15 37 Cnc	6
Saturn	07 52 Gem	5
Uranus	01 35 Gem	4
Neptune	00 30 Lib R	8
Pluto	05 00 Leo R	7

John Major 3 April 1943 03:00 London (Source: AA)

It is more than likely that John Major's rising sign is Capricorn, with Moon in Capricorn, which suggests an unusually cautious and self-controlled Aries. Jupiter in the Sixth House indicates a genuine interest in serving the public and fulfilling obligations. The Capricorn emphasis in the chart implies a person who takes his responsibilities seriously. The planet Mercury is never more than one sign away from the Sun in any chart, and the Aries politician invariably has Mercury in Aries. Mercury rules speech, communication and the expression of ideas; Mercury-in-Aries natives enjoy speaking in public, and are adept rhetoricians, capable of speaking passionately and persuasively. Neil Kinnock's chart has Mercury in Aries, as do those of Queen Elizabeth II, Lenin and Hitler.

Like Hugh Hefner John Major's chart includes a Capricorn Ascendant and Eighth House Neptune (relates to sex) and Seventh House Pluto (also sex). John Major, an Aries playboy? According to recent revelations concerning Major's secretive love life, the comparison is not so unlikely as it first seems.

Alan M Sugar

Whereas the prominent Aries politician, actor and entrepreneur frequently has the Mercury in Aries placing, Alan M Sugar, the publicity-shy multi-millionaire, has Mercury in Pisces. Pisces favours the sidelines rather than the limelight, and Alan Sugar guards his privacy with a zeal unusual for the attention-hungry Aries.

Mercury in Aries fortifies the Aries Sun; they seek public approval, speak with flair and conviction, and bask in the illumination of public exposure. Mars, the ruling planet of Aries – the Arian 'energizer' like Mercury – is tucked away in Pisces in the chart of Alan Sugar, coming to the forefront when least expected. In 1986 Sugar, 40 years old, bought out the computer business of Clive Sinclair, Britain's 'whizz-kid' industrialist, who, the previous year, had over-reached himself in the production of the ill-fated Sinclair electric car (see Leo).

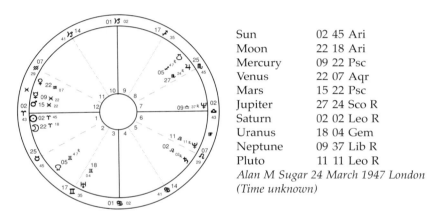

Sun	02 45 Ari
Moon	22 18 Ari
Mercury	09 22 Psc
Venus	22 07 Aqr
Mars	15 22 Psc
Jupiter	27 24 Sco R
Saturn	02 02 Leo R
Uranus	18 04 Gem
Neptune	09 37 Lib R
Pluto	11 11 Leo R

Alan M Sugar 24 March 1947 London (Time unknown)

Sugar began selling communications electronics (Venus in Aquarius) and expanded into satellite TV dishes before the established companies had mobilized themselves into the market. By the 2000s Sir Alan Sugar had branched out into a range of telecommunication enterprises, with Amserve, Amsurf, Amschat. Like so many other Aries entrepreneurs, the burden of continuity is placed upon the shoulders of the offspring: in the case of Amstrad it is Simon Sugar, Commercial Director of Amstrad, who takes the company into the twenty-first century.

Other prominent Arians: H C Andersen, Warren Beatty, Anthony Wedgwood Benn, Otto von Bismarck, Lucretia Borgia, Marlon Brando, Charlemagne, David Frost, Harry Houdini, Thomas Jefferson, Neil Kinnock, Nikita Kruschev, Eugene McCarthy, Wilhelm Reich, David Steel, Peter Ustinov, Vincent Van Gogh.

Leo

23 July – 22 August
Ruling planet: Sun
Element: Fire
Quality: Fixed
Symbol: The Lion

The Sun-sign descriptions of Leo are generous, passionate, proud; Leos love being the centre of attention and basking in the public eye. Kind, compassionate, benevolent – they like dogs and small children. With a reputation like that you can bet it is tough being a Leo. What an image to maintain!

When author Kurt Vonnegut turned his vitriolic Scorpio pen to the subject of astrology he wrote that astrology is good because 'it makes people feel vivid and full of possibilities... Take a seemingly drab person born on 3 August, for instance. He's a Leo. He is proud, generous, trusting, energetic, domineering, and authoritative! All Leos are! He is ruled by the Sun! His gems are the ruby and the diamond! His colour is orange! His metal is gold! This is a nobody?'

This lonely-looking human being, continues Vonnegut, shares birthdays with Alfred Hitchcock, Dorothy Parker, G B Shaw, etc, etc. The arts, he says, like astrology, use frauds in order to make human beings feel more wonderful than they really are. But notice that Vonnegut did not take up Capricorn or Pisces to illustrate astrology's 'fraudulence', because everyone knows that Leos are bright, sunny, cheerful souls who enjoy dressing up in colourful clothes and throwing wild parties with champagne and caviar. You see how tough it is being a Leo? Can you image the trauma and guilt Leos experience if they want to stay in one Saturday night and watch a film on television?

But creativity, individualism and being centre-stage, the traditional Leo attributes, can manifest themselves in a variety of ways. Madonna Ciccione and Mae West express these characteristics in one way, Clive Sinclair and the ill-fated Sinclair electric car in another, and the proud and protective lioness-like mother to five children, parading her well-dressed offspring to constant public exposure, exhibits them in yet another. Leos love 'family' – if they do not feel part of the one they are born into they will be quick to create one of their own, whether it is a business, an amateur theatre group or a dance ensemble.

Norman Schwarzkopf, Henry Ford, Alfred Hitchcock, Mick Jagger, Benito Mussolini, Napoleon Bonaparte and many other figures in politics and public office exhibit the Leonine traits of centre-staging, and commanding respect while combining them with the image of the playful Homo Ludens, man-the-player, practical joker, eternal youth figure. For Leo life is a drama and it is up to the players to make it colourful and exciting, with grand gestures and good dinners.

Just as the Sun is the focal point of the solar system around which the planets revolve, and the heart (ruled by Leo) is the physical centre of the body, Leo's natural domicile is right there in the middle of things. Leo creates a family to be exposed to the world (the preceding sign, Cancer, creates a family as part of creating a home – behind closed doors and drawn curtains). The Leo business is an extension of the 'family': Madonna with her entourage of male dancers, Mae West surrounded by body-builders and ex-prize fighters, Mick Jagger and his moving feast of epicurean indulgence, still commanding centre-stage after 30 years, all exemplify this trait.

But there are other ways of commanding centre-stage. In the late 1800s, Leo personality Joseph Merrick, better known as the Elephant Man, wrote to carnival entrepreneurs asking to be put on exhibition at sideshows throughout England. He spent a lifetime under the scrutiny of the public eye, as a sideshow freak and as a medical phenomenon. Beneath his deformed exterior, as doctors discovered, was a kind and warm-hearted soul, who, despite his unhappy lot, expressed to his dying day an innate trust in life. He wrote:

> *'Tis true my form is something odd,*
> *But blaming me is blaming God.*

Leo is a fixed sign – resolute, unyielding, stubborn. It is the sign of voracious sexuality. A male lion can mate 20 times in a day, then forget about mating for a fortnight. The animal kingdom metaphor clearly illuminates another aspect of the Leo personality – the pursuit of pleasure for pleasure's sake that may well lure Leos into complacency and self-indulgence. A domestic cat in the woods is a killer, but in front of the fireplace at home, Tiddles is only the tyrant of the armchair.

Unprovoked, Arian rams can lower their heads and charge at tree stumps for the sheer joy of it, but it can take a fire to get Leos out of the armchair. Then they'll roar. It is part of the image.

Curiously, no group is more fiercely proud of their Sun-sign than the Leos. Ask Leos what sign they are, and watch the proud smile spread from ear to ear. Even while professing that astrology was nonsense, Mick Jagger emblazoned the Leo motif across the heart of his stage outfit. Leos, it seems, love being Leos.

Leo as Leader

Leadership goes with Leo like crowns go with kings, but just as there are mad kings and ill-fitting crowns, a Leo Sun-sign is no guarantee of benevolent authority and smooth sailing on the stormy waters of commerce. The Leo Sun-sign in most respects defines the quality of leadership – authoritative, parental, protective. Leo leaders affect to know what is best for everyone else, and often have the charisma to get away with it, as Italy under Mussolini discovered to its cost.

Leos embody the celebration of the individual. Frequently it is their own individuality they are intent to glorify, but balanced Leos, comfortable in the role of leader, have a genuine flair for bringing out the individualism of others, thus inspiring loyalty and encouraging talent within the ranks. Leos' parent-like concern over the well-being of employees bodes well for a harmonious working environment. In times of plenty Leo leaders enjoy sharing the rewards of success. However, Leos' trust in the self, and their implicit faith in the undying loyalty of the team, including those close to the hub of power, makes for a vulnerable target for betrayal. When things are going well, Leos soon become pussy cats instead of jungle lions, and in ill-guarded moments of complacency, suddenly find themselves upstaged.

Aesop told a fable about a lion that spared a mouse, and, when trapped in a net, was in turn saved by the mouse. The wise Leo nurtures such relationships. It is the quiet and unassuming colleague that is often the salvation of a Leo blind to disloyalty and to his or her own shortcomings.

Leo as Manager

Leos are connoisseurs of elegance and beauty. The Leo woman chooses beautiful men, the Leo husband has a stunning wife to show off in public places. Leo managers are choosy when it comes to staff. Hard work and dedication are fine, but looking the part is paramount. A company representative had better look good, a company receptionist's qualifications include allure.

When Leos work hard everyone works hard, and well-centred Leo managers have the capacity to make hard work fun. The rewards can be great – Leo managers are benevolent and generous with praise when deserved. There is a tyrannical side to the Leo management ethic, though some see this quality as benevolent dictatorship and are quick to point out how well Florence flourished under the Medicis. A Fixed sign, even the most relaxed Leo has a strong stubborn streak, which can drive a reasoning Air sign colleague to exasperation. The Leo smiles benignly and will not budge. Compromise? What's that?

Leos love games. A Leo sales manager for a large UK magazine company arranged a sales conference where sales targets for respective area managers were pinned to the front wall. In the middle of the conference table was a large bowl of eggs. At the end of the Leo manager's pep talk concerning increased sales, he concluded by picking up an egg and declaring: 'All right, boys. What are we going to do with our sales targets?' Encouraging his salespeople to do likewise he enthusiastically cast an egg at one of the charts. 'We're going to smash 'em!' he screamed. And the entire assembly of area managers hurled raw eggs at their respective sales targets. This is a true story.

Leo managers like to make conferences 'theatrical' and fun, arranging for participants to contribute in one way or another, and keeping the Virgo statistical stuff to a minimum. Stories abound that in companies involved in less cerebral pursuits than magazine publishing, Leo managers arrange conference sessions where enormous cakes are wheeled into meeting rooms, and then at an appropriate moment provocatively-clad women emerge with erupting magnum bottles of Lanson Black Label.

Leo also like practical jokes. But if it is your company, check the expenses. The joke might be on you.

Leo as Employee

Just as the Leo manager is particular about who is employed, the Leo employee is equally selective when choosing whom to work for. Working for someone is not a Leo strength at the best of times, and Leos require the employer's support to allow them to take initiatives and assume charge of an area, no matter how small to start with. Even the lion cub demands its territory.

Leo salespeople are uncomfortable with the title 'company representative', and will work much harder and far longer hours for the same pay under the title 'area manager', or 'sales executive'. Leos like games and treat the most serious work as a form of play. A sales area becomes a game-board, and the office is like a playground. Leos might call it 'serious play' or 'hard fun'. The ambitious Leo career climber is especially adept at a game called Monopoly.

At conferences it is always wise to allow the Leo employees to give a short talk on something, in order to ensure that they will remain attentive for the rest of the proceedings. When anyone else is centre-stage, Leos tend to feel hard done by. 'It's me. I should be up there,' they reflect bitterly. Leos need free rein to 'perform', and even shy Leos (they exist), once pushed into the limelight, discover a new dimension to their personality. They enjoy being in the public eye, and relish the prospect of a new opportunity for exhibition and for gaining attention.

When it comes to pay Leos are particularly demanding. Leos cost. They have a strong sense of self-worth and pay is as much an issue of pride as a necessary means to finance their not necessarily uncomfortable lifestyle.

Leos have a strong creative drive and a vivid imagination, particularly when it comes to spending other people's money.

A Profile of the Leo Manager

The Office

Check out this office. This is the showpiece of the building. Look at the chair. It is enormous. It is even larger than the Aries chair. It is throne-like and grand – positively regal. The desk is elegant, well-polished and large. Seating accommodation for visitors is plentiful, gracious, comfortable and noticeably lower than the Leo manager's chair. This is to enforce the grandeur of the Leo company manager's presence.

Here all is space, elegance and style. Practical office furniture, like the filing cabinet, is discreetly tucked away or has been transformed into something magnificent. Photographs of self, surrounded by smiling subordinates, or family, are elegantly framed and prominently displayed.

The Leo office is equipped with a generous mirror and well-stocked bar – Chivas Regal, pina coladas and at least one bottle of champagne awaiting that special triumph, that inevitable victory, when colleagues and subordinates will be called in to share a very precious Leo-orientated moment.

The Company Car

The gleaming chauffeur-driven Rolls-Royce. Not many managers would say no to a chauffeur-driven Rolls, but whereas for most people this decadent mode of transport lies in the realm of fantasy and make-believe, the Leo manager considers it as a birthright. It is only a matter of time before due recognition is accorded and the Leo manager is being driven smoothly to the best restaurant in town, sipping colourful tropical cocktails from the backseat bar of a Silver Shadow or Corniche. The Leo manager will not be miserly with this perk, being only too pleased to entertain and to share the fruits of success at well-chosen moments with loyal and ingratiating subordinates. Bad luck, betrayal or the incompetence of underlings are all that stand between the ambitious Leo and a blue-capped driver opening the Rolls door, and bidding good morning with a respectful smile.

In the real world Leos frequently have to make do with less in the company car stakes, but there will always be a practical and inviolable need for the GXL, the Super, or the Ultra, when everyone else has to make do with the standard model. Leos go for well-padded and colourful seat covers and luxury designer executive accessories. There will always be a reason for these extras, which will include the specially imported stereo system with CD option, and custom designed mobile telephone. Leos' sense of their own importance simply demands the best.

The Business Lunch

Dress well if your luncheon appointment is with a well-to-do Leo, for you will not be subjected to the blandness of the company canteen, but to an extravagent affair at the Ritz, the Waldorf, the Regent or that unbelievably popular yet exclusive little place where Egypt's most celebrated belly dancer just happens to give lunchtime performances.

The Leo business lunch is an event, a celebration. You may find you are not the only guest (as you will have been led to believe) – Leo enjoys company. Nor will you be sitting in some quiet corner tucked away out of sight behind a pillar – it will be the centre table – and with a Leo as host or hostess you need not worry about being ignored by nonchalant waiters.

The Leo Business Venture

Providing they are at the top Leos can cope with just about anything, and the number of Leos in top company positions is disproportionately high. Leos favour the enterprise that is in the public eye, so they in turn have the opportunity to 'perform' centre-stage. Even Leo film directors, with a vocation located firmly behind the camera lens, have a curious knack of becoming 'stars' in their own right, sometimes more prominent than the actors they employ. Alfred Hitchcock, Cecil B de Mille, Roman Polanski and Peter Weir are a few examples.

The Leo Natal Chart

Bill Clinton

A country is not its president, a company is not its CEO. Yet isn't it fascinating how our perception of a country or company is shaped by the person at the top. The perception of the US since 2001 is quite different to the Clinton years 1993–2001. Does astrology affect these perceptions? Well, consider... Cancer and Leo are the two signs most strongly related to family, and the shaping of family identity as a clan or a tribe. The USA under George W Bush (see Cancer) corresponds to the US as one big family; let's take care of ourselves and we don't care about the rest of the world. The USA under Bill Clinton also corresponds to the US as one big family, but with a perception of: look at us, everybody, this is what we can do! Leo basks in the sunlight; Cancer withdraws into internal processes of self-sufficiency and tribalism. So if George W might be good for Americans, William J found more popularity abroad.

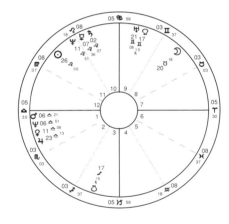

Asc	05 30 Lib	
MC	05 59 Cnc	
Sun	26 00 Leo	11
Moon	20 18 Tau	8
Mercury	07 36 Leo	10
Venus	11 06 Lib	1
Mars	06 21 Lib	1
Jupiter	23 13 Lib	1
Saturn	02 07 Leo	10
Uranus	21 08 Gem	9
Neptune	06 51 Lib	1
Pluto	11 51 Leo	11

Bill Clinton 19 Aug 1946 08:51 Hope AR
(Source: ADB)

Which is strange, considering that during the Clinton administration, the US enjoyed more peace and economic wellbeing than at any time in its history. He was the first Democratic president since Franklin D Roosevelt to win a second term. He could point to the lowest unemployment rate in modern times, the lowest inflation in 30 years, the highest home ownership in the country's history, dropping crime rates in many places, and reduced welfare roles. He proposed the first balanced budget in decades and achieved a budget surplus. He was also the first president to be impeached since Richard Nixon, and, although acquitted, left a country divided over issues of moral conduct and political credibility.

As a delegate to Boys Nation while in high school, he met President John Kennedy in the White House rose garden. JFK was not only the inspiration for young Bill to enter politics but provided a presidential style that he tried hard to emulate. But whereas Kennedy's extra-marital indiscretions remained obscured to the public eye (see Gemini), Clinton's most certainly did not. Had he shown the foresight of another former president (see Reagan, Aquarius) and sought astrological advice, he would have understood how Kennedy maintained the secrecy that so eluded Bill Clinton.

Clinton has Sun in Leo with Libra Ascendant, and Moon in Taurus. This combination represents a sense of style and smooth charm. Venus (relationships) and Mars (sexuality) together with two other planets, are in the First House. The First House depicts image and appearance, and the part of the personality that is on display for all to see. Venus and Mars in the First House are not the placings for secret relationships. (In Kennedy's chart Mars is in the Eighth House, the house of sex, death and much that is hidden to the conscious mind.)

Clinton's involvement with Monica Lewinsky in 1998 led to a number of statements and denials that critics of Clinton see as lies, yet for the creative Leo these statements could be construed as an imaginative gift for fiction. Leo has innate talent for story-telling.

Monica Lewinsky

Sun in Leo and Libra Ascendant, and Moon in Taurus. Sound familiar? The same positions as in the chart of Bill Clinton. Yet why is Monica Lewinsky included in a study of astrological management? Because Monica Lewinsky is more than a bit-player in the drama of Clinton's career; she is a young entrepreneur running a successful and high-profile global enterprise, The Real Monica Inc. Her designer line of handbags and accessories is, according to an interview in 2002, 'doing better than ever and so is she. She's poised, confident and conscious of making all the right moves.'

Of course, detractors may argue that the publicity around Lewinsky in the late 1990s would ensure success for anyone. But it takes a particular kind of personality to emerge from the wrath of the American moral Right and establish a remodelled and reshaped media-friendly identity. And the Fire-Earth-Air combination (Leo Sun, Taurus Moon and Libra Ascendant) that Lewinsky shares with Bill Clinton provides a solid foundation. But take a look at that First House. Bill has everything there, most conspicuously, Mars and Venus. Nothing stays hidden. In Monica's chart it is Uranus in the First House, conjunct with the Libran Ascendant. Uranus is the archetypal symbol of disruption, change and chaos; the bolt of lightning that creates havoc, ensuring any state of affairs will never be the same again. Only in Monica's case, it would change the affairs of state.

At the height of the Clinton-Lewinsky affair, political analysts denounced the media preoccupation as a distraction from the serious business of world politics and local governance. Yet it could be argued that the media exposure of the Lewinsky affair placed a new perspective on the role of the feminine in a dangerously over-patriarchal arena. Astrologer Graeme Jones notes that the Monica Lewinsky affair 'represents a significant moment in the revolutionary emergence of the Goddess archetype in American culture…'.

For Monica Lewinsky, the affair represented an intensely personal battle against the media, against the US legal system, against the people she held in trust. 'In the face of stress you either want to fight or flight,' she told CNN's Larry King in 2000. 'And the thing to do if you can't fight or flee is to just flow …'.

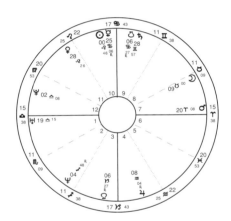

Asc	15 38 Lib	
MC	17 43 Cnc	
Sun	00 46 Leo	10
Moon	09 00 Tau	7
Mercury	25 06 Cnc R	10
Venus	28 26 Leo	11
Mars	20 08 Ari	7
Jupiter	08 04 Aqr R	4
Saturn	28 57 Gem	9
Uranus	19 15 Lib	1
Neptune	04 48 Sgr R	2
Pluto	2 05 Lib	12

Monica Lewinsky 23 July 1973 12:21 San Francisco CA (Source: ADB)

In 2002 Lewinsky invested in a play called *Tick Tick Boom*, about the trauma of turning 30 without realizing your dreams. She was just about to enter the year of her Saturn return, so it is pertinent that the *Los Angeles Times*, in the same year, writes: 'If Monica Lewinsky is living proof of anything, it's that suffering is good for the soul.' This is how many astrologers define the Saturn return process. This transformation was most evident in the HBO documentary, 'Monica in Black and White'.

Talking to her clients about the development of her company, Lewinsky says: 'Reawakening my creative senses has helped me cope during an almost unendurable time in my life. As I have learned from this extraordinary experience, I hope that you recognize the importance of being free-spirited with your creativity.' Creative self-expression is central to Monica Lewinsky's sense of identity, showing her to be a true Leo.

Norman Schwarzkopf

With Ascendant Sun, Mercury and Venus all in Leo, you can bet that General Schwarzkopf comes across as an 'archetypal' Leo. This 'lion of the desert' declared in patriarchal benevolence that he would not subject a single UN forces' soldier's life to unnecessary risk – these were 'his boys' out in the sand, massed against the forces of evil and tyranny, and he was going to look after them. 'Not one of my men will die – that's my aim,' he announced before the land offensive in the 1991 liberation of Kuwait.

Schwarzkopf made frequent visits to the field – he was a moral support for the soldiers, and an uplifting focus for the folks back home. The General was not camera-shy. His performances, both in the field and before the world's press, were masterly. Back home pressure began to mount for him to run as a US presidential candidate.

2Asc	21 36 Leo	
MC	13 59 Tau	
Sun	28 36 Leo	1
Moon	24 40 Cap	5
Mercury	24 37 Leo	1
Venus	05 46 Leo	12
Mars	24 45 Cnc	11
Jupiter	20 11 Lib	3
Saturn	24 31 Aqr R	7
Uranus	01 21 Tau R	9
Neptune	11 36 Vir	1
Pluto	25 13 Cnc	11

Norman Schwarzkopf 22 Aug 1934 04:45 Trenton NJ (Source: AA)

Schwarzkopf's chart features Jupiter in Libra, expressed through the Third House – communication – highlighting the contrast of a 'pacifist' ideology and the role of military leader. Jupiter in Libra suggests ideals based on fair play, justice and the peaceful resolution of conflict. Schwarzkopf's Sun, Mercury and Neptune in the First House emphasize his role as a public figure, sensitive (Neptune) yet powerful – Venus, the 'feminine' side, is discreetly tucked away in the Twelfth House. Certainly the Schwarzkopf image is that of the benign patriarch taking care of his 'boys', rather than that of a charmer of young women.

He was sent to military school by his father at the age of 10, cheerfully boasting to his mother that he would return a general – and then he would have to be taken seriously! A West Point colleague claimed the youthful Norman's aspiration was to be a military leader in the style of Alexander the Great – and that one day he would lead the US army into battle. Schwarzkopf thought it would be in Vietnam. Under the Reagan administration he was assigned to 'protect US and free world interests and secure access to oil reserves in the Middle East'. On 2 August 1990 Iraq 'annexed' Kuwait.

During the Gulf crisis and the Gulf war, Schwarzkopf spent eight months in the Gulf in command of one million men. When the war began he was just six months away from his pension. On 28 February 1991, Kuwait was liberated. A hundred men in the UN forces had died in battle against an estimated 100,000 Iraqis. Schwarzkopf's military strategy, aimed at minimizing the risk of casualties on the allied side, devastated the enemy forces. He exhibited the ruthless fury of an enraged beast – an armchair puss transformed into the fierce and protective lion.

Once on stage, Schwarzkopf proved a brilliant media-manipulator, outclassing professional press aides, newspeople and television personalities. When the war was over Norman Schwarzkopf had, according to the polls, the admiration of 93 per cent of all Americans. A New York PR expert declared: 'Schwarzkopf is a winner, a man's man, everything this country could ask for, giving America a new feeling of pride and enforcing the view of the US as a police force to the world.'

The following year the general wrote his memoirs for an advance of $5 million, declining invitations to get involved in a political career. Having been centre-stage and, in fine Leo style, performed superbly, the general succeeded in turning his back to the public eye. The allure of family life and the affordable elegance of a $5 million advance was quite probably enough to calm the Leo beast.

Sir Clive Sinclair

In 1984 Clive Sinclair was ranked by *The Sunday Times* as the sixth wealthiest businessman in Great Britain with a fortune of about £100 million. It was all his own work. He left school at 17 to become a journalist for various electronics publications, working as an inventor in his spare time. He soon discovered that the only way to market his own inventions was to do it himself.

'You can't separate the inventor and the businessman,' he said in an interview. 'The way you turn your invention into something is to start a company and to get your own invention off the ground.'

Sinclair progressed from an electronics mail order company in 1962 (Sinclair Radionics) to consumer electronics, calculators, digital watches, pocket televisions, followed by the founding of Sinclair Research in 1979 and the launch of the Sinclair ZX80 and ZX81. The 'home computer' had arrived. It cost under

£100, underpricing competition from the US and Japan, and took the UK market by storm. Leos are creative people and Sinclair had been very creative.

In 1984 Sinclair launched the C5 electric car. It was intended to revolutionize the transport industry. It would mean the end of inner-city traffic jams, carbon monoxide pollution and fossil fuel exploitation. It was cheap, easy to drive, easy to park, and quiet. The publicity campaign was grandiose. But no one bought it. In November 1985 Sinclair Research produced end-of-year figures which showed an £18 million deficit.

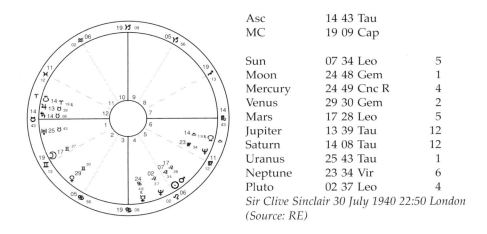

Asc	14 43 Tau	
MC	19 09 Cap	
Sun	07 34 Leo	5
Moon	24 48 Gem	1
Mercury	24 49 Cnc R	4
Venus	29 30 Gem	2
Mars	17 28 Leo	5
Jupiter	13 39 Tau	12
Saturn	14 08 Tau	12
Uranus	25 43 Tau	1
Neptune	23 34 Vir	6
Pluto	02 37 Leo	4

Sir Clive Sinclair 30 July 1940 22:50 London
(Source: RE)

The following year Sinclair sold the computer business to Alan M Sugar – AMS Trading, Amstrad – retaining control over Sinclair Research. Now, in the early 2000s, Sinclair and Amstrad computers are history; Alan Sugar is Sir Alan and Sir Clive has returned to the role of 'inventor'.

He describes himself as a poor manager, but one who delegates well, surrounding himself, he claims, with those who manage better than he does.

With both Sun and Mars in Leo, and in the Leo Fifth House, Sir Clive's creative energy is closely tied to his individuality. This is not the chart of a personality content with working for someone else. 'I can only concentrate if I can do what I want,' he once said.

The Jupiter–Saturn conjunction in Taurus in the Twelfth House, the House of 'undoings' and 'matters undisclosed', suggests that responsibilities are taken seriously, and that unforeseen circumstances lurk in the darkness, with Saturn prepared to take back the prosperity meted out by Jupiter.

As far as Sir Clive's public image is concerned, Uranus is prominent in the First House – the planet which rules Aquarius and creates the image of the inventor, the 'little professor', the eccentric genius, and suggests a preoccupation with electronics, communications, things original, and things bizarre. The chart makes an interesting comparison with that of Thomas Edison (see Aquarius), the man who invented the twentieth century single-handed.

Henry Ford

In 1893 Henry Ford produced the first car driven by petroleum. He founded his own company in 1899 in Detroit, designing his own cars, and in 1903 founded the Ford Motor Company. He pioneered the 'assembly line' mass-production techniques with the Model T (1909–15) – 15 million of them were produced up to 1928.

Ford branched out into aircraft and tractor manufacture, and with the backing of the fortune he had amassed, made public-spirited attempts to negotiate world peace in the wartorn Europe of 1915. 'History is bunk', he declared, and considered himself a pacifist. He published anti-Semitic pamphlets and in 1938 was awarded a medallion by Adolf Hitler.

Biographers describe Ford as a man who 'treated people with contempt and alienated his friends', yet was 'inherently magnanimous'. He was a benevolent employer who shortened the working day, doubled the minimum wage and created the five-day week to increase productivity.

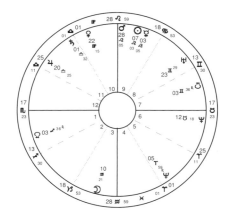

Asc	17 03 Sco	
MC	28 59 Leo	
Sun	07 03 Leo	9
Moon	10 21 Aqr	3
Mercury	03 05 Leo	9
Venus	22 15 Vir	10
Mars	28 05 Leo	9
Jupiter	20 25 Lib	11
Saturn	01 32 Lib	11
Uranus	23 20 Gem	8
Neptune	05 59 Ari R	4
Pluto	12 18 Tau	6

Henry Ford 30 July 1863 14:05 Greenfield MI
(Source: JK)

Ford's policy of paying his employees more than a normal rate led to conflict with the Roosevelt government's recovery programme pay codes in the 1930s, following the 1929 stock market collapse. Ford was continually in tension with the unions, whom he fought with 'terror tactics'. No one could tell Ford what to do, with the exception of one recorded incident when his devoted and otherwise subservient wife, Clara Jane, pleaded with him to reconcile with the unions in order to avoid bloodshed. For once, he acquiesced. Clara Jane continued darning Henry's socks long after he had become a millionaire. Former Ford employee Lee

Iacocca (see Libra) claims that 'When the car business started there was just one key figure: Henry Ford. With all his quirks and idiosyncrasies – and with all his bigotry – the original Henry Ford was an inventive genius...'. Iacocca insists Ford's innovative pay rates were not due to Ford's generosity or compassion – he just wanted his workers to earn enough to afford to buy the cars they were making.

Ford was an uneasy mix of benevolence and opportunism, of generosity and tyranny – a character of the 'well-intentional' patriarchal tyrant, firmly believing his dictatorial actions were in the best interests of all concerned. When Ford set up overseas subsidiaries they were regarded as autonomous companies, feeding profits back into the self-contained subsidiary rather than sending off cheques to the Detroit head office.

The Henry Ford story is an American saga of a poor country boy with an idea and a vision, and the resolve to actualize the 'dream'. The reward is untold riches. What matter if a few toes were tramped upon along the way? He died a billionaire in 1947.

Mae West

The daughter of a heavyweight boxer, Mae West spent her life surrounded by boxers and body-builders, preferably black. She wrote, directed, produced and starred in her first play, *Sex*, in 1926, which played on Broadway till police closed down the show. She was charged with obscenity and sentenced to 10 days in jail. This was not to be the last time Mae West came into conflict with the custodians of moral rectitude.

In her Hollywood film career in the early 1930s Mae West collided with the censors, and to elude prosecution she mastered the art of the

Asc	17 28 Leo	
MC	08 25 Tau	
Sun	24 52 Leo	1
Moon	22 23 Gem	11
Mercury	10 02 Vir R	1
Venus	14 30 Cnc	11
Mars	09 01 Aqr R	6
Jupiter	24 55 Ari R	9
Saturn	28 33 Vir	2
Uranus	02 36 Sco	3
Neptune	11 06 Gem	10
Pluto	09 44 Gem	10

Mae West 17 Aug 1892 04:35 Brooklyn NY
(Source: AA)

double entendre. She wrote her own lines and collaborated on most scripts. In 1935 Mae West was the highest-paid woman in the United States – a corporation in her own right. In World War II sailors named their inflatable life vests after her, in honour of her substantial bosom.

In contrast to the many actresses devastated by the ruthlessly commercial Hollywood star system, Mae West exploited the system to her own advantage, taking full control of the merchandizing of her own sexuality. Constantly in the public eye, condemned by moralists, she performed with the same flamboyance off camera as on camera. The indignation of moral guardians served only to fire the enthusiasm of her performance.

With Moon in Gemini and Mercury in Virgo, her mastery of innuendo-filled banter and sure-fire repartee demolished critics and delighted audiences. In the 1950s, over 60 years old, she began a nightclub act surrounded by musclemen, and loaded it with the sexual *double entendres* that were her hallmark.

She starred in two more films, *Myra Beckinridge* (1970) and *Sextette* (1978).

Madonna Ciccione

Madonna wasn't kidding when she sang 'Like a Virgin'. She is a Leo with a Virgo Ascendant and Moon, Mercury and Pluto all in Virgo. Hence the predilection for white dresses and body shaping. Let's look pristine.

Like Mae West, Madonna is not just a performer, she is an enterprise. Mae West successfully exploited the Hollywood system, and in a very similar way, Madonna Ciccione, when she emerged on the pop scene of the 1980s with pre-packaged coyness and marketable sexuality, quickly took over the business of 'merchandizing' herself. Within a few years she was controlling and managing the plethora of companies set up to market the Madonna brand throughout the world.

School friends from Michigan comment that Madonna was always a prima donna, that stardom was no big deal, because she always acted like a star anyway. The Madonna anomaly is that by exploiting her own sexuality she has become a promient feminine role model for young women, and at the same time a sex symbol for male adulation.

As in the chart of Mae West, there is a strong Mercurial side to Madonna: like Mae West she is a master of acid-tongued innuendo, and also writes her own scripts and song lyrics. As is often the case with personalities whose images become public property, Madonna has the Sun in the Twelfth House, whereas the Moon, representing feelings, instincts and moods, is openly exposed in the First House – the House of the projected image. Madonna is disarmingly open about displaying her feelings to public scrutiny, as her film *In Bed with Madonna* revealed, to the extent that two dancers from her entourage took legal action, protesting that too much 'mood' and 'personal feeling' had been exposed. Actor Warren Beatty expressed similar views.

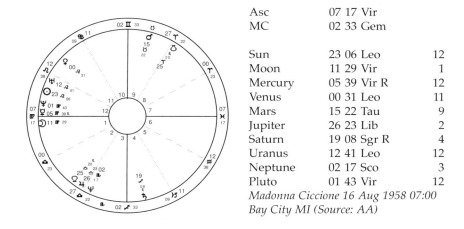

Asc	07 17 Vir	
MC	02 33 Gem	
Sun	23 06 Leo	12
Moon	11 29 Vir	1
Mercury	05 39 Vir R	12
Venus	00 31 Leo	11
Mars	15 22 Tau	9
Jupiter	26 23 Lib	2
Saturn	19 08 Sgr R	4
Uranus	12 41 Leo	12
Neptune	02 17 Sco	3
Pluto	01 43 Vir	12

Madonna Ciccione 16 Aug 1958 07:00
Bay City MI (Source: AA)

A decade later another film placed Madonna in the media spotlight, *Swept Away* (2002), directed by husband Guy Ritchie. Criticism against her Bond film signature, *Die Another Day* (the least popular of all Bond signatures according to a UK poll), Madonna dismisses: 'It was time Bond went techno.' No one tells Leo how to behave and stays around very long. Madonna has already occupied centre-stage in the media world for nearly two decades, and her innate sense of image and swift changes of style stand her in good stead for commanding the limelight for decades to come.

Other prominent Leos: Princess Anne, Neil Armstrong, Lucille Ball, Stanley Baldwin, Helena Blavatsky, Napoleon Bonaparte, Mata Hari, Alfred Hitchcock, Mick Jagger, C G Jung, T E Lawrence, Cecil B de Mille, Benito Mussolini, Roman Polanski, G B Shaw.

Sagittarius

21 November – 21 December
Ruling planet: Jupiter
Element: Fire
Quality: Mutable
Symbol: The Centaur

Ian 'Jack' Channel, a bearded long-haired character known to millions of Australians and New Zealanders simply as the Wizard, has been proclaiming since the early 1970s that he would be the first man in this astrological age (about 2000 years) to levitate into the centre of the universe. He was born under the sign of Sagittarius. Now in his sixties, his convictions remain resolute. The Wizard can be seen on New Zealand television performing 'levitation' warm-up exercises.

Sagittarius is the centaur, half-man, half-beast. Like the other mutable signs, Gemini, Virgo and Pisces, it is a dual sign: the animal half of the creature has four feet firmly planted on the ground (Sagittarians are notorious for bluntness, even crudity), while the human half aims the bow and arrow into the heavens (Sagittarians are great philosophers).

If the Leo Sun-sign regards life as one glorious theatrical drama, and its own role in it as providing the most colourful model, the Sagittarian perceives life more as a cartoon. The most profound dilemmas of human existence can be outlined and resolved in a three-frame comic strip. Charles Schultz (*Peanuts*) is a Sagittarian, so is Walt Disney, as is Monty Python animator, Terry Gilliam. The life of American cartoonist/humorist James Thurber (born 8 December 1894) has a particularly Sagittarian twist. He was blinded in one eye at the age of six when his brother accidentally shot him with a bow and arrow. He was completely blind by 45 and forced to give up cartooning and concentrate on humorous writing. He continued writing funny stories until his death in 1961.

Sagittarians are optimists. Like the other Fire signs, Aries and Leo, they have an innate trust in life. For Sagittarians, people are like animals, and animals are like people – the world is populated by animated archetypes and cartoon caricatures. A life crisis can be reduced to a Calvin and Hobbes cartoon strip – sometimes there is a resolution, sometimes not.

Sagittarians take their philosophical disposition with them into their careers and, being of a Mutable sign, exhibit a good deal more flexibility than their Fire sign (Aries and Leo) colleagues. They are not motivated by the same urgency to compete, nor by the need to triumph in a battle of wills. Winning or losing is not the primary consideration: Sagittarians need to believe in the business they are involved in. Even selling a case of tomatoes must somehow be imbued with ideological conviction.

Though the instinctive Sagittarian optimism often seems to bring them good fortune, life sometimes becomes too dark, and Sagittarians tend to evade problems rather then dealing with them. This may explain the self-destructive side to the Sagittarian personality. Very few Sagittarians succeed in committing suicide, but a lot of them attempt it – a kind of last-ditch spontaneous act, that says 'to hell with everything.' They can be optimistic just so much of the time, and there comes a point in every Sagittarian life when reality is a severe impediment to having a good time.

Sagittarians are the master expounders of ideas, and you may experience difficulty interrupting a Sagittarian monologue-style conversational flow. If you succeed, it may not make a great deal of difference – Sagittarians are notoriously bad listeners. When you speak to a Sagittarian, make it sound exciting; monthly budgets are best presented as mighty challenges of cosmic significance.

In general, Sagittarians rarely allow anything to come between themselves and having fun. It is quite possible the New Zealand Wizard will succeed in levitating into the centre of the universe, wherever it may be.

Sagittarius as Leader

In the film *Local Hero* (1982) Burt Lancaster plays the part of Felix Happer, an eccentric, fatalistic and highly successful President of a Texan oil company. When not making millions he winds back the ceiling of his penthouse office and gazes at the stars. He is an amateur astronomer. When the company representative flies off from Houston to a small village on the eastern Scottish coast, Happer tells him to pay particular attention to the constellation of Virgo. A comet is due.

Mac the oil company representative persuades the local people to sell off their village, with the exception of one old man who lives in a shack and owns a key stretch of beach. Happer himself flies over, clambers into the old man's shack and the two men extol the beauties of the night sky, and make a deal.

This is an idealized portrait of the Sagittarian leader, but no less valid for that. One moment lost in the realm of abstracts and the profundity of the universe, the next coming down to earthly business, and signing contract papers. Sagittarians are the grand visionaries: poor on detail, but capable of an overview that few manage to grasp. Business deals are a kind of cosmic game, and though success is a simple affair for Sagittarians, they are not driven by the same compulsion as their Leo and Aries colleagues to win at all costs. Sagittarians look beyond the personal contest to the grand plan of life. Win or lose, something else will turn up.

Sagittarius as Manager

Sagittarian managers, when they're around, abound with patriarchal concern and make excellent counsellors in times of duress and uncertainty. They rarely mince words, are forthright, open, perhaps a little clumsy, but speak out with brazen honesty. Expressions such as 'You stupid idiot', 'You've really put your foot in it', and 'You're fired', come readily to the Sagittarian manager. Words of praise come less easily, which makes them all the more worthwhile when expressed, for they are expressed with sincerity and without ulterior motive.

The general good humour and buoyancy of Sagittarian managers must be taken alongside the Sagittarian tendency to boastfulness, extravagant claims and unrealistic demands. 'Of course you can cover every account in the North East in three days. What are you waiting around here for?' Mars-dominated Sagittarians will bully underlings to get the results they want, and may even, Scorpio-like, enjoy provoking volatile situations. 'Nothing like a good argument to clear the air,' says Sagittarius, beaming.

The Sagittarian bully is transparent, however, and the employees who give as good as they get will soon win the esteem and confidence of the Sagittarian manager, quaffing beers and shooting pool together after work.

A Sagittarian buyer for a provincial outlet greeted a first-time (Libran) sales representative with the words: 'Get out. I haven't time to waste with the likes of you!' The Libran salesman turned and fled in terror, stopped outside the door, and reflected over the injustice of the situation. He returned to the buyer and said, 'I haven't done anything to you. We have an appointment.' The buyer invited the representative to take a seat, smiled mischievously, and said, 'I do that to all the newcomers. Sorts out the riff-raff.' The Libran salesman went home with the largest order of his trip. This is a true story.

The Sagittarian manager is the 'Tigger' (of *Winnie the Pooh* fame) terrorizer of board meetings.

Sagittarius as Employee

Easy-going, relaxed and optimistic – these may sound like ideal characeristics for the successful job interview. And although these represent some of the more well-known Sagittarian personality traits, they do not always work to the Sagittarian's advantage. Too much self-confidence, for example, can often be misinterpreted by the interviewer as boastfulness.

There is another reason why Sagittarians often find job interviews so difficult. Their fear of committing themselves to a life-long career, combined with an easy-going and jovial disposition, gives an impression of nonchalance. But do not be fooled. Sagittarians have a strong belief in themselves, never flinch in the face of adversity, and, providing the prospects look like good fun, are quite happy to leap before looking. In short, Sagittarian employees can be powerful allies, tackling tasks less capable vassals would shirk.

Sagittarian salespeople have a tendency to give extravagant promises and generous discounts, but they are expert in establishing solid customer relations – they can get on with just about anyone.

Sagittarian employees are game for anything, so long as it is not routine, and would jump at the chance of anything that sounds adventurous enough to take them away from the confines of the office. Should they encounter the Sagittarian manager who suggests visiting every account in the North East in three days, Sagittarian employees would accept eagerly.

The customary Sagittarian reply in any given situation is: 'OK. Why not?'

A Profile of the Sagittarius Manager

The Office

Empty. The chances of finding your Sagittarian colleagues at the office desk are slim. They like roaming. This will provide you with an opportunity to have a look around. The Sagittarians won't mind. They pride themselves on having nothing to hide. Firstly, you'll see a large map of the world pinned to a wall, with faraway places circled in red ink; perhaps a travel poster or two; a bikini-clad nymph or bronzed young man on a South Sea island beach; prominent photographs of Sagittarian self with celebrities. There is a hint of the groupie in Sagittarians – they like to be seen with people who like to be seen. Perhaps there are artefacts from foreign lands haphazardly arrayed. A shark's tooth from Manly Beach, a silly hat from Mexico, or a few photographs with funny bubbles written in.

The ambience in the room is relaxed, informal, the furnishings modest – perhaps a hammock is the only noticeable eccentricity. If they can arrange for them to be looked after during prolonged absences, there may be a collection of exotic plants – palm trees or wild bushy things. Sagittarians need space – either for the sense of freedom which space instils, or for more practical reasons. A Sagittarian managing director for a major UK publishing house used his extensive office floor space to lay out the railway track for his model trains.

Check out the door as you go in. Chances are you will find a comic strip or cartoon selected by the Sagittarian as a motif for the apparent absurdity of life. If the Sagittarian is in you might find a large, cheerful-looking dog looking up at you from the corner. He won't bite.

The Company Car

Some Sagittarians will not drive. They claim driving makes people stupid. Otherwise they favour some kind of horse-drawn open chariot of the type seen in the Ben Hur films. A contemporary equivalent might be a large flamboyant car with wide seats and tail fins, which feels less confining than most automobiles.

Sagittarians are extravagant types, and if they've got it, they invariably flaunt it: MDs will opt for the custom-designed Daimler Bentley, or wide-seated limousine, with the sunroof or fold-down roof an obligatory feature. Many Sagittarians are uncomfortable with high technology, however, and an especially unpopular Sagittarian MD interrupted a 60-mile journey to head office in the afore-mentioned Daimler Bentley convertible (in order to inform employees of a 20 per cent cut in staff) to pull into an automatic car-wash. Unfortunately, water splashed on to the electrical circuits controlling the automatic windows before the MD had managed to close them. With the roof down this superb vehicle quickly filled with water, and the MD arrived in a singularly bad temper, commanding subordinates to arrange for a change of clothes.

In general the Sagittarian favours alternative modes of transport: a horse, a bicycle, an ocean liner or an intercontinental Jumbo jet.

The Business Lunch

Sagittarians always eat out. If the weather is right, they will probably fix up a nice outdoor place with plenty of trees, where they grill steaks on a barbecue. Sagittarians have expansive eating habits, rather than expensive, so if the place can do an entire cow on a spit, so much the better. Otherwise Sagittarian hosts favour exotically foreign establishments with palm trees and tropical aquariums. Tibetan, Tahitian, Tongonese, Somalian – the more foreign the better.

Sagittarians are flexible types and always open to suggestions, in contrast to Arians, say, who will take a vegetarian to an Argentinian steak house and fight with the waiters until they agree to prepare a non-meat steak. Because Sagittarians are restless types, regularly visiting restaurants (Sagittarian and public-shy Woody Allen eats out in New York restaurants every night, for example), they will have an excellent repertoire of places to go, and will delight in introducing their guests to the correct way of devouring Mongolian appetizers or flaming Uzbekistani shish kebabs.

Sagittarians are animated talkers, with wild gesticulations, and they are notoriously clumsy to boot. Watch the wine glasses, bottles, pepper and salt cellars, and assorted table artefacts during the course of lunch. Fortunately (for them), Sagittarians are extraordinarily insensitive to their clumsiness and will probably make a bawdy joke when they unintentionally spill a bottle of red wine on you, on themselves, on the waiter, or on an entire party of guests at a neighbouring table.

Be on guard, too, for the Sagittarian tendency to join in other people's conversations, sometimes leading to heated exchanges, and the articulate Sagittarian's superb command of the insult. The Sagittarian business lunch may not always be productive but it will certainly be entertaining.

The Sagittarius Business Venture

Sagittarians favour enterprises imbued with a sense of adventure and expansion, either physical or philosophical. Publishing and preaching are good Sagittarian careers, as are mountain climbing and managing an Olympic sports team.

Unlike Earth signs, Sagittarians are not keen to commit themselves to enterprises dealing in tangibles. They are poor concrete salespeople. Cement, steel, long-term building projects and the like suggest long-range commitment and severe restrictions on the Sagittarian need for freedom. Motor car companies, however, the travel business, teaching and legal affairs are appropriate Sagittarian enterprises, allowing Sagittarians full rein either to go places, or to expound wisdom on any given subject.

Sagittarians make excellent bartenders.

The Sagittarius Natal Chart

Jeff Bezos

Sagittarians are risk-takers, and what bigger risk than setting up a global market place on new and risk-filled technology? Jeff Bezos created one of the best-known e-commerce sites on the Internet, Amazon.com, originally set up to sell books to members of its carefully cultivated community. Amazon.com was the first major bookseller on-line to offer visitors a way to search among more than a million books, by author, title or subject. Readers can investigate a title through reviews, a sample chapter, even author interviews.

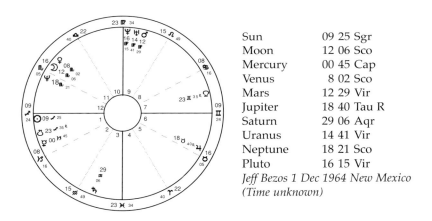

Sun	09 25 Sgr
Moon	12 06 Sco
Mercury	00 45 Cap
Venus	8 02 Sco
Mars	12 29 Vir
Jupiter	18 40 Tau R
Saturn	29 06 Aqr
Uranus	14 41 Vir
Neptune	18 21 Sco
Pluto	16 15 Vir

Jeff Bezos 1 Dec 1964 New Mexico
(Time unknown)

An on-line global bookshop includes all the hallmarks of the Sagittarian personality: the dissemination of ideas and information, the possibility of reaching all parts of the globe, an avoidance of being tied down to a single shop, office or venue, and an enterprise which is a huge gamble and has the potential to expand into unprecedented proportions. Jeff Bezos has created a viable model for doing business on the Internet. He understands the technology that makes it possible, and it seems, has an insight into the motivations and needs of the customers who come to it. Amazon.com's high repeat business ratio reveals a strong sense of brand loyalty, achieved through creating a community of readers, writers, booksellers, book-buyers and publishers.

Is there is a catch to this Utopian Sagittarian concept? Maybe two. The expansive Sagittarian mind has difficulty acknowledging limitations. From books, Amazon has ventured into just about everything, including on-line auctioning. Will over-expansion stretch customer loyalty to breaking point? And secondly, Amazon has an enormous turnover, but so far, little profit. Amazon's losses, it could be argued, are a sign of the New Economics of Internet commerce. These new rules spring from the idea that in the new global marketplace whoever has the most information wins. Amazon has a lot of information. Every time we, the customers, click on to the site, we are welcomed with personal greetings, personal recommendations, and customized special offers.

How much of Jeff Bezos is ingrained in the Amazon concept? A solar chart shows us Sun in Sagittarius and a Moon–Venus conjunction in Scorpio. This Moon–Venus placing suggests getting beneath surfaces, delving deep both on collective and individual levels. In this Amazon has succeeded.

Jeff Bezos graduated from Princeton in Electrical Engineering and Computer Science in 1986, began his career with FITEL, a high-tech start-up company in New York, and two years later joined the Bankers Trust Company, New York. He led the development of computer systems that helped manage $250+ billion in assets and became their youngest vice-president in February 1990. In 1992 he became the youngest senior vice-president for D E Shaw & Co., New York, then left in 1994 to set up Amazon in Seattle. 'The ubiquity of the Internet is more important than the technology of the Internet,' he said in an 1998 interview; but the Internet is not just everywhere at once, but everything at once. In former times the marketplace was not just a place for buying and selling, but the centre of social interaction, information and inspiration. Jeff Bezos returns the values of the medieval marketplace to the new twenty-first century global village.

J P Getty

The chart of J P Getty, at one time the richest man in the world, shows a Sagittarian Sun with a Capricorn Ascendant. In contrast, the millionaire Howard Hughes had a Capricorn Sun and an array of planets in Sagittarius. He got involved in the film industry and in aviation (test-flying planes which he designed himself), and spent the last years of his life as a recluse. If Hughes was the disciplined Capricorn 'out of control', then Getty was the expansive Sagittarian very much 'in control'.

John Paul Getty inherited his father's oil business, and, following the Wall Street crash of 1929, bought up cheap stock in the 1930s and made millions. In 1954 he founded the J Paul Getty Museum in Malibu, California, with an endowment of $750 million, making it the richest museum in the world. He left America to live in a mansion at Sutton Place, near London, from 1962 until his death in 1976.

Getty appointed his lawyer and trustee, Lansing Hays, to control the vast Getty Oil empire. When he died in 1982, Getty's three surviving sons began a contest over who should run the company. The family in-fighting, litigation and the leadership of the ill-suited Gordon Getty resulted in the largest US merger to date (1984), when Gordon sold the company to Texaco.

As his chart suggests, J P Getty was a complicated and contradictory character – generous and benevolent in his philanthropic work, yet so miserly on the home front that he installed pay phones in his own house, to prevent guests taking liberties when making telephone calls.

Uranus in the Tenth House indicates a public image of an eccentric and a trouble-maker: he terrorized business adversaries and family members alike. Getty boasted the world's largest collection of dolls' houses. He gave away millions to benevolent trusts, the arts and charities (Sagittarian expansion), and at the same time oversaw the meagre allowances to his offspring with dictatorial rigidity (Capricorn control, caution and restriction).

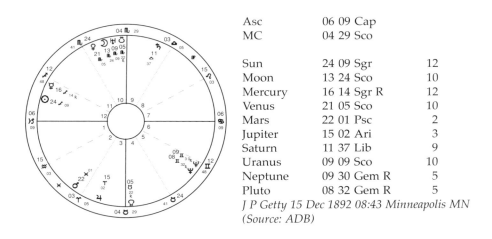

Asc	06 09 Cap	
MC	04 29 Sco	
Sun	24 09 Sgr	12
Moon	13 24 Sco	10
Mercury	16 14 Sgr R	12
Venus	21 05 Sco	10
Mars	22 01 Psc	2
Jupiter	15 02 Ari	3
Saturn	11 37 Lib	9
Uranus	09 09 Sco	10
Neptune	09 30 Gem R	5
Pluto	08 32 Gem R	5

J P Getty 15 Dec 1892 08:43 Minneapolis MN
(Source: ADB)

Getty's vision was a company, a family and a museum all intertwined. As one biographer wrote, 'The old man had intended for tens of thousands of Getty Oil employees, several generations of the Getty family, and one of the richest art museums in the country somehow to share the same destiny.' Neptune and Pluto, in a powerful conjunction in the Fifth House (Leo), the House of family, procreation and creativity, suggests just such an all-embracing vision, subtly shaped by the shadows of the Plutonic underworld. The transforming effect of Pluto is often a sinister one, but only Getty himself could judge the influence his family had upon the spiritual and universal aspects of his life.

Gordon Getty, the fourth son of John Paul, after the death of company lawyer and trustee Lansing Hays in 1982, became one of America's richest men, inheriting $25 million a year in income from his father's fortune. The eldest son, George, died in Los Angeles from an overdose of barbiturates in 1973. The second eldest, Ronald, was estranged from his father, and got a settlement after protracted court cases, but was left without a say in the running of the company. The third son, John Paul Jnr, a registered drug addict, chronically ill, dependent on heroin and other substances in a London hospital, received millions annually from the Sara Getty Trust, set up in 1934. His involvement with company affairs was also minimal.

Gordon, described as vague and forgetful, with not a trace of business acumen, but a talented musician, spurred on by the ambitions of a dominant and strong-willed wife, was placed in control of the multi-million-dollar Getty empire after the death of Lansing Hays. His position was short-lived. In 1984 Texaco Oil 'persuaded' Gordon Getty to sell Getty Oil for $10 billion. Getty Oil, nearly a century old, and 10 years prior to this one of the world's richest companies, was no more. Two years later Texaco itself was on the verge of bankruptcy due to a legal conflict with Pennzoil.

Gordon Getty was unaffected by the loss of Getty Oil: 'I have no feeling on that score. I assure you my father wouldn't have either. My father loved nothing better than buying in a low market and selling in a high market.'

Sir Stanley Unwin

In 1914, Sir Stanley Unwin bought in to George Allen publishers to form the company Allen & Unwin. When philosopher Bertrand Russell was imprisoned for conscientious objection during World War I, many publishers refused to consider his work. Sir Stanley, a champion of free expression, became his publisher. He was also the first publisher to issue the works of Marx, Engels and Sigmund Freud in the English language.

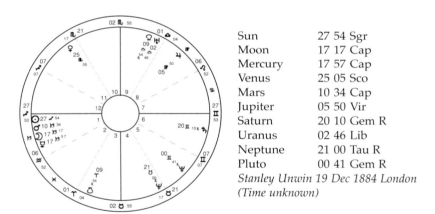

Sun	27 54 Sgr
Moon	17 17 Cap
Mercury	17 57 Cap
Venus	25 05 Sco
Mars	10 34 Cap
Jupiter	05 50 Vir
Saturn	20 10 Gem R
Uranus	02 46 Lib
Neptune	21 00 Tau R
Pluto	00 41 Gem R

Stanley Unwin 19 Dec 1884 London (Time unknown)

Inspired by Thor Heyerdahl's *Kon Tiki* expedition in 1948, Stanley Unwin secured the rights to Heyerdahl's account of the journey, which became an international bestseller and compulsory reading for school pupils throughout the world.

His arrangements with authors often involved profit-share contracts instead of standard royalty percentages, which proved generous for successful authors, and disastrous for the less successful, who found themselves without even an advance. One author to benefit from this arrangement was an Oxford Professor of Anglo-Saxon, English Language and Literature who submitted a curious tale about a hairy-legged creature who lived in a hole in the ground. Professor Tolkien was encouraged by Stanley Unwin to write a sequel to *The Hobbit* (published 1937), which turned into the three-part novel *The Lord of the Rings*.

Sir Stanley is remembered today as the British publisher who in a lifetime of world travelling succeeded in visiting every major bookseller in the world. He travelled every continent, opening the way for British publishers throughout the Far East and Eastern Europe. He visited bookshops from Ouagadougou to Reykjavik, long before the days of jumbo jets and charter travel, customarily beginning calls (with Sagittarian bluntness and Capricorn parsimony) by stretching out an arm across the cash-till and demanding payment for outstanding bills. He set up a scholarship fund, the Stanley Unwin award, which enables young booksellers or publishers to travel abroad and gain overseas experience in their chosen field. His book, *The Truth About Publishing*, first published in 1960, is still recommended as a standard introductory text for aspiring publishers.

Known internationally for his philanthropy and campaigns that promoted freedom of expression, to the staff of the company's office in London's Museum Street he was zealously restrictive concerning expenditure and extravagance of any kind. He admonished office workers who were careless with paper clips. Paper clips represented money, he said.

As in the chart of J P Getty, the predominant influences are Sagittarius and Capricorn (Moon, Mercury and Mars in conjunction), and Sir Stanley was a combination of the philanthropic visionary, upholding freedom of expression, and the despotic workaholic employer, fists clenched around company purse strings. Also, as in the chart of J P Getty, this Sagittarius–Capricorn dualism enables the fiery and expansive vision of Sagittarius to be brought down to earth and transformed to material reality through the pragmatic and determined energy of Capricorn. Note, too, that in Sir Stanley's chart, Jupiter (career and opportunities) is in Virgo – the sign associated with words and publishing.

The favourite Sir Stanley anecdote among members of the British book trade describes a Saturday morning when Sir Stanley was at work in his Museum Street office (he always worked Saturdays and made sure his employees did likewise) and saw smoke rising from a nearby building. He telephoned publishing colleague Hamish Hamilton and remarked, 'If you worked Saturdays, like we do, you'd know that your building is on fire.'

Though considerably less dramatic than the demise of the Getty empire, without the vision of Sir Stanley and relying on past triumphs such as Tolkien, Bertrand Russell and Thor Heyerdahl, his company faltered during the 1970s after his death. Sir Stanley's son, Rayner (Capricorn – born on the same day as Tolkien, and Sir Stanley's adviser on the publication of *The Hobbit* at the age of 10), and grandson, Merlin (Taurus), ran the company with Earth-sign caution. By the 1980s the company was famous for having a stable of successful deceased authors, and not a single living one. Medium-sized publishing houses, like any other medium-sized corporations, either innovate or perish. Unable to compete with the huge publishing houses that emerged in the late 1980s, Allen & Unwin became first Unwin Hyman, then in 1990 was absorbed into Rupert Murdoch's publishing acquisition, HarperCollins. Like Getty Oil, Allen & Unwin ceased to be.

Walt Disney

Young Walt delighted in drawing animal cartoons and began his career as a commercial illustrator. His first animated cartoon featured Oswald the Rabbit and his breakthrough came in 1928 with a character called Mortimer Mouse, who starred in a 10-minute sound-synchronized film entitled *Steamboat Willie*. The ingenious use of sound effects and music made the film as influential as *The Jazz Singer* in hastening the end of the silent film era. Mortimer's name changed to Mickey and the Disney studios, under Walt Disney's firm and patriarchal leadership, began producing cartoons that gained worldwide popularity. Sagittarius is scarcely the sign associated with the painstaking and laborious process of cell-animation, but Disney's Virgo Ascendant is notably shared by the contemporary animator Terry Gilliam, of Monty Python fame.

Asc	24 40 Vir	
MC	23 46 Gem	
Sun	12 26 Sgr	3
Moon	09 07 Lib	1
Mercury	27 30 Sco	3
Venus	29 42 Cap	4
Mars	08 27 Cap	4
Jupiter	15 23 Cap	4
Saturn	14 40 Cap	4
Uranus	16 49 Sgr	3
Neptune	00 33 Cnc R	10
Pluto	17 47 Gem R	9

Walt Disney 5 Dec 1901 00:30 Chicago IL
(Source: JK)

Disney introduced the animated feature, beginning with *Snow White and the Seven Dwarfs* in 1937. In keeping with a morally wholesome and uncomplicated Sagittarian world view, the sinister aspects of this brooding Brothers Grimm tale were rejected in favour of a sweet-faced Snow White amidst chirping birds, cute-faced rabbits and cuddly, playful dwarfs. Today, the term 'A Walt Disney Film' describes a kind of entertainment that is wholesome for children and appreciated by adults. Good invariably triumphs over the forces of chaos and disorder – the unwitting perpetrator of mischievous deeds can find redemption. The Disney film is a celebration of childhood's innocence, avoiding the moral complexities of the adult world.

Sagittarius is the sign of the 'eternal youth', and with four planets in Capricorn, Disney succeeded in actualizing the lofty idealism of his Sun-sign. Significantly, Walt Disney's head is in a deep freeze unit, waiting for the progress in medical science that will bring him back to life. He died following an operation in 1966.

Steven Spielberg

His favourite film is *Bambi*, and for cinema-goers throughout the world he is Disney's successor. Spielberg, like Disney, a Sagittarian with Venus and Mars in Earth signs, had directed three of the top ten grossing films before the age of 40.

Like Disney, Spielberg's film successes and Sagittarian vision led to a host of spin-offs. Also like Disney, Spielberg has an enormous public following and a critical circle who regard his films as sentimental and uncomplicated. But his action films, and collaborations with Taurean George Lucas (such as the Indiana Jones films) are major successes. Like a true Sagittarian, he delights in exotic locations because of the travelling opportunities. His one big flop, *1941*, was considered 'too extravagant', even for a Spielberg film.

Sun	25 44 Sgr
Moon	1 00 Psc
Mercury	16 48 Sgr
Venus	22 12 Cap
Mars	5 03 Vir
Jupiter	12 12 Sgr
Saturn	22 30 Leo R
Uranus	24 04 Gem R
Neptune	12 47 Lib
Pluto	14 44 Leo R

Steven Spielberg 18 Dec 1947 Cincinnatti OH
(Time unknown) (Source: ADB)

Other prominent Sagittarians: Woody Allen, Jane Austen, Ludwig van Beethoven, Busby Berkley, William Blake, Tycho Brahe, Leonid Brezhnev, Andrew Carnegie, Noam Chomsky, Winston Churchill, Joseph Conrad, Noel Coward, General Custer, Kirk Douglas, Friedrich Engels, Jane Fonda, Charles de Gaulle, Bob Hawke, Jimi Hendrix, Toulouse Lautrec, Harpo Marx, Sir Robert Menzies, Edvard Munch, Nostradamus, Kerry Packer, Bhagwan Shree Rajneesh, Charles Schultz, Frank Sinatra, Aleksander Solzhenitsyn, Spinoza, Jonathan Swift, Mark Twain.

Earth Signs

Taurus

Tony Blair
Elizabeth II
W R Hearst
Orson Welles
Adolf Hitler
Saddam Hussein

Virgo

Alexander Korda
Samuel Goldwyn
Joseph Kennedy

Capricorn

Howard Hughes
Ari Onassis
John De Lorean
Richard Nixon
Al Capone

Taurus

20 April – 20 May
Ruling planet: Venus
Element: Earth
Quality: Fixed
Symbol: The Bull

People with Sun in Taurus are often described as slow-thinking, reliable, loyal types with healthy appetites. Once these are satisfied, Taureans are happy. However, a lot of philosophers are born under the sign of Taurus, which does not fit with the conventional portrait of either the contented construction worker with lunchbox in hand, or the Tom Jones (Taurus Ascendant) type with unbuttoned shirt, a degree in coal-mining and a voice to drive women to exultation. Cher is the feminine countertype, with remodelled body, the lingerie to reveal it, come-hither lips and a bedroom smile – the earthy sensualist, in other words.

Despite the complexities of the seemingly straightforward Taurean character, the 'earthy sensualist' is an accurate soubriquet. Taurean philosophers, for example, are pragmatists, even sensualists, in the true meaning of the word. They philosophize about ideas that relate to the five senses: 'This is a table, I can touch it, it's real.' When Albert Einstein (Pisces) drafted the theory of relativity, Bertrand Russell (Taurus) rewrote it so that it could be understood by the lay person. When Gautama the Buddha despaired of his followers and their lowly ways, he disappeared into the forest for weeks on end, to commune, he said, with the creatures, trees and plants of nature. Krishnamurti, sponsored by well-meaning Theosophists to come to the West and impart the wisdom of the East, horrified his patrons by denying reincarnation and the eternal life of the soul, and proclaiming that when you die, you die and that's it. Still lecturing in the early 1980s, when he was in his mid-eighties, Krishnamurti delighted in goading followers of Sagittarian Bhagwan Rajneesh. 'You put on red robes, call yourself a silly name, and claim you've found religion,' he would say. Even Buddha taught that all that awaits you at death is the 'void', nothingness.

Marx, Freud, Kierkegaard, Kant, John Stuart Mill, Teilhard de Chardin and the Dalai Lama are just a few Taurean thinkers, all sharing the pragmatism that singles out the distinct Taurean philosophy.

The Taurus type relates to external stimulation; Freud (Sun, Mercury, Uranus and Pluto in Taurus, Scorpio Ascendant and Moon in Gemini) based his psycho-analytical theory of the human psyche on the individual's instinctive drive for pleasure (Eros), or death (Thanatos). The Taurean conflict lies between gratifying the senses on the one hand, and constructing tangibles on the other – namely, building something of permanence and purpose that will endure after death.

Taureans are rarely good politicians: they tend to tell it 'like it is' with a bluntness that puts off voters. Taurean former Australian Prime Minister Malcolm Fraser was quickly voted out of office when, in the midst of the 1970s economic crisis, he declared to the Australian people: 'Life wasn't meant to be easy!'

There are two sides to the Taurean character that are important to bear in mind: the Ferdinand the Bull syndrome, and the bull-in-the-china-shop syndrome.

Ferdinand the Bull was content to sit under his favourite cork tree and smell flowers. Then he was happy. A special delegation from Madrid singled him out for a bullfight, but, once in the arena, he sat still, smiled and smelled the flowers. He was sent back to his cork tree and smelled flowers happily for the rest of his days. The Venus side of Taurus likes simply to enjoy life's basics – seeking pleasure through the gratification of the senses. Taureans like to keep their pantries full, and they enjoy the role of provider.

In a china shop, the Taurean presence can have a somewhat different effect. Even a small, lithe and delicate Taurean (Margot Fonteyn, for example), when roused to anger, can do lots of damage. Taureans *need* to throw plates. Pehr G Gyllenhammar, for 20 years Chairman of Volvo, Europe's most successful automobile corporation, throws plates and is proud of it.

In the film *Citizen Kane*, Taurus Orson Welles, in a fit of rage, smashes his girlfriend's room to a thousand fragments: he claimed the scene was based on a real-life incident from the career of Taurean W R Hearst. However, Welles' producer, John Houseman, claims it was in fact an incident from Welles' own life. 'Orson likes to throw things,' he said.

Sometimes Taureans in the china shop, or the delicate situation, or in the midst of intricate company negotiations, do not intend to wreak untold damage – but they are clumsy, lack social graces, and fail to think through a situation to its possible consequences. They feel more at home on a piece of turf in a pair of Wellington boots, spade in hand, than amidst the subterfuge and double-dealing of boardroom politics. Here the 'bull-in-a-china-shop' syndrome may function in a positive manner. 'Let's cut through the bullshit' is a favoured Taurean expression (Taurean expletives frequently refer to bowel movements, a favoured Taurean pre-occupation). Taurean executives have an uncanny knack of getting down to basics.

Taurus as Leader

Pehr G Gyllenhammar, the plate-throwing Taurus Chairman of Volvo, published a book in 1991, entitled *Even With Feelings* (*Även med känsla*; Bonniers), in which he claimed that feelings, what he called 'gut-response', steered industry and business far more than most people realize. For all the Taureans' pragmatism and 'bottom-line' considerations, Taurus leaders' major decisions are either part of an ongoing process of consolidation and accumulation, or, as Pehr Gyllenhammar suggests, a decision straight from the heart. What would you expect of a sign ruled by Venus?

Taurean leaders are no strategists – they like to get things done with a minimum of fuss. Taurus is a Fixed sign, steadfast and resolute, even stubborn. Taurean leaders favour steady progress over quick success.

Taureans are adept at accumulating things, and, having once embarked upon an enterprise, become increasingly territorial. Slowly, cautiously, step-by-step, if unhindered Taureans will take over the entire building. Taureans are an illustration of the idea that having more creates an appetite for more still. Volvo's steady expansion in its 20 years under Gyllenhammar's leadership, for example, has included the absorption of medical, chemical and pharmaceutical companies; in 1992 he became involved in the single largest takeover bid of a state-owned company in Swedish history, which would make Volvo owners of a range of companies that produce just about everything to be found in the Swedish householder's everyday shopping basket.

Taureans have difficulty letting go of accumulated fortunes and amassed treasures, and one can speculate that a high percentage of 1929 Wall Street skyscraper casualties were Taureans. Geminis might have shrugged their shoulders, packed up the briefcase and moved to Santa Monica to start a career in politics.

Taurus as Manager

Do not be subtle with a Taurean manager in a job interview. Blunt, straightforward, down-to-earth answers are the key to success here. If you have written 'fluent French and German' on the application form, be prepared to meet Mademoiselle Du Pont from accounts and Werner from the car pool, who under gentle but firm Taurean direction will ensure your claims are accurate.

Nor is it recommended to ask Taurus managers, 'What's your Sun-sign?' (if you do not know it already, ask a Scorpio or Pisces in the personnel department for a sneak peek at the files). The Taurus manager will either cast a suspicious glance in your general direction, or demand 'What do you want to know that for?' Taureans are not impressed with 'waffly mumbo-jumbo astrology', or with any other kind of abstract human thought, unless it can be put to some practical use.

Taurean managers cannot and will not be rushed into a hasty decision, and if you are waiting for the result of your interview, be patient. If you are capable, honest and look people straight in the eye, your chances are good.

The Taurean's conservative side does not take kindly to change and rapid staff turnover. Taureans are loyal and benign managers who take pride in looking after staff – and in times of personal or professional crisis, the Taurean ear is as sympathetic as you are likely to find. But Taurean bluntness prevails when confronted with staff who are unreliable, unproductive and unscrupulous. It is a bluntness expressed in phrases like, 'You're fired.'

Taurus as Employee

Taurean workers are thorough, methodical, not easily distracted from a task once commenced and appreciate the structure and order of routine. The security of knowing that morning tea is at precisely 10:30 am, that post must be ready for the 4:00 pm postbag, and that going-home time is precisely 5:30 pm, instils Taureans with a general well-being that will contribute greatly to a contented work environment. A department with unhappy Taureans is not a fun place to be.

Taureans have an unjust reputation for having difficulty contending with intellectually demanding jobs. Taureans might take a little longer with the balance sheets but that is only because they are thorough. In their schooldays many large-sized and slow-thinking Taureans cultivate a 'minder/little professor' relationship, usually with a diminutive but intellectually versatile Pisces or Aquarian (unlike Gemini or Libra, so good at talking their way out of a conflict situation). The 'little professor' would meet the Taurus 'minder' once a week, Monday mornings. 'Here's your history homework,' says the little professor, 'and here's your English homework... and here's a list of the guys I want you to work over!' Such a relationship functions admirably in a school environment, but in a work situation Taureans may need coaxing and encouragement in certain cerebrally demanding situations.

Taureans are best motivated by tangibles. A fancy title does not mean much, but an increased pay cheque goes a long way in securing Taurean loyalty. Perhaps the greatest benefit an employer can bestow upon the Taurean employee is an extended lunchtime. Taureans eat slowly.

A Profile of the Taurus Manager

The Office

The decor is conservative, yet cosy, with little indication of extravagance or non-functional furnishings. It contains chunky rustic furniture, preferably wood, elegant in its simplicity. The chair is designed for comfort – high tech status-imbued office furniture is not to the Taurean taste. There may well be a couch. A short nap after a well-deserved lunch and a good-quality full-bodied Bordeaux recharges the Taurean batteries for the afternoon ahead. The couch is also an essential element in psychoanalysis, the system initiated by Taurean Sigmund Freud (with its typical Taurean preoccupation with bowel movements).

Colours are subdued, and the ambience quiet and dignified. Photographs of the spouse and kids are on the desk. A visitor is made to feel at home, and unlike a visit to an Aries office, you will not have to take your own chair. Only one or two guest chairs, however, as Taureans do not take kindly to having too many visitors at any one time or during any one day. There will probably be a table – 'Well, we're here to work, after all' – but afternoon tea will always be laid on.

The Company Car

A Range Rover, or large four-wheel drive. Now the Range Rover is not everyone's choice of company car, and only a select few Taurean managers are likely to fulfil such aspirations. However, should the Taurean realize that such a vehicle is a *need* rather than a mere whim, and succeed in convincing upper-level management likewise, the Range Rover is as good as in the garage – Taureans make sure they get what they need. And why a Range Rover? Taureans like sitting up high, feeling powerfully aloof from the snappier, sportier vehicles whizzing by. Slow and steady wins the race, as they say. Chances are the Taurean manager has a patch of land somewhere not too far from the office, and the Range Rover is ideal for transporting sackloads of fertilizer, building materials and oversized dogs.

The Business Lunch

Astrologically aware managers, anticipating with salivating palate the prospect of a business luncheon at the expense of a Taurean colleague, cognizant of Taureans' epicurean demands on the great feast of life, may be surprised and dismayed to find themselves seated at the corner table of the local pub, tucking into a hot dog, lubricated with a glass of beer. True, Taureans love a good dinner, but they are practical people favouring value-for-money over needless extravagance. Lunch at Claridges can wait until the Leo from marketing is imbued with benign consideration for his colleagues, keen to bring a little colour into their otherwise dreary lives.

When it comes to the special occasion, however, the deal that must go through, you can rely on Taureans to know whether the Michelin rating of that place down the road is credible or not. There are Taurean managers known to have accepted a job with a particular company because of its proximity to an eating establishment of repute.

The Taurean Business Venture

Construction, hotels, restaurants, money. Taureans like to deal with tangibles – things that can be touched, grasped, lived in, slept on and eaten. Taureans do not trust ideas, though idealism is fine if it makes people productive. Taureans are uncomfortable with an entrepreneurial role that demands mobility, flexibility and constant change. Rather a chain of bakery shops than an advertising agency or management consultancy.

There are proportionately few travelling salespeople born under the sign of Taurus – it is not a sign well suited to constant movement and adapting to new environments and uncertain routines. One notable exception was the celebrated sales representative who declined a head-office desk job in favour of globetrotting on behalf of the company. His motive, it transpired, was the frequent opportunity for staying in five-star hotels in capital cities (always the best) and ticking off all the restaurants in the Michelin guide. At the same time he was compiling his own guide to the world's top restaurants. His chief source of entertainment on these trips was admonishing or praising an establishment for repasts satisfactory or not, as the case may be. This is a true story, and the restaurant guide is now published.

The Taurus Natal Chart

Tony Blair

In 1997, Tony Blair won Great Britain's general election with a landslide majority – the largest in Labour Party history – and soon became one of the most popular prime ministers in recent British history. In his second term of office, Blair's star began to wane: criticism centred on his seeming lack of political ideology. Was he a Labour prime minister, or a thinly disguised Conservative? 'Well to the right of Al Gore's disastrous tilt at the US presidency', wrote political analyst Andrew Roth (March 2001) 'Blair favours a new self-made entrepreneurial elite. So, of course, did Margaret Thatcher.'

Andrew Roth's analysis considers various approaches to unravel the enigma of Tony Blair, the person.

Asc	04 51 Gem	
MC	26 03 Cap	
Sun	15 22 Tau	12
Moon	11 29 Aqr	10
Mercury	26 23 Ari	12
Venus	15 01 Ari	12
Mars	03 27 Gem	12
Jupiter	29 11 Tau	12
Saturn	22 20 Lib R	6
Uranus	15 16 Cnc	3
Neptune	21 54 Lib R	6
Pluto	20 48 Leo	5

Tony Blair 6 May 1953 06:10 Edinburgh
(Source: AA)

A behavioural psychologist might argue that the prime minister is a right-wing social democrat who succeeded in capturing the victory-starved Labour party from within. An analytical psychologist would consider Blair's background: as the son of Leo Blair (a leader of the pre-war Glasgow Young Communists), Tony Blair has brought more left-wingers into government than even Harold Wilson, and revolutionized the constitution. A synthesis of both would see Tony Blair as a former member of the legal profession who has no rooted ideology whatever – 'a political weathervane subject to any puff of hot air'. A geneticist might consider Tony Blair's heredity: Mr Blair's father made the jump from pre-war Young

Communist League to the Conservative ethos and, when he became a law lecturer after the war, he hoped to become a Tory MP and was only stopped by ill-health. Is Tony Blair's lack of ideological commitment in his genes?

What about simple empirical observation? 'We've seen him give countless speeches and read thousands of words about him. But why does no one seem to know the man behind the smile? Who is the real Tony Blair?' asked *The Guardian* newspaper prior to the 2001 general election. American political writer Joe Klein went in search of the answer following the campaign trail in June 2001.

Klein left his question unanswered, comparing his journalistic quest to the US election of 1992: 'Within months of his election the "Who is Bill Clinton" stories had disappeared – we knew exactly who he was.'

So who is Tony Blair, the person? What can astrology tell us? Tony Blair's Sun-sign, Taurus, is the sign of conservatism (as in maintaining the status quo) and consolidation. Compare the unfailing principles of Blair's counterpart, Queen Elizabeth II.

Blair's Rising Sign is Gemini – mercurial, flexible, communicative and a strong contrast to Taurean solidity and inflexibility. (Astrology works like 'wave theory', where the characteristics of each sign are the opposite of the preceding sign.) Mercury is in Aries – a strong placing for any politician, as it signifies the skills of oratory and the art of persuasion. Many salespeople have this placing. But the key to unlocking the psychic depths of Blair's personality, most astrologers would argue, is in the Twelfth House. There are five planets placed here – Sun, Mercury, Venus, Mars and Jupiter. The Twelfth used to be known as the 'House of Undoing', and it is associated with sacrifice, secrets, and the will of the collective. Several books have been written on the Twelfth House, attempting to unravel its hidden qualities.

Compare the charts of Madonna, Orson Welles, W R Hearst, Ari Onassis, Xaviera Hollander, Al Capone – all strong Twelfth House natives featured in this study. What you see is what you don't get. The Twelfth House is the House of Pisces, and suggests a strong sense of empathy on a broad collective level. In the case of an artist such as Madonna, it suggests a quality that keeps her in tune with her public and one step ahead of what's going on. A strong Twelfth House native has an uncanny knack of picking up 'the vibe' – if they are in a position of authority, they can 'give the public what they want'. This was the catchphrase of Chicago entrepreneur, Al Capone, in the 1920s (see Capricorn) and the ideology of Xaviera Hollander, 'the happy hooker' (see Gemini).

But there is a catch; the gift of insight does not come cheap. The Twelfth House is also the House of uncertainties, self-doubt, insecurity. Many actors have strong Twelfth House issues – rather than suffer the torment of anxiety or lack of self-confidence, they perform. In his biography of Blair, John Rentoul quotes David Kennedy, who taught Blair at Fettes College: 'He was so affable that you couldn't call him reserved, but you never saw his real self. He didn't like to expose himself in case someone spotted a weakness... He has always been conscious of how he appears to other people, the facade is always there. He is very intelligent and calculating. Don't forget that he was a superb actor.'

Elizabeth II

It was one Tony Blair's 'superb performances' that helped heal an ailing nation – a country in shock over the death of Princess Diana in 1998, and stunned by the seeming callousness of a monarch long revered.

In 2002 the British Queen commemorated 50 years on the throne. Destiny is not always kind to monarchs, but in the case of Queen Elizabeth the natal chart is well suited to sovereignty. The Capricorn Ascendant suggests taking royal responsibilities seriously, a Leo Moon indicates a royal and imposing bearing. The Taurus–Leo (both Fixed signs) and Capricorn combination imply not only authority but a seriousness of intent. Protocol and tradition at all costs. Individual wishes must bow to the responsibilities of office.

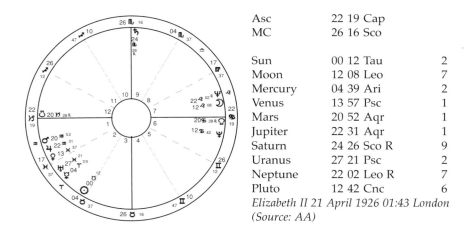

Asc	22 19 Cap	
MC	26 16 Sco	
Sun	00 12 Tau	2
Moon	12 08 Leo	7
Mercury	04 39 Ari	2
Venus	13 57 Psc	1
Mars	20 52 Aqr	1
Jupiter	22 31 Aqr	1
Saturn	24 26 Sco R	9
Uranus	27 21 Psc	2
Neptune	22 02 Leo R	7
Pluto	12 42 Cnc	6

Elizabeth II 21 April 1926 01:43 London
(Source: AA)

The producer and director of the 1992 BBC documentary *Elizabeth R* commented: 'Mystique is what matters most to the royal family. If they don't have it what have they got? The hardest part about making this film was pushing the frontiers back slightly, which is acceptable, without destroying the mystique, which is unacceptable.' Yet now, in the twenty-first century, it is the mystique that is unacceptable. We find ourselves in an age of media manipulation which requires new skills from our public figures. Tony Blair has the skill, so did Princess Diana; the Queen may have tradition and resilience of her side, but not the media.

The chart of Queen Elizabeth is focused on tangibles – Earth signs and Earth houses. Three planets, including the Sun, located in the Second House concern money and wealth; three planets in the First emphasize the image projected to the outside world. The prominent First House accentuates public image: in her 50-year reign the Queen has been responsible for the royal family's transformation from private, remote family, closed off from the outside world, to a family on public display. The Queen, realizing how persausive public image is, has allowed television cameras to come closer to scrutinize the monarchy, which, after all, has had its share of critics during her sojourn – while ensuring that the institution of the monarchy retains dignity and continues to command respect. Just like any modern chief executive, she has had to balance effectiveness – getting the job done – with a delicate sensibility towards public appearance and the image of her 'corporation'.

W R Hearst

Before Rupert Murdoch, Robert Maxwell and the media barons of the late twentieth century, there was William Randolph Hearst. Hearst's life was well documented, albeit unofficially, by Herman Mankowiecz and Orson Welles in the film *Citizen Kane* (1941).

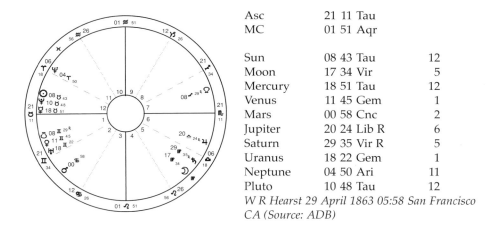

Asc	21 11 Tau	
MC	01 51 Aqr	
Sun	08 43 Tau	12
Moon	17 34 Vir	5
Mercury	18 51 Tau	12
Venus	11 45 Gem	1
Mars	00 58 Cnc	2
Jupiter	20 24 Lib R	6
Saturn	29 35 Vir R	5
Uranus	18 22 Gem	1
Neptune	04 50 Ari	11
Pluto	10 48 Tau	12

W R Hearst 29 April 1863 05:58 San Francisco CA (Source: ADB)

His father had made a fortune in mining, and bought his son a newspaper, the San Francisco *Examiner*. Hearst was 28, and this Saturn return marked the beginning of a 60-year career as media mogul. Today's popular press is largely the result of Hearst's innovations – banner headlines, lavish illustrations, sensationalism; indeed the term 'yellow press' was invented by Hearst's critics to describe his new brand of populist journalism. In 1895, aged 32, he took over the New York *Journal*, trebled its circulation and became head of a national syndicate of newspapers and periodicals. Hearst's editorial influence virtually forced the US government into the Spanish–American War, and was instrumental in the election of Theodore Roosevelt in the early 1900s and Franklin D Roosevelt three decades later, whom he advised in regard to suitable government appointments.

'He so mistrusted the world that he created one of his own,' is a line from *Citizen Kane*, describing Kane's compulsion to construct the fictitious Xanadu. Hearst's palatial San Simeon Towers on the Californian coast became his private kingdom of 270,000 acres (109,000 hectares), where imported giraffes, buffalo, elephants and kangaroos roamed freely. The fantasy newsreel of *Citizen Kane* highlighting Kane's extravagances is inspired by actual newsreel footage from San Simeon. Additional Hearst properties included a 100-room 'beach house' at Santa Monica, a mock Bavarian village on the north Californian coast, and a luxurious New York residence.

Taurus, ruled by Venus, is the sensualist of the zodiac, requiring affection as well as acquisitions. Hearst had a wife and five sons but in 1917, aged 54, he met a young chorus girl, Marion Davies, and although the couple never married, they lived together, mainly at San Simeon, until Hearst's death. To realize his vow to make her Hollywood's most famous actress (fictionalized as Susan Alexander in *Citizen Kane*) he created Cosmopolitan Pictures, which lost a total of $7 million between 1919 and 1923. Hearst insisted scriptwriters rewrite stories in order to give 'Muggins' additional screen exposure.

Hearst made annual visits to Europe, where he would buy up a wide range of art and antiquities: statues were a special interest, and the bells of Bruges cathedral, along with many other artefacts, found a home at San Simeon. Meanwhile Hearst's media empire grew to 30 newspapers and dominated the US media for 50 years.

In 1935 the Hearst empire suffered a financial setback; Hearst was 72 years old, and Marion Davies provided $1 million to help Hearst overcome his fiscal troubles. Hearst was nonetheless forced to relinquish the empire. San Simeon was never completed, and in 1951, at the age of 88, he died.

Orson Welles

Citizen Kane may have been inspired by the life of W Randolph Hearst, but it is as much the story of Orson Welles, and his own Taurean preoccupations. For while Hearst spent a lifetime investing his amassed fortune in power, either over an entire population through his newspaper empire, or over an individual through his projected aspirations for Marion Davies, Welles' life was dogged by the relentless pursuit of money to finance his 'filmed' dreams of power.

Welles' Taurean extravagances included the financing of Dolores del Rio's collection of exotic underwear, reputedly the most formidable in Hollywood. His creative output was restricted by lack of funds and in his later years Welles concluded that most of his career had been tied up in pursuing money. Neptune – the planet representing dreams and illusions – is in the Second House ruling money and material wealth. Saturn conjunct with Pluto in the First indicates prominence in the public eye, public struggles and a strong-willed temperament. Mars and Venus in Aries suggest a certain recklessness and impulsiveness both in work and in personal relations, and, as is often the case with planets in Aries, a struggle against odds.

Welles often considered himself a casualty of the remorseless Hollywood machinery, but, like anyone, he was as much victim as benefactor of his own characteristics. The Welles myth of a 'wunderkind' who produced his greatest work at the age of 26 (*Citizen Kane*) and went steadily into decline is grossly inaccurate, and yet it is a myth perpetuated as much by Welles himself as any of his critics. He presented himself as the creative genius persecuted by the Hollywood dictates of commerce and profit – a victim of West Coast philistinism.

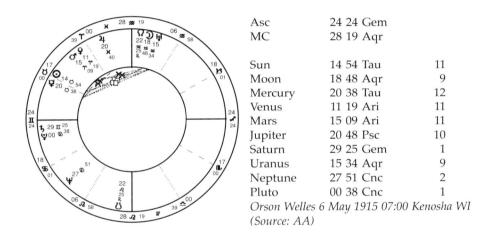

Asc	24 24 Gem	
MC	28 19 Aqr	
Sun	14 54 Tau	11
Moon	18 48 Aqr	9
Mercury	20 38 Tau	12
Venus	11 19 Ari	11
Mars	15 09 Ari	11
Jupiter	20 48 Psc	10
Saturn	29 25 Gem	1
Uranus	15 34 Aqr	9
Neptune	27 51 Cnc	2
Pluto	00 38 Cnc	1

Orson Welles 6 May 1915 07:00 Kenosha WI
(Source: AA)

The Welles story began in earnest after his success as a stage and radio dramatist, and the infamous *War of the Worlds* broadcast in 1938. The following year Welles and his Mercury Theatre troupe were summoned to RKO Studios, Hollywood, where he was given *carte blanche* to make movies. Welles was 24 and enjoying the expansive effects of a Jupiter return. After the success of *Kane*, he completed *The Magnificent Ambersons*, and was on assignment making a film in South America when studio executives intervened and re-edited the film, eliminating half of the material. Funds for the South America project were halted, and Welles, 29 years old, found himself experiencing a career crisis for the first time, manifested in the restrictive effect of the Saturn return making severe inroads into the natal chart's First House of self-image and identity,

Welles' portrayal of Harry Lime in *The Third Man* became part of his public image – a likeable rogue with a propensity for good living. The latter part of his life was spent financing film projects through advertising for Sandeman's sherry, cigars and consumer goods for the epicurean. It was a role he played with relish.

Adolf Hitler

Hitler's phenomenal rise to power and the dire consequences of this rise are often taken as an example to 'debunk' the claims of astrology. How is it possible that the Venus-ruled Taurean, with a Venus-ruled Libran Ascendant, should rise to such awesome power, and, after a 12-year dictatorship, leave behind a continent so devastated that even now, 60 years later, the scars remain? Had Hitler found success as an artist on the streets of Vienna, would Europe have been spared catastrophe?

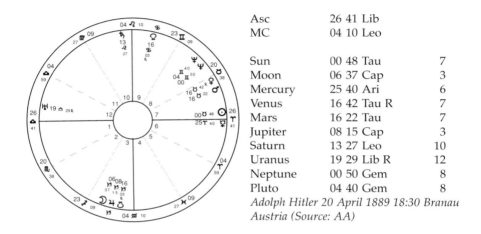

Asc	26 41 Lib	
MC	04 10 Leo	
Sun	00 48 Tau	7
Moon	06 37 Cap	3
Mercury	25 40 Ari	6
Venus	16 42 Tau R	7
Mars	16 22 Tau	7
Jupiter	08 15 Cap	3
Saturn	13 27 Leo	10
Uranus	19 29 Lib R	12
Neptune	00 50 Gem	8
Pluto	04 40 Gem	8

Adolph Hitler 20 April 1889 18:30 Branau Austria (Source: AA)

Like Napoleon, Hitler had an interest in the occult, believing himself a 'man of destiny'. Hitler consulted astrologers, but how much influence they exercised over his political and military operations is open to speculation. What the natal chart shows is a prominent Venus influence; Venus rules both Taurus and Libra, and there are three planets in the Venus-ruled Seventh House, including Venus. Venus stands for harmony, peace and contentment through material pleasure.

That Venus is so dominant in the chart suggests an imbalance, and an emphasis on a less attractive side of the Venus attributes. Venus likes to have things. Venus holds material values high, likes to accumulate possessions, and is unable to 'let go'. The chart of W R Hearst is another example of Venus 'gone mad'. Hearst constructed an entire kingdom, complete with the monuments and antiquities of Europe, for his own indulgence and self-gratification, attempting to satisfy the insatiable demands of an ill-favoured Venus.

A natal chart can never explain someone like Hitler. A horoscope is a record of a particular moment in time, nothing more. But a chart reveals the qualities of a personality; Neptune and Pluto in the Eighth House indicate self-destructive, mystical and transforming qualities, and the prominent Venus describes a person who 'wants things'. Three planets in the Seventh House signifies the projection of one's own identity on to another identity. In Hitler's case it was the identity of a new Germany and the Third Reich.

Saddam Hussein

The time of birth provided by an Iraqi official indicates the same Libra Ascendant as in Hitler's chart. However, the time, even the exact day, as with so much of Hussein's past, is uncertain. Nonetheless, Hussein's Sun-sign is Taurus and the negative sides of the Taurus character are manifest. Like Hitler, Hussein's concern over public image reveals Venus-like attributes – a desire to be seen with young children, or smiling jovially with colleagues and subordinates.

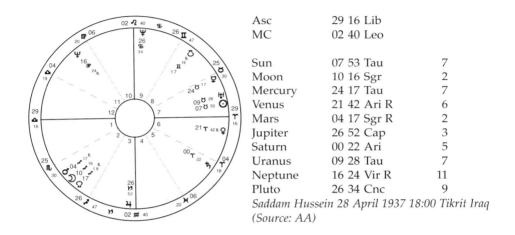

Asc	29 16 Lib	
MC	02 40 Leo	
Sun	07 53 Tau	7
Moon	10 16 Sgr	2
Mercury	24 17 Tau	7
Venus	21 42 Ari R	6
Mars	04 17 Sgr R	2
Jupiter	26 52 Cap	3
Saturn	00 22 Ari	5
Uranus	09 28 Tau	7
Neptune	16 24 Vir R	11
Pluto	26 34 Cnc	9

Saddam Hussein 28 April 1937 18:00 Tikrit Iraq (Source: AA)

And what was the Gulf War about? Kuwait had oil and Hussein wanted it. For all the historical complexities and the absurd injustices imposed upon the Middle East by Western powers, the Gulf War was Saddam Hussein's personal war of greed. In July 1990, Hussein threatened Kuwait, then on 2 August launched an invasion, later annexing the country as an Iraqi state. In January 1991, after repeated ultimatums and demands that Iraq's troops withdraw, the UN forces launched an air assault, and in late February initiated a land offensive. By the end of February Iraq was defeated and Kuwait liberated. At Hussein's initiative over 100 Kuwaiti oil fields were set alight. 'If I can't have them, then you can't either.'

In 2002, Hussein won the country's elections with 100 per cent of the vote – he was the only candidate – and continued to dismiss threats of an invasion on Iraq, even after it began in April 2003. The demise of Hussein, as his rise to power, bears uncanny similarities to that of Hitler.

Other prominent Taureans: Dante Alighieri, Johannes Brahms, Carl XVI Gustaf of Sweden, Teilhard de Chardin, Oliver Cromwell, Henry Fonda, Sigmund Freud, Gautama the Buddha, Immanuel Kant, Soren Kierkegaard, Krishnamurti, Leonardo da Vinci, Sir Thomas Lipton, Nicola Machiavelli, Karl Marx, John Stuart Mill, Vladimir Nabokov, Jack Nicholson, Eva Perón, Bertrand Russell, William Shakespeare, Barbra Streisand, Piotr Tchaikovsky, Harry Truman.

Virgo

22 August – 21 September
Ruling planet: Mercury
Element: Earth
Quality: Mutable
Symbol: The Virgin

As well as having to endure endless jokes about their sex lives, Virgos have a somewhat unattractive reputation as unimaginative, critical nitpickers. Not that they mind too much – Virgos can analyze and discuss any subject, precisely and endlessly. However, even in the most intimate of revelations there is always something untouched, unspoken, and private in the Virgo character; if Virgos broach too sensitive a subject, they are adept at talking around it, rather than going to the heart of it. They won't shut up, anyway.

As far as Virgos being virgins is concerned, and the relentless teasing that poor Virgos have to put up with at work, it may be a comfort to know that the word 'virgin' originally referred to a woman who did not belong to a man – the independent feminine spirit, in other words. The Virgo character highly values privacy and independence – there is always a part of Virgo you feel you can never get to know. Virgo actresses like Greta Garbo, Ingrid Bergman and Sophia Loren have this 'don't get too close to me' quality.

Virgo is an Earth/Mutable sign, and 'Mutable' represents a duality. Other dual signs are self-evident – twins, two fishes, half-man half-beast – but the Virgo duality is more subtle, representing the conflict between form (especially the physical form of the body) and the intellect (Virgo is ruled by Mercury).

The Virgo symbol is the harvest-bearing maiden, pure and pristine in a long white dress and with an ethereal smile. In her hands, however, she holds stalks of grain which she has dug up herself from the soil. For, in spite of appearances, Virgo enjoys grovelling in the dirt. Watch Virgo infants in sandpits, in the garden, in the flower-bed. The only way to know something is to taste it – and smiling, innocent young Virgo mouths are soon filled with gravel, soil and sand as part of their enthusiastic quest for information and 'knowing things'.

Later in life Virgos become fascinated with rubbish tips and street-containers, and providing no one is watching they enjoy a good poke around just to see if there is anything of interest. This is an invaluable attribute in the professional life of Virgos. Everything is examined, all possibilities are considered, nothing is discarded needlessly. Virgos like to collect.

For this reason Virgos are often gifted entrepreneurs, organizers and managers. As far as work is concerned, people are also commodities, and Virgos like to collect talented people, organize them into a system, and create a team that is both productive and socially stimulating. Opportunism? Or perhaps just good sense. Virgos can put anything to good use, and they appreciate useful objects and useful people. Inevitably this means that Virgos must be useful themselves. Consequently, Virgos like work.

Virgos like working behind the scenes, taking care of practical details, systematizing, organizing, coordinating. Virgos are not big on ego, and, on finding themselves centre-stage, prefer to perform on behalf of a company, an organization, a cause, or, in the case of, say, Michael Jackson, a family. Many entrepreneurs in publishing, politics and business are born under this sign: they can manipulate other more ego-driven talents to promote their views and fulfil their aims. As Peter Sellers (Virgo) remarked 'in character' in his last film, *Being There*: 'I like to watch.'

As observers, Virgos develop an acute critical faculty, directed both at themselves and at others. Their incisive and always well-formulated, acid wit leaps into the fray where more timid souls would perish and die. When words wound, Virgos are the circus knife-throwers *par excellence*, aiming for the parts that others miss. The Virgo critique is not always intended as scathing, but Virgos discriminate, and imprecision and inaccuracy offend the Virgo preoccupation with purity. For Virgos the task is sacred – if you are going to do something, do it properly or incur the wrath of Virgo's persistent and sharp-edged tongue.

As an Earth sign Virgos' quest for purity extends to physical matters – Virgos are most fastidious about what they put inside their bodies, with a predilection for health foods and carrot juice. You can bet that the chain-smoking Virgo has reasoned out a solid argument for smoking cigarettes, that the wall of smoke prevents people getting too close, for instance. Larry Hagman (JR of the TV serial *Dallas*, and a Virgo) pulls out a pocket fan which returns the toxic fumes in the direction of the smoker, daring anyone to light up a cigarette in his presence. He has written a book, produced a videotape and heads a US campaign directed against cigarette smokers. As Sue Ellen in *Dallas*, Linda Gray (also Virgo) made a fortune selling sexy underwear, but as real-life Linda she has made a fortune promoting healthy living and natural beauty.

Virgo as Leader

The Virgo boss sees everyone as a resource and is terrible at firing people, 'because you just never know when they might be useful.' But Virgos are adept at relocating staff. Perhaps the Aries accounts manager with a propensity to altercations with colleagues is just the man we need in Ougadougou, and lo! – three months later, record sales are achieved in Africa. Virgo company leaders are discreet, working hard and non-stop behind the scenes, interfering in organizational matters only when necessary. Virgos are rarely ruthlessly ambitious for their own sakes, and so may come into power by default, called in to clear up the mess left by an aspiring but failed predecessor. In this situation Virgo leadership is in its element: reorganizing, restructuring, analyzing the situation and staff, delegating and finally making order of chaos. When Caligula met his fateful end, leaving Rome in political anarchy, the stammering and timid Claudius, a Virgo, was pushed reluctantly into power. During his rule, he restructured and reorganized; reason and order returned to the Roman Empire.

There is, however, an opportunistic streak in the most well-meaning of Virgo leaders, and if the right opportunity comes along you just might find that the company to which you have devoted 10 years of working life has been sold from under your feet.

Virgo as Manager

The Virgo manager is unobtrusive, but, more often than not, highly effective. Virgos are the coordinators, the team builders, the organizers. Virgo managers, under inspired leadership, are formidable allies, who are just as concerned for the well-being of employees as for increased figures and higher productivity. Virgos disdain status tags and refer to 'the team', and themselves as 'team members' rather than team leaders. Virgo managers are the communicating managers *par excellence*.

Check out your folders, files, sales kits, and presentation kits at the company conference. They are complete in every way. You might get too much information from Virgo managers but never too little. Ask a simple question and you will get a complicated but precise answer, encyclopaedic in scope, rich in detail.

Virgo managers are service-orientated in all directions, keen to serve the company that employs them, and just as keen to serve the subordinates they manage with discretion and tact. Virgo managers take obligations and duties with earnest intent.

In times of crisis Virgo managers worry, convinced that everything is their fault. 'If only I'd worked harder'; 'If only I'd filed those letters'; 'If only I hadn't spilled carrot juice all over the MD's desk,' etc, etc. All these and more are constant concerns, and just as Virgo managers look after the 'team', considerate 'team-members' are advised to steer them away from the bar at lunchtime, and toward the health food counter with plentiful supplies of carrot and celery juice. Worried Virgos drink, and when they drink they don't eat, and after two months of work environment crisis, they get stomach ulcers. They'll hurt like the devil, but Virgos won't complain much.

'I'll take care of it', is a favourite expression of Virgo managers, and they always mean to do just that. However, since they may have uttered the same words to about 37 other people in the past hour, it is prudent to make sure that they have done what they promised. Virgos always mean well, they are just overworked.

Virgo as Employee

At the job interview Virgos will do more asking than the interviewer, gleaning item after item of information necessary to make a correct assessment.

The interviewer might get questions like: 'May I start at six am instead of at nine? I just find those extra three hours, without distraction and interruption, so productive.' Is this a ruse thinks the interviewer? Should I consider this applicant, should I call in security and have this lunatic thrown out, or should I just hand over the key to the building and say 'start tomorrow'?

Virgos can be bashful: they like to observe proceedings from a safe distance which enables close scrutiny and analysis without getting too involved. You can be certain that the Virgo representative felt slightly awkward in the egg-throwing target-smashing exercise organized by the Leo sales manager. Virgos like to watch.

If the job meets expectations, Virgos love to work. They also genuinely enjoy grumbling (Virgo writer J B Priestley confessed that grumbling was one of his favourite pastimes: 'I enjoy a good grumble, that's all there is to it!'), so the manager need not take Virgo criticisms too much to heart. It is just Virgos' idea of a good time. Anyway, listening to a complaint or two is a small price to pay for someone who puts in voluntary overtime without pay.

Virgos are born worriers and need reassurance from time to time. You will never quite quell their anxieties, but communication does help. Small but precise words of praise work miracles with the diminutive and sheltered Virgo ego.

Unlike their more practical Taurus and Capricorn Earth-sign colleagues, many Virgos are keen on astrology. Except for the fact that they themselves get such bad press, astrology is fantastic: a system for classifying and organizing different personality types, providing an endless source of fun and fascination for the entrepreneurial Virgo.

A Profile of the Virgo Manager

The Office

There may be some spare slippers by the door, so you do not soil the carpet of the pristine Virgo office, but if your feet are clean you will certainly be welcome, as Virgos thrive on social intercourse.

But as you sit and listen, being shown through the computer print-outs, tables of figures, and analysis reports, have a look around. Looks pretty ordered, doesn't it? Books, catalogues and files are all neatly arranged in chronological or alphabetical order. Perhaps they are arranged in a system you would never have thought possible. By colour, by size, by fragrance, perhaps in a sequence grading the value of information contained in each file, from the 'indispensable' to the 'decorative and superfluous'.

There is also the messy Virgo office with piled-up papers, scribbled-in appointment diaries, and overflowing In Trays, Out Trays and Pending Evaluation trays. This is not necessarily a sign of a slovenly Virgo (although they exist); it may also be the sign of a busy Virgo, too occupied with tasks at hand. Virgos 'juggle balls' – why be busy with one task when you can have 20? But you can reckon that inside that feverishly occupied manic Virgo brain, speeding through a maze of intellectual processes at a cool 90 miles per hour, is a finely-honed system into which all that disorder and all those papers are already sorted and filed. On the desk you will find anything from five to 15 telephones – Virgo managers are obsessive about 'team-mates' calling up and 'communicating'. A salesman out in the field might have lousy figures, but if he phones in three times a week to 'analyze situations' he will have a job till Christmas at least.

A very sociable Virgo manager (and all Virgos are *quite* sociable), will even insist on sharing the office with colleagues in order to improve communications and efficiency. Virgos have embraced computer technology with a passion (or the nearest equivalent to 'passion' with which Virgos can respond) and a multitude of computer items feature prominently. Office gadgetry is almost on a par with that in the Gemini office, but is more discreet, less vulgarly arranged, and with the irritating electronic bleep noises either turned down or off.

Guests are only going to mess things up so extra chairs are unlikely, but when the visitor does arrive, Virgos will go to extraordinary lengths to be amenable hosts, even sitting on the edge of the paper-filled desk, insisting that the guest occupy the chair. They will even offer to share lunch with you, which is fine if you are keen on celery sticks and carrot juice.

The astrologically aware Virgo manager may well have a large sign on the closed outer door – Aries By Appointment Only.

The Company Car

A BMW would be fine, but the company car is not a big issue for Virgo managers, and as a gesture of team solidarity, Virgo managers are just as likely to drive a small car from the pool, and will do so with a wave and a smile. Hired cars are perfectly agreeable too – Virgos are restless spirits, and a little variety on the automotive side is no bad idea.

But if the managers are coerced into quality ('A BMW? For little old me? You shouldn't have. I'll take it!') then a BMW is the car to have. They appreciate a machine with precision engineering, unadorned with pretentious extras, and of a size that is practical but restrained, pristine and not too ostentatious.

Regardless of vehicle the car-pool mechanic will soon be on first name terms with the Virgo manager, rectifying annoying rattles, strange squeaking noises, or a window that will not close properly, and adjusting the tuning at least twice a week. 'Almost, almost... but still not quite right... yes, yes. Almost had it that time... one more time!'

The Business Lunch

Virgos are health-food devotees, but just when you expected to spend a lunchtime analysing the latest computer print-out with your Virgo colleague at the Health Bar, you end up at the sleaziest place in town. 'What's going on?' muses the astrologically aware colleague, well versed in the Virgo attributes of perfectionism, pedantry and the holy war on bacteria of all categories. But there is another side to Virgos. In their emotionally controlled and purely clean heart of hearts, Virgos relish the sleaze, the decadence, the disorder of places like Johnny's Back Street billiard hall eating annex, or Louis' all-night greasy hamburger place, or the subdued lighting of the unnamed kebab place in the Turkish quarter. In such establishments the analysis of computer print-outs is not only a joyful task, but an adventure. But watch as the Virgo manager places his lips to the porcelain rim about to consume a mouthful of Turkish coffee. A tissue is produced and the vessel wiped thoroughly, appeasing Virgo's fastidiousness, if not actually destroying germs. Then, next week, it is back to clean plates, carrot juice and holistic macrobiotic celery and lentil soup. And adequate lighting to read the computer print-outs with precision.

The Virgo Business Venture

According to some astrology books, it seems that Virgos are only good for proof-reading and statistical analysis, but there are many more strings to the Virgo bow than ploughing through pages of printed words and numbers, correcting, modifying, altering, improving and criticizing. Many more strings? Well, at least one more string. Certainly publishing, printing and any calling related to the printed word beckon strongly to the analytical and exacting Virgo mind. But the organizational talents of Virgos also find their way into any sort of business where the entrepreneur can shine: finance, stockbroking, corporate troubleshooting where restructuring is required, and consultancy of any kind are favoured Virgo enterprises. Virgos get anxious stuck under the limelight for prolonged periods, and prefer positions where manipulation can take place behind the scenes, unhindered by the scrutiny of the public gaze.

They are also excellent watch repairers.

The Virgo Natal Chart

Alexander Korda

The two major entrepreneurial talents of the early sound era in the movie industry were East European émigrés born a year apart, both under the sign of Virgo.

The British film industry has always been an industry in crisis. Hungarian émigré Alexander Korda saved it from ruin in the 1930s, and, his critics claim, left it in tatters in the 1950s. He began his career as a journalist, then directed his first film in Hungary in 1916. In 1926 he moved to Hollywood, and in 1930 he settled in England, where he founded London Films. The ailing industry, dominated by Hollywood imports, welcomed Korda with open arms. He built the Denham Studios and for the first time England had a film industry of quality.

Sun	23 30 Vir
Moon	01 47 Sgr
Mercury	19 52 Vir
Venus	29 04 Lib
Mars	19 33 Vir
Jupiter	01 25 Gem
Saturn	13 03 Lib
Uranus	08 16 Sco
Neptune	13 33 Gem R
Pluto	10 47 Gem R

Alexander Korda 16 Sept 1893 Budapest Hungary (Time unknown)

Korda quickly capitalized on the British predilection for their own history, and produced and directed *The Private Life of Henry VIII*, revealing a major British talent, Charles Laughton. Having established contacts in Hollywood, he launched the film in America, and using profits from this relatively low-budget film he financed further film projects, including *The Scarlet Pimpernel* and *The Four Feathers*. He then abandoned directing and became consumed by organizational matters. A practitioner of brazen nepotism, he was shameless in employing his brothers, Zoltan and Vincent. He also imported an entourage of Hungarian friends and relatives, providing them with various jobs (including non-English-speaking scriptwriters), which became a source of some irritation to his British colleagues.

Korda's singular ability to survive deceits, debts, debt-collectors, writs and legal action won him both admiration and notoriety. He insisted that his great love was making films, but that he found himself tied down to an entrepreneurial role and fund-chasing, activities from which he was unable to extricate himself. He instigated co-productions, including *The Third Man* in 1949. He continued as executive producer in the 1950s, but the British film industry was once again swallowed up by US imports, US distribution buy-outs and the stifling conservatism of J Arthur Rank. Now a Knight of the Realm for services rendered, Sir Alexander Korda died in 1956, aged 61, shortly after the release of Laurence Olivier's *Richard III*, which he helped produce.

Virgo is the sign of the worker behind the scenes, rather than in public view. It is the sign of the organizer and the strategist – the sharp-minded individual who schemes and plans, able to envisage and exploit talents with precision. In the case of Korda, as well as those of Samuel Goldwyn and Joseph Kennedy, we see individuals who achieved fame not for their own creative efforts, but through organizing and arranging the talents of others.

Korda's own films were witty and elegant, but never profound: he did not have the conviction in himself as an artist to devote himself solely to film directing. His great role was as an entrepreneur – recognizing and encouraging talented people, and co-ordinating them to create the most productive period of British film history.

The conjunction of Mars, Mercury and Sun in Virgo, all within a 4 degree orb, suggests a personality of strong will, driving ambition and an ability to adapt readily to new and demanding situations.

Samuel Goldwyn

'The trouble, Mr Goldwyn, is that you are only interested in art and I am only interested in money.' And so G B Shaw rejected Goldwyn's offer for the rights to one of his plays.

One year and 19 days senior to Korda, Samuel Goldwyn, born Goldfish, left Poland aged 11, travelling unaccompanied to England, where he worked as a blacksmith. He emigrated to America, worked in the glove business, then went into films in 1913. With Cecil B de Mille and Jesse Lasky, he made the first Hollywood film, *The Squaw Man*, in 1914. The film's success inspired other film companies to move west, and Hollywood was born. It was also the beginning for De Mille and Goldfish.

In 1916 Goldfish went into partnership with the Selwyn brothers – and with a choice of company name between Goldwyn or Selfish, Goldwyn stuck. As Goldwyn, he bought himself out in 1922 and became an independent producer. In 1924, 42 years old, he sold out to Metro, to become the G of MGM, vowing never to go into partnership again. 'A verbal agreement isn't worth the paper it's written on,' he claimed. He formed his own independent Samuel Goldwyn Productions, free now to produce what he liked.

In Goldwyn's chart, Mercury and Uranus form an almost exact conjunction in Virgo. While Korda's Mercury–Mars conjunction indicates strength and force-fulness of expression, Goldwyn's Mercury–Uranus aspect highlights eccentric and bizarre forms of expression. Goldwyn's free and original style of thinking was reflected in his wide-ranging and seemingly unrelated film projects, as well as his independent and autonomous approach to leadership.

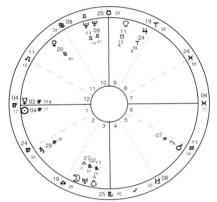

Sun	04 17 Vir
Moon	27 17 Lib
Mercury	02 23 Vir R
Venus	20 40 Cnc
Mars	07 28 Aqr R
Jupiter	24 39 Ari R
Saturn	29 39 Vir
Uranus	02 57 Sco
Neptune	11 13 Gem
Pluto	09 47 Gem

Samuel Goldwyn 27 Aug 1882 Warsaw Poland (Time unknown)

Goldwyn never wrote or directed films, but, like Korda, he had a knack of putting together the right team, with an unduly high regard for screenwriters. For 30 years the 'Samuel Goldwyn Presents' epithet was synonymous with the quality Holly-wood entertainment film, as identifiable as the Walt Disney label was to become.

He died in 1974, and the MGM studies are now owned by Rupert Murdoch.

Joseph Kennedy

The grandson of an Irish Catholic immigrant, and son of a Boston publican, Joseph Kennedy was educated at Harvard and, as a financier in the 1920s, he amassed a fortune. He entered the film business in the 1920s. In 1926 he bought out a film distribution and production company, became executive producer for Gloria Swanson and financed her own film company. In 1928 he sold off his film company interests in RCA, acquiring an interest in Pathé Exchange. He was president and director of the company until it merged with RKO in 1930.

In 1936 he worked as special adviser for Paramount Pictures, but became increasingly engaged in behind-the-scenes political activities as a staunch supporter of President Roosevelt's 'new deal'. He was ambassador to the UK between 1938 and 1940. But for all his business and political achievements Joseph Kennedy is today most remembered as the patriarch of the Kennedy clan, which, for a period in the 1960s, was the most powerful family in America.

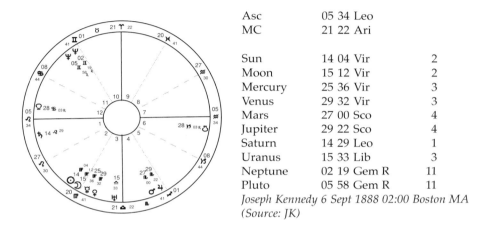

Asc	05 34 Leo	
MC	21 22 Ari	
Sun	14 04 Vir	2
Moon	15 12 Vir	2
Mercury	25 36 Vir	3
Venus	29 32 Vir	3
Mars	27 00 Sco	4
Jupiter	29 22 Sco	4
Saturn	14 29 Leo	1
Uranus	15 33 Lib	3
Neptune	02 19 Gem R	11
Pluto	05 58 Gem R	11

Joseph Kennedy 6 Sept 1888 02:00 Boston MA (Source: JK)

Where is the ambition and drive represented in Kennedy's chart? With four planets in 'behind-the-scenes' Virgo? However, Mars (ambition) and Jupiter (opportunity) are in tight conjunction in Scorpio (willpower) and in the Fourth House (family). It is also worth noting the Leo Ascendant – an attraction to glamour, flamboyance and wealth – which Jospeh Kennedy sought in America's two most prominent forms of show business: Hollywood and politics.

Kennedy married Rose Fitzgerald in 1914; they had nine children, including four sons. Whereas his own political aspirations had only moderate success, he was determined to ensure greater success for his sons' political careers. After the eldest son, Joseph, was killed in World War II, Joseph senior invested his energies as manager, fixer and entrepreneur for John (born 1917, Gemini) and Robert (born 1925, Scorpio), contributing his multi-millions towards their political campaigns.

In 1960 John F Kennedy was elected President, then assassinated in Dallas in 1963. Robert ran for President in 1968 and was assassinated before the elections were held. Senator Edward Kennedy (born 1932, Pisces), strongly tipped as a presidential candidate in the 1970s, ended his chances in an overturned, submerged car, facing allegations of negligence. Joseph Kennedy died in 1969.

Other prominent Virgos: Sir Richard Attenborough, Ingrid Bergman, Sean Connery, Roald Dahl, Frederick Forsyth, Greta Garbo, J W Goethe, William Golding, G W Hegel, James Hilton, Christopher Isherwood, Michael Jackson, Lyndon B Johnson, Stephen King, Arthur Koestler, D H Lawrence, Sophia Loren, J B Priestley, Oliver Stone, Mother Theresa, Leo Tolstoy, H G Wells, Deng Xiaoping, Lee Kuan Yew.

Capricorn

21 December – 20 January
Ruling planet: Saturn
Element: Earth
Quality: Cardinal
Symbol: The Goat

The main reason Capricorns are averse to astrology is not because they are practical, conservative, down-to-earth kill-joys, but because all the astrology columns describe them as practical, conservative, down-to-earth kill-joys. The truth is, of course, that even Capricorns can have fun (well, providing it is on the schedule and does not cost too much).

The Capricorn motif of a mountain-climbing goat is misleading, perhaps even erroneous. In old books the Capricorn symbol is a goat-legged creature with devilish horns – a satyr. The satyr of Greek mythology was a grinning half-man half-goat with a permanent erection. The satyr was insatiable – he could never get enough.

In every Capricorn lurks a devil waiting to get out and satiate its desires, but held back by the restraining shackles of social convention. What happens to Capricorns when those conventions are swept aside? The grim examples of Stalin, Al Capone, Idi Amin, Mao Tse Tung, J Edgar Hoover and even multi-millionaires like Howard Hughes and Aristotle Onassis spring to mind. More wants more. Capricorns become insatiable.

Capricorns are driven people and one often has a sense of power and energy beneath the calm and composed facade of the Capricorn personality. There is an uneasy feeling that if Capricorns lose control all hell will break loose, and those who have witnessed a Capricorn tantrum may testify to this being the case. However, this same energy, harnessed by self-discipline and a sense of purpose, urges Capricorns into succeeding where lesser souls fall by the wayside. Capricorns are persistent.

Capricorns are masters of 'worst possible' scenarios, and you can bet that whatever ambitious and fun-filled project you might have dreamed up, Capricorns can think of 10 good reasons why you should forget it. It is a marvellous game and nothing cheers up a depressed Capricorn more quickly than a good contest of who can imagine the most hideous consequence:

Capricorns will question any new project with ruthless persistence until you are ready to abandon the enterprise altogether, convincing you it was a stupid idea anyway. Then they will shock you by saying 'OK. Let's do it!' at the last minute and risk the dire consequences they have impressed upon you so forthrightly. Capricorn is, after all, a Cardinal sign, and full of enterprising ideas and strong urges for business success. It is just that Capricorns are not favourably disposed toward risks. Nor do they like the idea of not being in complete control.

Capricorns are fiercely independent. They like to be in control: in control of their feelings, in control of situations, and even in control of others. Control reduces the risk of the unexpected. Capricorns loathe the unexpected. They may drop their mask. The devil might be freed.

Capricorns are old when they are young, and get younger when they are older. They hope for the best, and expect the worst. Where others yield, Capricorns persevere. Capricorns work to long-range plans with realizable goals. Capricorn pragmatism excludes time-wasting on idle dreams or implausible ventures.

So when success for its own sake is an all-consuming preoccupation, failure becomes all the more difficult to bear. Capricorns are adept at wearing a social mask which may conceal deep-rooted insecurity. What if I fail? What if I don't fail? But Capricorns' greatest fear is the fear of being boring. It is a fear that makes some Capricorns do outrageous things. Who really lurks behind that Capricorn mask? Capricorns find the personality that is 'right' for the situation. Elvis Presley found his 'right' personality, after trying out a few unconventional ones; David Bowie changes 'persona' every few years, still searching for the 'right' one.

Capricorn conservatism is often a disguise born out of concern for doing the right thing at the right time. All this, just to keep back the satyr that is straining to get free. No wonder Capricorns seem so serious.

Finally, before insatiable male Capricorns leap off in search of insatiable female Capricorns, it is worth bearing in mind that Capricorns have an overriding sense of social propriety: in dining rooms we eat, at the office we work, and in the bedroom, and only in the bedroom, if we are not sleeping, then we have sex, regardless of how insatiable our appetites may be.

Capricorn as Leader

Capricorns at the top are happy Capricorns. It means they are as much in control as they will ever be. Of course, up there on the top floor, that is where the real worries are, and although responsibilities hang about the Capricornian neck like a dead albatross, Capricorns would have it no other way. Capricorn leaders, having 'arrived', need to make sure they stay 'arrived' and so are now more resistant to change than ever before.

'Hm. Sounds like a dead duck to me,' is the Capricorn chairman's favoured catchphrase when confronted by yet another ambitious and success-hungry manager, with the blueprints to 'an exciting new project'. So if you have an idea that is going to save the company, or is destined to make millions, you had better have researched it well, and have lots of documentation to clarify and prove your points.

Curiously enough, although Capricorn leaders have had a lifetime's training in saying 'no', they are really yearning for the opportunity to say 'yes'. Capricorn bosses can articulate every one of a scheme's impracticalities, and will probably be right. But given the concrete evidence, given the opportunity for actualizing some crazy lunatic scheme, given pudding-type proof... for all the sombre and head-shaking glances, the Capricorn executive-in-chief has an insatiable satyr lurking within, goading. And after all, just because Stalin, Nixon, Mao Tse Tung, Idi Amin, Al Capone and Attila the Hun were all Capricorns, it does not mean that the head of your company has to be a bloodthirsty tyrant. Capricorns simply have excellent motivational qualities.

Beware the Capricorn chairperson who shows up unexpectedly at company conferences. The motives are two-fold. Firstly, to check up – particularly regarding unnecessary expenditure that is extra to budget; and, secondly, to brag to the sales representatives about the holiday in Turkey, where chairperson and spouse stayed in hotels costing less than the price of a cup of coffee. The salespeople shuffle their feet, and look at the carpet, fumbling expensive hotel receipts in their pockets.

Capricorn as Manager

Best to keep cool during the interview with a Capricorn manager. Ignore the long meaningful silences, the staring eye, the rustling through files as the Capricorn interviewer reads a line on your application form, looks at you with a suspicious gaze and nods fatefully. Hm. Your future is hanging by a thread. You wonder nervously what are the thoughts going on behind that poker face?

All the time Capricorns are thinking – can you be controlled? Are you restrainable? Will you be trouble? How useful can you make yourself? In this situation it is best to stick to facts rather than suggest way-out crazy million-dollar ideas. Save those for later, when you have got the job. They will amuse the Capricorns no end as you describe your next plan with gusto and enthusiasm. Capricorn managers will chuckle discreetly, shake their heads and say, 'Forget it.'

Similarly, if you stroll into a Capricorn manager's office and present a new scheme (refining budget expenses or advocating improved staff / management relations), Capricorn managers will growl despondently and slowly shake their head. More trouble. More grief. Why do I bother?

Capricorns are organizers – both in regard to their own lives, and to other people's. Capricorns strive for success, not through chance or risk-taking, but through application and hard work. What motivates Capricorn managers? Public acclaim and self-esteem; an article in the trade paper proclaiming that hard work and perseverance has paid off; a Capricorn success. Any other motivations? Yes. The position of chairman.

Capricorn as Employee

There are two distinct kinds of Capricorn employee. There are the worrier-type Capricorns, who walk despondently about the building, with bowed head and lowered voice apologizing for everything and staying to work a few hours extra in the evening. These are the slightly gloomy Capricorns who are diligent, serious, hard-working and well-intentioned. These Capricorns stay in at lunchtime with a sandwich and a cup of tea, and manage a bit of extra work.

The other type of Capricorns are also hard-working, but ambitious, and often outgoing and boisterous, with a dry sense of humour. These Capricorns are in the bar at lunchtime, telling jokes or organizing a trade union affiliation to make sure management does not get away with too much.

Both types of Capricorn require a desk full of tasks. A Capricorn without a task in hand is – in a word – redundant. Don't advise the Capricorn to take it easy, relax or not work so hard. They will only get annoyed. Capricorn workers are persistent and unyielding. Providing the prestige is sufficient and the pay is right, Capricorns will gladly work to the death. What motivates Capricorn employees? Hard work is its own reward, they say. Are there any other motivations about which they are keeping quiet? Yes, there is certainly one thing: the position of manager. Your job.

A Profile of the Capricorn Manager

The Office

No extra frills here. Solid block-like furniture, a somewhat Spartan ambience, discreet, sober decor. Where everyone else has computer terminals Capricorn managers have old-fashioned typewriters on the desk, to type those very special letters they do not want their secretaries to see. In the corner is a fireproof and burglar-proof safe, for those special files in case of redundancy.

There will be one guest chair, and an office lamp will be directed into the eyes of the seated visitor, like a scene from a 1940s detective film where the brutal policeman gives the victim 'the third degree'. Capricorn managers often are not aware that they are doing it – they are just born inquisitors.

The rest of the office is filled with filing cabinets, lots of filing cabinets, lots of files. You just never know when this sort of information might come in useful. Of course it works both ways. Capricorn President Richard Nixon tape-recorded all of his conversations: it caused him no end of trouble.

The Company Car

A Volvo 780 Estate: the car of the successful yet discreet manager with a tendency to pragmatism rather than outlandish fantasy fulfilment. In Australia estate drivers, especially in Volvos, are referred to unkindly as the Kamikaze squad, alluding to the fact that in the case of less-than-peaceful exchange between two vehicles the Volvo driver will emerge unscathed, and the other driver won't. Australian cars have a reputation for folding at the merest bump of a Queensland cane toad, but the Australian Volvo driver, acutely cognizant of the Volvo's patented rigid steel caging system, has developed reckless driving habits.

Thus the Volvo has strong Capricorn appeal. Capricorn managers appreciate safety, good internal design and solid construction. Furthermore, Capricorn managers, fantasizing about the day they might lose control, forget discipline and become reckless enough to career through the city square at 4.30 on a Friday afternoon at 50 miles per hour, might find some comfort in commanding a vehicle capable of transforming red Lamborghinis into scrap metal with just a touch of the power steering wheel.

The Business Lunch

Capricorn managers have an undeserved reputation for limiting culinary experiences to the nearby Berni Inn, Howard Johnson's, or established chain Steak House of good repute. If such is the case, it is often out of consideration for clients and the usual Capricorn concern for not wishing to impose with a suggestion too outré or adventurous. Caution is the key word here.

Capricorn managers may be restrained in the business lunch department, but, with a keen eye for quality and value for money, Capricorns will have a list of tried and trusted superior establishments, albeit traditional, excelling in food, service, value and, above all, reputation. Capricorns are rarely extravagant, and even more rarely succumb to the influence of intoxication (proud of their ability to conceal such transgressive lapses with credibility); they disapprove of frills and unnecessary excesses, but always appreciate an establishment distinguished by a name of repute.

If you are attending a European trade fair, be sure to meet up with Capricorns who know the ropes. You can bet they know the best place to get pig's knuckles and sauerkraut. A cheap value-for-money dinner that will fill you up in no time.

The Capricorn Business Venture

Capricorn is an Earth sign and thus favours enterprises that deal in tangibles. Money is a good tangible. So are buildings, construction companies, and real estate. As masters of the 'worst possible scenario', Capricorns practically invented insurance, and if they are not selling insurance, they are running insurance companies or investigating insurance claims. Capricorns enjoy uncovering frauds almost as much as Scorpios, making up in perseverance what they may lack in malice.

Capricorns are achievers, and having once experienced success, like to go on and experience more. Consequently Capricorns make excellent corporation presidents, world rulers, researchers, and social services job interviewers.

Quality control, like insurance, was virtually created by and for Capricorn, and positions involving either quality or control are high up on the Capricorn list of preferences.

The Capricorn Natal Chart

Howard Hughes

If Capricorns are conventional then what about Howard Hughes? This most eccentric of tycoons was, even by the standards of Hollywood, where he spent many years, a decidedly odd character.

The Sun is conjunct Uranus in Capricorn (Uranus is unconventional); Moon, Mercury and Venus are in Sagittarius (freedom, travelling and ideologies), and the Ascendant is Virgo (health, work and entrepreneurial wheeling and dealing).

We see five planets in the Fourth House, relating to the home and family commitments; like it or not, Hughes found himself in the 'family business' like Prince Charles, Rupert Murdoch, and other Fourth House natives. At the age of 18 Hughes inherited and took over the management of the Hughes Tool Company founded by his father. The company produced oil-drilling equipment and, with the inheritance, Hughes became a millionaire.

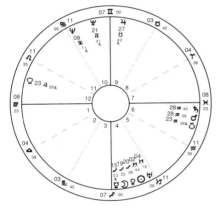

Asc	08 23 Vir	
MC	07 00 Gem	
Sun	02 44 Cap	4
Moon	19 23 Sag	4
Mercury	15 02 Sag R	4
Venus	20 28 Sag	4
Mars	28 04 Aqr	6
Jupiter	27 42 Tau R	9
Saturn	28 40 Aqr	6
Uranus	04 16 Cap	4
Neptune	09 11 Cnc R	10
Pluto	21 31 Gem R	10

Howard Hughes 24 Dec 1905 21:30 Houston TX (Source: MP)

As a very young millionaire Howard Hughes headed for Hollywood and began producing films in the late 1920s. He personally directed the spectacular aerial sequences of the World War I aviation film *Hell's Angels* in 1930, while plot and dialogue scenes were left in the more capable hands of an eccentric British director, James Whale.

Hughes produced several more aviation films, then quite suddenly in 1932 he left Hollywood and under the assumed name of Charles Howard got work as a co-pilot with American Airways at $250 a month. He left after two months, claiming he now knew everything he needed to know about commercial aviation, and began a career as aviator and airplane designer, before finally buying an airline company of his own. In 1935 he broke the world speed record in a machine of his own design, and the following year broke the transatlantic speed record.

The next year, 1937, he broke his own record, and in 1938 he set a world record, flying around the world in 91 hours. He was given a hero's welcome in New York and received a congressional medal from the American government.

There are some parallels here with the career of the Virgin wunderkind Richard Branson (see Cancer); Hughes seemed determined to control what he could on the ground (Capricorn) while at the same time seeking escape in the freedom of the blue skies (Sagittarius). The Virgo health issues, which were to dominate his later life, were already manifest in a number of bizarre phobias, which many claim he inherited from his hyperphobic mother (also Fourth House).

In the late 1930s he returned to Hollywood and more earthly pursuits. He began filming *The Outlaw*, personally selecting Jane Russell for the lead role, and preparing three pages of detailed notes outlining the design for a specially-shaped brassière to enhance Russell's bosom. Indeed, so enhanced was her bosom that in the face of moral indignation Hughes withdrew the film immediately after its initial release in 1940, waiting six years before he relaunched the film in a wave of publicity and controversy.

During the intervening war years Hughes designed and built a warplane, the Hercules, nicknamed the Super Goose, which was a wooden seaplane and at that time the largest aircraft ever flown. After five years and $18 million of government money it was flown only once. In 1947 Hughes piloted the mammoth craft himself in a brief test flight, after which the Super Goose was stored away in a government hangar.

In July 1946, Hughes crashed a plane of his own design during a test flight, and was severely injured. He recovered but returned to Hollywood, according to his associates, a changed man. He became a zealous anti-Communist (Sagittarian ideology) and when he bought RKO Studios in 1947, he immediately sacked what was left of the left-wing elements. These were the studios that had made the 'social conscience' films of the early 1940s, for which some of the people involved (Edward Dmytryck, Dore Sharey) were imprisoned by the House Un-American Activities Committee. RKO was also the studio where, seven years earlier, Orson Welles created *Citizen Kane*, the protagonist of which Hughes was beginning to resemble.

During his Hollywood sojourn Hughes hired operatives across the country to seek out new actresses, and starlets to be considered for screen tests were accommodated in one of Hughes' many LA houses. According to one operative, Hughes had over 100 files of possible starlets/mistresses, favouring large-busted brunettes in the Jane Russell mould.

He made his last public appearance in 1947 before a US Senate committee that was investigating the Hercules fiasco. As the head of RKO Studios he was never seen, and the company slid rapidly into decline. He produced, *in absentia*, some more flying pictures, seven films with Jane Russell, and one of the most vehement anti-Communist pictures ever made, *The Woman on Pier 13*. Finally, in 1955, he sold off RKO to television for a $10 million profit.

Like the fictitious Kane, and in common with the magnate archetype – Hearst, Kreuger, Maxwell, Murdoch, etc – the image that emerges of Howard Hughes is of a man striving to elude reality through illusion. Unlike many of the Hollywood moguls, Hughes' productions at least adhered to specific themes: motifs of aircraft, brunettes, large breasts and world-weary heroes. Hughes paraded his family of sub-personalities for all the world to see – the mother (Virgo and Fourth House), the father (Capricorn), and the eternal little boy finding freedom and solace in the heavens (Sagittarius).

In 1966 he disappeared from public view completely to live as a recluse in the penthouse suite of the Desert Inn Hotel, Las Vegas, where he was served and sheltered from the outside world by five Mormon male nurses. He continued to run his $2.5 billion empire by telephone, buying up hotels, an airline company, a TV station, virtually controlling the economy of the entire city.

On one occasion he assembled the world's press at a conference and then spoke to journalists separately by telephone from his room, because he was so worried about contamination.

The Mars–Saturn conjunction in the Sixth House in opposition to the Virgo Ascendant now dominated Hughes' life. During this period his phobia of germs led him to fear physical contact with anyone or anything. He covered the floor with paper and picked things up with paper tissues. His life consisted of drug-taking and watching TV.

In 1971 the 'authorized' Hughes biography was published, which transpired to be one of the most expensive hoaxes in publishing history. Author Clifford Irving and his wife went to gaol for fraud, and the Hughes enigma deepened.

In 1976 he was removed from the hotel suite. He had become an emaciated, frail shadow of a man with long white hair and a long white beard. He was taken to hospital, where he died shortly afterwards.

Hughes left an estate worth millions, which was quickly inundated with fake wills and claims to the fortune.

Ari Onassis

The son of a well-to-do Greek tobacco merchant, Ari Onassis earned the nickname 'King Midas' after the Greek king who turned everything he touched to gold, including his only real treasure, his daughter. When Ari was 16, the family moved from Turkey to Athens, and young Ari travelled to Argentina, arriving in Buenos Aires with a few hundred dollars, where he set up in the tobacco business and branched out into shipping. By the age of 25 he was a millionaire. He invested in oil tankers and amassed a fortune. In business he attained the reputation of a man who always got what he wanted through sheer tenacity – no obstacle could hinder him.

This tenacity extended to his private life. At the age of 13, the story goes, he lost his virginity to his 25-year-old French teacher, claiming: 'Mam'selle, you are arousing me against my will. Nothing can stop me from violating you.'

With a Capricorn Sun, Capricorn Ascendant and three planets in Capricorn, Onassis kept tight control over all his dealings, both financial and private. After many mistresses, he married, aged 40, the 17-year-old daughter of a rival ship owner, who bore him two children. But his most famous affair was a life-long liaison with opera singer Maria Callas.

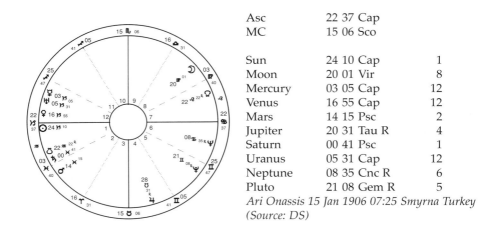

Asc	22 37 Cap	
MC	15 06 Sco	
Sun	24 10 Cap	1
Moon	20 01 Vir	8
Mercury	03 05 Cap	12
Venus	16 55 Cap	12
Mars	14 15 Psc	2
Jupiter	20 31 Tau R	4
Saturn	00 41 Psc	1
Uranus	05 31 Cap	12
Neptune	08 35 Cnc R	6
Pluto	21 08 Gem R	5

Ari Onassis 15 Jan 1906 07:25 Smyrna Turkey
(Source: DS)

He was for a time the richest man in the world – 'everything he touched turned to gold' – and in 1968, five years after President Kennedy's assassination, he married Jacqueline Kennedy (Leo). He was 62 and she was still in her thirties. For his remaining years the couple were subjected to the camera lenses of the world press. After 10 years of marriage, he confided to Maria Callas that Jacqueline's extravagances were wearing him down, and in accordance with a pre-nuptial contract the couple never shared a bedroom. Onassis' wife was beyond his reach, and, just like the story of King Midas and his golden touch, Ari Onassis could never touch her. He died in 1975.

Conrad Hilton

There is a Hilton Hotel in most major cities around the world, even the most far-flung outposts. The hotel buildings commissioned by the Hilton company are architecturally uniform: solid block-shaped rectangular buildings. The impression is one of solidity, even power – there is nothing ornate about the modern Hilton Hotel.

The Hilton name is associated with comfort, quality and service, and for US travellers especially the guarantee of a room and an ambience where the guest will feel at home and at ease is the hallmark of the Hilton Company. The Hilton is conservative, comfortable and far removed from whatever kind of Second or Third World reality may exist beyond the window.

It is this very conservatism that is the essence of the Hilton success, appealing to as broad a clientele as possible. Conrad Hilton, a self-made man who went into the hotel business in late middle age, had Sun in Capricorn, and a Sagittarius Ascendant, indicating a direction in life related to travelling and foreign countries. Capicorns like solid structure, and Mercury in the First House represents the projection of the self – the Hilton name will be seen far and wide.

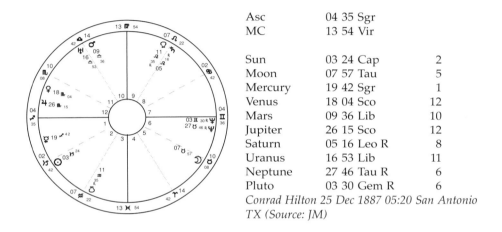

Asc	04 35 Sgr	
MC	13 54 Vir	
Sun	03 24 Cap	2
Moon	07 57 Tau	5
Mercury	19 42 Sgr	1
Venus	18 04 Sco	12
Mars	09 36 Lib	10
Jupiter	26 15 Sco	12
Saturn	05 16 Leo R	8
Uranus	16 53 Lib	11
Neptune	27 46 Tau R	6
Pluto	03 30 Gem R	6

Conrad Hilton 25 Dec 1887 05:20 San Antonio TX (Source: JM)

Pluto and Neptune (collective planets) in the Sixth House, relating to work, obligations and service, in this instance denote serving others on an abstract and collective level; and the Moon in Taurus, Fifth House, indicates individual creative efforts centred on creating a 'home'.

John De Lorean

A Capricorn–Aries combination is an 'image-conscious' combination, both personal and public. When he became group Vice-President of General Motors, at barely 40 years old, John De Lorean underwent 'facial improvements' (plastic surgery) and began a stringent fitness course in body-building.

The Japanese author, Yukio Mishima, also Capricorn with Aries rising and also born in 1925 (on 13 January), and like De Lorean a frail and small-framed youth, likewise became obsessive about fitness and body-building at the onset of middle age. Both men embraced the body cult with vehemence: Mishima, though married, enjoyed the company of young men, while De Lorean sought the company of young girls.

After a number of jobs with various companies in the automobile business De Lorean quickly advanced through the ranks at General Motors to become the company's youngest-ever manager of the Pontiac Division. He was promoted to the prestigious Chevrolet Division, and from there he moved to GM world headquarters as group Vice-President.

During this period he was divorced and then married the 19-year-old daughter of an American football star. De Lorean was 45. Several years later he divorced again to marry a fashion model 28 years his junior. Capricorns are 'old' when they are young and get 'young' when they are old.

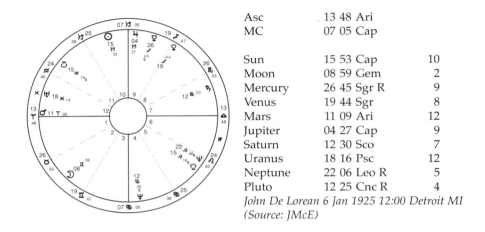

Asc	13 48 Ari	
MC	07 05 Cap	
Sun	15 53 Cap	10
Moon	08 59 Gem	2
Mercury	26 45 Sgr R	9
Venus	19 44 Sgr	8
Mars	11 09 Ari	12
Jupiter	04 27 Cap	9
Saturn	12 30 Sco	7
Uranus	18 16 Psc	12
Neptune	22 06 Leo R	5
Pluto	12 25 Cnc R	4

John De Lorean 6 Jan 1925 12:00 Detroit MI
(Source: JMcE)

In 1973, aged 48, De Lorean left GM amid rumours that he had been receiving 'inducements' from Chevrolet dealers. In 1976 De Lorean was a contender for Chairman of American Motors. Gerald Meyers, who finally got the job, describes his impression of the man who nearly took it away from him: 'He was a vision in Gucci loafers, a fine Italian-tailored suit, and locks of hair that were tousled just enough to avoid looking set. Slim and elegant . . . he seemed destined to succeed at anything he tried. He looked good and that is what mattered.' Meyers also describes him as 'a man who tripped over his own ego'.

A year earlier De Lorean had set up the John De Lorean Sports Car Partnership to build a two-seat sports car with extensive safety features. After missing the American Motors chairmanship he pursued the project further and found backing from the Labour government in power in the United Kingdom to build a plant in Northern Ireland. The scheme would bring dollars to recession-hit Belfast and provide jobs for the unemployed. De Lorean received a government grant of $30 million, with a $20 million incentive if employment targets were reached. In addition he was granted a $12 million loan to build the plant.

In 1980 British journalists and government accountants began investigating an unaccounted $17.5 million, and De Lorean's precarious and dubious financial dealings finally led to receivers being appointed in 1982. On the verge of bailing himself out with borrowed money, he was charged by the FBI and Drug Enforcement Agency for selling cocaine, a transaction they had recorded using video cameras. Incredibly, De Lorean was released on a legal technicality, leaving behind the ruins of an automobile company that had produced a grand total of 1000 vehicles in six years while running up debts amounting to $250 million.

Now in his seventies, repenting the misdemeanours of his past, De Lorean has become a devout Christian and has retired from public life.

Richard Nixon

Nixon began his career as a lawyer. He was elected to the House of Representatives in 1946 and became a senator in 1950 (aged 37: Jupiter return), and Vice-President in 1952. Analysts attribute his meteoric rise to a combination of astute opportunism and politically-expedient forthrightness during his period as a member of the House Un-American Activities Committee.

In 1960, as Republican Presidential candidate, he was narrowly defeated by Kennedy, but returned to win the Presidential Election in 1968, and was re-elected in 1972.

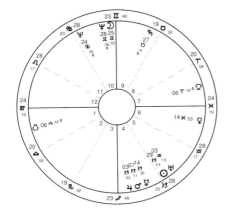

Asc	24 19 Vir	
MC	23 48 Gem	
Sun	29 34 Cap	5
Moon	25 55 Gem	10
Mercury	14 35 Cap	4
Venus	14 53 Psc	6
Mars	07 11 Cap	4
Jupiter	03 53 Cap	4
Saturn	27 14 Tau R	9
Uranus	03 16 Aqr	5
Neptune	24 29 Cnc R	10
Pluto	28 28 Gem R	10

Richard Nixon 19 Jan 1913 21:30 Yorba Linda CA
(Source: JMcE)

During his years as President, the Vietnam War escalated in the name of defeating Communism: as a senator in the 1960s Nixon had even advocated the use of nuclear weapons to put an end to Communist expansion. He is also remembered as the President who sent in the National Guard to quell student demonstrations. The Nixon years signify a time when elements of youth and change confronted the establishment, the status quo and the conservatism of middle America. Nixon's Capricornian endeavours to contain radical and subversive elements extended to the attempted control of the legal opposition, and corruption in his election campaigns. In 1974, during an official investigation into an attempted break-in at the Democratic Party's headquarters at the Watergate Hotel in Washington, Nixon was finally implicated in a cover-up. He resigned in August that year under threat of impeachment.

Together with the aftermath of the Vietnam War, the affair seriously demoralized America, and, according to opinion polls, what shocked the American people most was the President's use of bad language – the so-called 'expletives deleted' concealed by bleeps during the television playbacks of the controversial Watergate tapes that Nixon had for so long attempted to withhold. A month after his impeachment he was, incredibly, granted a full pardon by President Ford.

Nixon, a BBC television documentary produced nearly 30 years later, with access to much previously unavailable material, revealed the darker side of Nixon's character: his depressions, drinking and brooding spells. It also showed at the same time his determination to use his position for humanitarian deeds rather than self glory.

Al Capone

The subject of books and films spanning six decades, Capone achieved worldwide notoriety in the late 1920s during the Prohibition era in Chicago. He began as a small-time racketeer, and expanded quickly when the prohibition laws came into effect, selling illegal alcohol.

He quickly amassed a fortune, and with Stalin-like ruthlessness, eliminated any competition, broadening his empire into a multitude of illegitimate enterprises. 'I'm against violence,' he once claimed. 'It's not good business.' Yet at the same time that Stalin (also Capricorn) was securing his political position with party purges, Capone arranged the infamous St Valentine's Day massacre, at which his hirelings, dressed in police uniforms, gunned down a rival gang. Such was his power that, despite his known complicity in murder and extortion, charges could not be brought against him.

Reputedly generous to Chicago's poor, handing out $20 bills to needy people in the streets, he ensured a popularity and a following of sorts. Given also the unpopularity of the Prohibition laws, Capone saw himself as a businessman meeting consumer demands: for the frequenters of speakeasies he was a folk hero. Finally, in 1931 he was brought to trial on charges of tax evasion, and after protracted legal battles, was found guilty and sentenced to 10 years in prison. He died in 1947.

Asc	5 21 Cap	
MC	29 43 Lib	
Sun	27 10 Cap	1
Moon	12 05 Ari	3
Mercury	04 11 Cap	12
Venus	13 14 Sgr	12
Mars	29 20 Cnc R	7
Jupiter	08 05 Sco	10
Saturn	19 26 Sgr	12
Uranus	06 44 Sgr	11
Neptune	22 30 Gem R	6
Pluto	13 59 Gem R	6

Al Capone 17 Jan 1899 06:00 New York NY
(Source: MP)

Like Joseph Stalin, Capone expresses the shadow side of Capricorn's concern with power and control. With no external restraints, Capone developed his own corporate framework, allowing him to expand, extend and exploit his illegal business interests to the maximum, and to ruthlessly eliminate any variables – or adversaries – that stood between him and absolute control.

Other prominent Capricorns: Mohammed Ali, Shirley Bassey, Humphrey Bogart, David Bowie, Anton Chekhov, Marlene Dietrich, Marianne Faithfull, Federico Fellini, Benjamin Franklin, William Gladstone, Herman Goering, G I Gurdjieff, J Edgar Hoover, Janis Joplin, Johannes Kepler, Martin Luther King, Rudyard Kipling, David Lynch, Osip Mandelstam, Henry Miller, Isaac Newton, Dolly Parton, Louis Pasteur, Elvis Presley, J Arthur Rank, Albert Schweizer, Joseph Stalin, J R R Tolkien, Mao Tse Tung, Woodrow Wilson.

Air Signs

Gemini

Donald Trump
Robert Maxwell
Bjorn Borg
Karl XII of Sweden
Xaviera Hollander
John Kennedy

Libra

Anita Roddick
Lee Iacocca
Vladmir Putin
Margaret Thatcher
Mahatma Gandhi
Dwight Eisenhower
Alfred Nobel

Aquarius

Oprah Winfrey
Sven-Göran Eriksson
Ronald Reagan
Boris Yeltsin
Thomas Alva Edison
D W Griffith
Sergei Eisenstein

Gemini

21 May – 20 June
Ruling planet: Mercury
Element: Air
Quality: Mutable
Symbol: The Twins

Geminis' major problem is trying to understand why everyone else is not as reasonable as they are. Because Geminis are very reasonable. Geminis rationalize things, have good reasons for their actions, and they do not need to lose their tempers, because they are thoroughly reasonable. They can get on with just about anyone, even unreasonable people, because they are so very, very reasonable. Model specimens of humanity, in other words. So why is it that Geminis, being as reasonable as they are, get involved in such complex entanglements?

It is a curious paradox that such straightforward and reasonable people manage to have such complicated lives. It is related to Geminis' low boredom threshold. The Gemini spirit is a restless one, constantly seeking new forms of diversion. Geminis are ideas people – they think up ideas, are attracted to ideas, and fantasize about things that most ordinary people would not understand.

The Gemini personality is a split one, as the image of the twins suggests. While one half of Gemini is working out budget figures on the lap-top computer screen, the other half of Gemini is busy making transatlantic calls, tying up a major import deal. The two Gemini halves together are driving their open-roofed sports car along the freeway to the airport. There are even Geminis who make love and watch television at the same time.

The agile Gemini mind is capable of coordinating many activities simultaneously, but the Gemini disadvantage is that they prefer to do many things quickly. Haste makes waste, as they say.

It is a haste that extends to many arenas of the Gemini life, especially talking. Gemini President John F Kennedy holds the world record for the fastest ever delivery of a congressional speech, and cetainly critics of former Gemini US President George Bush Senior claim the man talks, not necessarily quickly, but non-stop, precluding any other activity on his part. All talk and no action, as they say. Concerning Cancerian son George W, on his election, the less kindly Washington journalists described him as 'all hat and no cattle'.

Among the profusion of anecdotes concerning the late Gemini media magnate Robert Maxwell is a cautionary tale demonstrating the inherent dangers of the Gemini tendency not to let the second party get a word in edgeways. Robert Maxwell noticed a young man chatting to one of his secretaries. When he came out of his office 15 minutes later the same young man was still there talking. In addition, he was smoking a cigarette, a Maxwell office taboo.

Maxwell: There's no place for time-wasters in this company, young man. What do you earn?

Young man: But I...
Maxwell: I won't have my secretaries bothered by idlers. (*Takes out a roll of notes*)
Young man: But I...
Maxwell: What's your weekly pay?
Young man: But I...
Maxwell: Come on, I haven't got all day.
Young man: But... well... about £100.
(*Maxwell counts out £400 and hands it to the young man.*)
Maxwell: That's a month's salary. Now take your things and go.

Maxwell returned to his office, and the bewildered young man pocketed the cash, picked up a parcel from the secretary's desk, put on his courier-company hat and left the building. There are several versions of this story, and at least one of them is certainly true.

Geminis are quick to learn, have a natural aptitude for languages and enjoy playing with words – naming things, and playing word and picture games. Terrible puns that make sane people wince are a constant source of amusement for Geminis. They have a quick verbal repartee, and mean-spirited Geminis (of which there are few – Geminis are, after all, reasonable people) are adept at cutting down an opponent with a few well-chosen barbed phrases.

As far as the written word is concerned, for Geminis the pen is a good deal mightier than the sword, and does not incite duel-seeking trouble-makers. Geminis loathe physical violence, and are averse to overt displays of sentiment and clingingly emotional scenes. Geminis prefer to remain detached. They like to observe, analyze, criticize and comment. Lots of comment. Geminis have a very highly developed sense of fun and have difficulty in taking things seriously, so that when depression hits Geminis it hits doubly hard. They cannot figure out why they're being unreasonable to themselves.

But even twins fall out from time to time.

Gemini as Leader

Leadership and the dual nature of Gemini make for a lively work environment. One moment fun, inspiring and a friend to all; the next, tyrannical, demanding and ruthless. Gemini leaders do not stand on formality, and first name terms are usually the rule in the Gemini company. Even Robert Maxwell had no objection to being called Captain Bob, so long as the emphasis was on the Captain.

But a casual and informal atmosphere does not mean relaxed. Geminis are hyper-active and expect the same from the rest of the firm. Geminis like ideas, change, new projects, and exploring possibilities, and Gemini leaders, when not talking on the telephone, are good listeners, providing you bear in mind two important provisos:
1. Keep your ideas succinct and to the point.
2. Make them entertaining.

The Gemini tolerance quota, when it comes to sustaining concentration on any one item, is limited to about two minutes. After that your Gemini chairman is either back on the telephone, or is destroying space creatures on a pocket Nintendo Gameboy.

Gemini bosses are unpredictable bosses, and the higher up the ladder of success Geminis get the more unpredictable they become. Geminis do not have 'moods'. Moods are for 'emotionally insecure' people, according to Geminis, so they have phases oscillating from one extreme of behaviour to another. Most people would call these 'moods', but Geminis are too rational.

Should you incur the wrath of a Gemini chairman at any stage, chances are it will be forgotten the next day. There are at least two people inside every Gemini, and although you will get on well with one of them most of the time, you might just irritate the devil out of the other one.

Gemini bosses are full of surprises. The responsibilities of leadership are an uneasy burden, so Geminis will invest their energies into a wide range of activities. Sometimes they are successful, but sometimes they can overstretch themselves. Too many ideas and too little time.

Gemini as Manager

The reason why Gemini managers seem to rush urgently from one task to another, and from one appointment to another, is because they are always a few minutes behind schedule. The Gemini day starts a few minutes behind schedule (as does the Gemini night: Geminis stay up late, they wouldn't want to miss anything, after all), and gets progressively later as the day proceeds. Geminis have a different concept of time to the rest of the world – a Gemini hour runs to about 75 minutes. The 60-minute hour refuses to allow for the diversity of activities it needs to contain. That does not mean a prospective employee should even think about showing up to an interview with a Gemini manager 15 minutes late. Rule Number One regarding Geminis: there are no rules. Geminis are unpredictable, and could even show up five minutes early when you least expect it.

As an interviewee you may leave an interview feeling confused. 'But I never got to say anything,' you will think to yourself. Imagine how confused Geminis feel. 'Another applicant who never said anything,' think Geminis. 'Twenty applicants and all of them as quiet as mice.

So, what are the Gemini criteria for evaluating a suitable candidate? Geminis disdain vulgarity and roughness in manner and dress. Geminis are fashion-conscious, and, as the great labellers of life, will classify people according to their clothes, hairstyle, taste in music, literature and films, and their intellectual ability. Appear intelligent and mentally stimulating and you will win the Gemini seal of approval.

On the one hand, Geminis are uneasy about having 'conflict' people on the team, but on the other, they are acutely aware that often those people – the stubborn types so unlike Geminis – are exactly the kind of people who can sort out the tangles and quandaries that Gemini managers have neither the time nor inclination to unravel.

So the key to winning over Gemini managers is a combination of intelligence and order. If you seem to have control over your own life, and order in your brain – without being overbearing about it – Geminis will be impressed. Order is what they want, but no matter how many systems they introduce, somehow they can never get enough of it. For Geminis 'order' is a good deal. And Geminis can never pass up a good deal.

Gemini as Employee

Geminis are fast-talking, quick-moving, versatile, adaptable and pride themselves on being able to get along with just about anyone. Gemini salespeople could sell tea to China if they stopped talking long enough to take the order.

Geminis have the 'gift of the gab' and like to flaunt it. Air signs are social signs and they thrive on social interaction: Geminis are communicators *par excellence*, especially verbally. It is the process of 'dealing' that stimulates Geminis.

Geminis like to mess about with lots of different things, and may have difficulty concentrating on one task for prolonged periods. A stimulating and varied environment inspires Geminis to great deeds; a less stimulating environment inspires gossip. Geminis love gossip and are excellent companions at conferences, where they can fill you in on all the salacious details concerning inter-office goings-on.

And just where are the Gemini employees when you have an urgent task at hand? Upstairs, downstairs, in reception, chatting with the chairman, or perhaps helping out the peron who has come to fix the photcopier, with rolled up sleeves and screwdriver in hand.

A Profile of the Gemini Manager

The Office

Geminis are restless spirits constantly seeking new diversions, so the office often contains hi-tech do-it-yourself-kit furniture (they like putting things together), easy to move about for when they switch offices. Geminis like moving offices – a different view, a new space, and an unfamiliar environment are all added stimulation for the over-active Gemini brain.

The most important piece of office equipment for Gemini managers is the telephone, together with an array of telephone accessories – the telephone bleeper, the electronic pocket dialler, the pocket electronic phone directory, the mobile telephone, and anything else from Japan or South Korea in communications technology. If you want to know the latest in office gadgetry, check out a Gemini manager's office. (It is rare that you actually find the Gemini manager *in* the office, but at least you can look around.) A 20-button memory is barely adequate for the Gemini office phone because Geminis know a lot of people and have contacts all over the place. A single telephone is totally inadequate – Gemini managers are quite capable of carrying on at least three telephone conversations simultaneously, while dictating letters into a pocket tape-recorder and slaughtering grotesque monstrosities by the thousand on the computer game screen.

The Gemini coffee mug (tea is too sedate for the speeding Gemini brain) is adorned with a whimsical but slightly obscene jokey motif. Invariably there is an entire range of such vessels as visitors parade in and out of the Gemini office with the easy familiarity of a bus station.

The abundance of clocks and time-pieces in the Gemini office does little to instil a sense of scheduled discipline into the lifestyle of Geminis as they live by their own idiosyncratic version of time – bedtime, in particular, is a concept they find hard to grasp. Robert Maxwell had a sleeping arrangement in his office for the 'all-night' sessions – lesser Gemini executives keep a sleeping-bag under the desk.

The Company Car

The convertible. With lots of buttons. If not a convertible, then at least a sporty little number with a sun-roof. Geminis appreciate versatility, and what better than a car that has a roof one day, and no roof the next?

Geminis love gadgets and things to play with, and need some intellectual diversion or distraction during the long motorway journeys, or when stuck in the evening rush. (Geminis rarely get stuck in early morning traffic – they get up too late.) The Gemini company car dashboard is an array of meters, dials, flashing lights, knobs, buttons and switches. The car has at least one sticker, usually more, alluding to the proximity of an approaching vehicle, or the application of the motor horn in case of a flush of sexual arousal ('If you can read this, back off', 'Honk if you're horny', 'Managers do it in their filing cabinet', etc) or any other variation of the motorist's witty epigram currently available from any reputable mail-order firm.

The Business Lunch

If you go out to lunch with a Gemini executive you can bet it will be a lively place, with lots going on, popular with the in-crowd, and where formality is at a minimum and does not interfere with the serious business of talking. You can also bet that your Gemini host knows the waiter, the chef and the owner – having no doubt 'fixed' something for them, either quite literally (the repair of a faulty cash register, a flickering light, an ineffective corkscrew), or metaphorically (a good tip on a horse or providing the name of a reliable contract killer).

The buffet is a favourite of Geminis, where they can walk around and talk to lots of different people. Here the emphasis is on variety – so Geminis can pick at things, play around with mustard and ketchup, and make interesting patterns on the plate. At the buffet, people, socializing and talking, are the main source of attraction, and if the food's good, well, that's OK too. And the best thing about a buffet, is that you do not get stuck at a table with Geminis' major dread, the boring guest. Boring types and emotionally depressed types are just plain unreasonable. 'After all', think Geminis, 'if I want downers I can take a tablet.'

The Gemini Business Venture

It is 'the deal' that stimulates Geminis, and any other form of interpersonal interaction. Wheeling and dealing, recruiting, headhunting, telephone marketing – any enterprise involving conversations, ideas and state-of-the-art forms of communication has added appeal. Any business involving mobile telephones, answering machines, hand-held computers and mail-order firms specializing in Taiwanese low-price electronics and communications merchandise are high on the Gemini priority list. (If you still haven't worked out how the percentage button on your calculator works, consult a Gemini colleague.)

Also publishing: magazines, books, computer games, computer programs, hi-tech and fashion journals. Geminis have a flair for layout and design and a knack of encapsulating a great deal of information in just the right image or slogan. The advertising business is a virtual parade of Gemini talent. Gossip column writer and radio disc-jockey are solid Gemini careers.

Geminis are adept at compiling word games and crossword puzzles: and for those wondering who composes the silly office slogans like 'We never make mistrakes', his name is Bert and he is a Gemini.

Geminis make excellent surgeons; they derive great pleasure from taking things apart and putting them back together again, and the stress of a life and death time limit is an added stimulation.

The Gemini mind is a cornucopia of ideas, constantly seeking stimulation – Geminis have difficulty discerning which ideas to follow through. Restlessly energetic, the principal Gemini flaw is overextending their resources. After all, when there are so many stimulating diversions with which Geminis can engage themselves, how is it possible to concentrate on only one?

The Gemini Natal Chart

Donald Trump

Traditionally, Geminis are the restless spirits of the zodiac, constantly seeking stimulation of the mind. Mental agility means quick thinking, a capacity to wheel and deal, and an ability to establish an instant rapport with just about anyone. On the down side, being a 'fast thinker' can lead to frustration with 'slow thinking' and thoroughness. A restless Gemini entrepreneur might initiate one brilliant idea, but rather than see it through to the end, prefers to move on to the next brilliant idea. How does this kind of mentally agile, fast-thinking, wheeling and dealing temperament fare in the corporate driving seat? Is it a bonus or a bind when it comes to running a company?

Donald Trump, American entrepreneur (Sun in Gemini, Leo Rising and Moon in Sagittarius), reveals many of these traditional Gemini qualities. He made a fortune by finding and buying losing properties and turning them around. In 2001, *Forbes* magazine estimated Trump's net worth to be $1.4 billion. According to Trump it is more like $3.7 billion. His broad range of interests includes real estate, gaming, sports and entertainment. The son of a self-made millionaire in real estate, and the fourth of five children, he grew up in Queens, New York. In 1968 he graduated from business school. In 1975 he made his first purchase of a run-down hotel, and began his history of renovations. Trump's career, however, has had all the ups and downs of a roller coaster ride: in the early 1990s the media had virtually written off Donald Trump. He was over $975 million in debt and nearly bankrupt. Over-extended, his empire began to crumble, leading to massive juggling of properties, buying and selling to stay afloat. The general opinion was that he would never bounce back.

But in 1997, at the age of 51, Trump declared in his third autobiography, *Trump: The Art of the Comeback*, 'I'm a firm believer in learning from adversity.' The media turned out to be wrong. In the 2000s Donald Trump is now stronger, richer and, in his view, wiser than ever before. 'My policy is to learn from the past, focus on the present, and dream about the future… often the worst of times can turn to your advantage – my life is a study of that.'

Trump's New York real-estate empire includes: the world-renowned Fifth Avenue skyscraper, Trump Tower; the majestic Plaza Hotel; the tallest building on the Upper East Side, Trump Palace; the elegant condominiums overlooking Central Park, Trump Parc; the luxury cooperative, Trump Plaza; as well as what is billed as the most important new address in the world, the Trump International Hotel and Tower. Other luxury properties include the Seven Springs Mansion in Bedford, New York, and the Mar-a-Lago Club in Palm Beach, Florida.

In Atlantic City, no less than three world-class casino hotels bear his name: Trump Plaza Hotel and Casino on the Boardwalk, Atlantic City's only four-diamond, four-star hotel; Trump's Castle Casino Resort in the Marina District; and the four-star Trump Taj Mahal, the world's largest and most luxurious hotel/casino ever. The Trump Organization is now the world's largest gaming hotel operator.

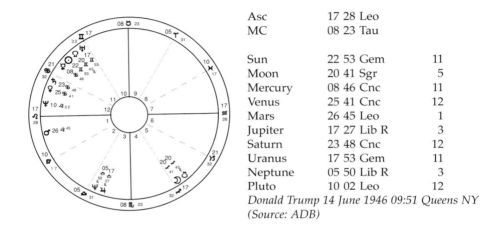

Asc	17 28 Leo	
MC	08 23 Tau	
Sun	22 53 Gem	11
Moon	20 41 Sgr	5
Mercury	08 46 Cnc	11
Venus	25 41 Cnc	12
Mars	26 45 Leo	1
Jupiter	17 27 Lib R	3
Saturn	23 48 Cnc	12
Uranus	17 53 Gem	11
Neptune	05 50 Lib R	3
Pluto	10 02 Leo	12

Donald Trump 14 June 1946 09:51 Queens NY (Source: ADB)

Donald Trump's Gemini Sun is most evident in his media appearances – he is positive, talkative and has a restless glance that seems to seek some new challenge, some new stimulation. The Leo Ascendant is projected into his flamboyant lifestyle: a $30 million yacht, a 118-room palace in Florida and a vast Manhattan apartment; he is 'a conspicuous consumer with a powerful mystique'. He sculpts his own persona with the aid of a press agent and has his name emblazoned on everything he touches. His well-publicized marriages include a 13-year one with Ivana, ending in 1991 with Ivana settling for a $3.5 million home and $14 million. His stormy relationship with Marla Maples ended in May 1997 with a settlement estimated between one and five million dollars.

Moon in Sagittarius points to the gambler, the risk-taker – and in the Fifth House of Leo, the stakes have to be big. It also suggests an impulsively generous spirit. A story published in a collection entitled *The American Dream* illustrates this less-publicized side of Donald Trump's character. Trump's limousine broke down one night as he was coming home from Atlantic City. An unemployed mechanic stopped by and fixed it and refused payment. Next day the mechanic and his wife received flowers and a certified letter saying their mortgage had been paid in full.

Uranus conjunct Sun suggests the sudden disruptive forces that bring about the Himalaya-like ups and downs of Trump's financial and domestic fortunes. What can the chart tell us about his leadership style? That in a typically Gemini way it is uncharacteristic; mercurial and unpredictable. The Gemini style can pay off with huge returns, or collapse like a house of cards, for all to see and wonder at, as we shall see in our next study of the Gemini leader.

Robert Maxwell

'This newspaper will go on investigating injustices, opposing privilege and standing alone among the popular dailies as the voice of the sensible left.'

Robert Maxwell's front page leader for his first issue of *The Daily Mirror*, on 14 July 1984, is strangely reminiscent of W R Hearst's first issue *Examiner* leader and Charles Foster Kane's *Inquirer* with its 'Declaration of Principles'. Maxwell's rise to media magnate, and control of a newspaper empire with political sway, also bears resemblance to the Hearst empire, right down to a financial over-extension which resulted in the collapse of both.

Maxwell's time of birth is unknown. Astrologer Roger Elliot favours a Scorpio Ascendant and a First House Jupiter. Some astrologers use a rectification system based on the exact moment of death, but in Maxwell's case, this too is unknown. All that is known is that he disappeared over the side of the luxury yacht *Lady Ghislaine* in the early hours of 5 November 1991, off Tenerife. He left behind debts estimated at £1.5–£2 billion, and in December 1991 insurance investigators claimed they had sufficient evidence to indicate suicide instead of the alternative theories, which ranged from heart attack or somnambulism to assassination by a government secret service agency.

The rise and rise of Robert Maxwell began when he emigrated to Britain during World War II. 'I was never young. I never had that privilege,' Maxwell claimed. Born Jan Hoch in abject poverty in a small Orthodox Jewish community in the Czech Republic close to the Romanian border, he lived on a diet of potatoes and never owned a pair of shoes till he was seven. He left home at 16 to seek his fortune in Bucharest when war broke out. Most of his family was killed by the Nazis. In the later part of the war he fought for the British and won medals and commendations for heroism. Colleagues described his exploits as reckless; the young Robert Maxwell lived on a razor's edge.

In England he changed his name, and after a variety of jobs, launched successfully into the sale, import and distribution of academic journals, an enterprise facilitated by his knowledge of the central European market, contacts in the Eastern bloc, and a remarkable aptitude for languages.

He set up Pergamon Press in Oxford, an academic publishing company which was to become the cornerstone of his publishing empire. In the 1970s a trade enquiry concluded that Maxwell deliberately suppressed information, was optimistic to the point of recklessness, and provided statements and figures either deceptive or deliberately misleading. He sold the company in the late 1970s, bought it back a few years later, and sold it again in early 1991.

But Maxwell's interests and activities were many: from 1964 to 1970, for example, he was a Labour MP with aspirations to the position of Prime Minister. His political career remained undistinguished, however, and he launched into another enterprise – newspaper publishing. In 1984 Maxwell bought *The Daily Mirror* and reduced staffing from 7000 to 3000, introducing new technology for printing, reporting and administration. It was the first UK daily to use colour. In November 1991 the Maxwell empire consisted of 20,000 employees in 28 countries working in newspapers, magazines, scientific journals, printing plants, databases, book publishing, satellite communications (including 50 per cent MTV Europe) and soccer. Suddenly they were without a boss. Within a month, following revelations of huge debts, the Maxwell empire was no more. Simultaneously the extent of financial ruin became apparent.

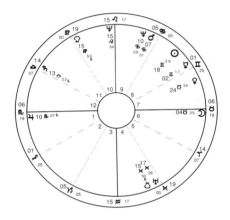

Asc	3 00 Sco	
MC	12 51 Leo	
Sun	18 40 Gem	8
Moon	4 36 Tau	7
Mercury	2 18 Gem	8
Venus	24 05 Tau	7
Mars	7 02 Cnc	9
Jupiter	10 7 Sco R	1
Saturn	13 24 Lib	12
Uranus	17 30 Psc	5
Neptune	15 55 Leo	10
Pluto	10 10 Cnc	9

Robert Maxwell (Jan Hoch) 10 June 1923 16:15
Slatinske Doly Czechoslavakia (Source: RE)

From 'the man who saved the *Mirror*' Maxwell was transformed into 'villain of the century', having transferred £4 million from the Mirror Group pension fund to his various private companies run from an inconspicuous office in Leichtenstein. By December 1991, only a month after his death, companies within Maxwell's three divisions were up for sale, including *The Daily Mirror*, *The European* and *The New York Daily News*.

Maxwell's financial empire consisted of Mirror Group Newspapers, Maxwell Communication Corporation (including Macmillan Inc., Berlitz, and Nimbus Records) and Maxwell's family companies. These included the RM Group, Headington Investments, *The European* and *The New York Daily News*. Maxwell had purchased the near-bankrupt *Daily News* earlier in the year for a token price. He had intended to make it a profitable concern, as he had done with *The Daily Mirror*.

Maxwell was a restless and energetic entrepreneur, quick-thinking, quick-talking and a man courting risk. Money was not his driving force, he confessed; he loved the game. 'He spins off ideas like a Catherine wheel sprays sparks,' said his wife Betty. And he liked to talk. He told Nelson Mandela, when he visited London in 1989: 'I've negotiated with every American president since Eisenhower and every Soviet leader since Stalin.'

Once a week he held lunches with his staff – attendance was obligatory, as was talking. Bluntness was encouraged, and evasive subordinates were fired. Robert Maxwell demanded loyalty. He spoke nine languages fluently, and had a brilliant mind for figures. His zest for dealing was as legendary as his reputation for changing terms continually in his own favour. His word was most definitely not his bond, which infuriated the City establishment. But not enough to stop them lending Maxwell a good deal of money.

His colleagues and associates describe him as a Jekyll and Hyde character who could be generous, flattering, humorous and charming – then transform into a menacing tyrant, contemptuous, vindictive and unforgiving. A man involved in so many enterprises that none of his colleagues could keep track.

A few weeks before his death, another side of Maxwell was revealed. Seymour Hersh in his book *The Samson Option* (1991) claimed that Maxwell was a member of Mossad – the Israeli intelligence unit – and was involved with arms deals on their behalf. Maxwell was juggling so many balls in the air that finally they all fell on top of him. He was a man who had challenged fate so many times, and won, that he was convinced he would never lose.

Björn Borg

In the summer of 1989 Borg's companies crashed. The bailiffs moved in and sold his luxury mansion outside Stockholm, a block of flats and anything else they could claim while he was in Monaco. He also lost custody of his son Robin. In the summer of 1991 authorities in Monaco closed down the last remains of a vast and complicated business empire. It was during this two-year period (1989–91) that the planet Saturn had completed its transit in opposition to Borg's Venus in Cancer and Uranus in Cancer.

At the same time Borg attempted a comeback in tennis. In March 1991 the tennis wunderkind who took five Wimbledon titles from 1976 to 1980 said on British television that he would reclaim the Wimbledon title. Journalists speculated he needed money. The magazine gossip-columnists speculated he needed a break from his Italian wife, ex-pop-star, Loredana. During his 1991 pre-Wimbledon matches in Monte Carlo, Loredana (Virgo) attempted suicide by taking an overdose of tablets. Borg cancelled the tour and returned to Italy. He had lost every match. He withdrew from Wimbledon. Six months earlier Borg himself had been rushed to hospital and had his stomach pumped: he later explained that this was a result of swallowing the incorrect medication. He had inadvertently ingested half a bottle of sedatives. Early reports suggested food poisoning. He denied all reports of attempted suicide – 'a misunderstanding', said Borg.

In November 1991, 298 Swedish creditors claimed 12,690,901:55 kronor – over £1 million – in unpaid debts. Borg's lawyer, Henning Sjöström, said of his client: 'Björn is a magnificent sportsman, but a hopeless businessman.' Sjöström had been extremely active in the Swedish courts during the previous 10 years filing libel suits and actions against a plethora of Swedish magazines, newspapers and journals exploiting Borg's sorrowful private life to increase circulation figures.

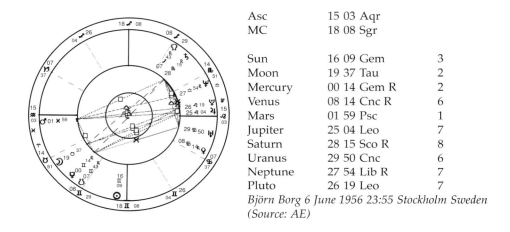

Asc	15 03 Aqr	
MC	18 08 Sgr	
Sun	16 09 Gem	3
Moon	19 37 Tau	2
Mercury	00 14 Gem R	2
Venus	08 14 Cnc R	6
Mars	01 59 Psc	1
Jupiter	25 04 Leo	7
Saturn	28 15 Sco R	8
Uranus	29 50 Cnc	6
Neptune	27 54 Lib R	7
Pluto	26 19 Leo	7

Björn Borg 6 June 1956 23:55 Stockholm Sweden (Source: AE)

Is Björn Borg another example of a Gemini businessman who overstretched himself? His companies included perfumes, aftershave, cosmetics, men's and women's clothing, sportswear and electronics: an overall diversity that might have bewildered even Robert Maxwell. Borg was mainly interested in the fashion companies, and even modelled the menswear himself, but his involvement in all his business ventures was limited. Most of the time they were run by associates, and in the ruins of Borg's business empire, arguments over who deluded whom cropped up frequently in the Swedish law courts.

In Borg's chart, apart from the Gemini Sun, we see a grand square between Mars, Saturn, Mercury and a strong Jupiter–Pluto conjunction. This combination indicates hardships, struggle and tenacity. Mars in the First House represents competitive will – clearly apparent in his sports career, whereas Moon in Taurus also suggests a strong conservative side to an otherwise innovative character (Sun Gemini, Aquarius Ascendant); a conservatism that means holding on to old ways. Sports analysts claimed the reason Borg lost all his 1991 Monte Carlo tennis matches was due to the fact that, when every professional tennis player in the world had gone over to playing with graphite rackets, Borg refused to give up his faithful wooden racket. But Geminis are adaptable. In a new comeback in the Nice Open tennis championships in April 1992, Borg played with a graphite racket.

Björn Borg remarried in the summer of 2002, bought a luxury apartment in central Stockholm, but spends a lot of time abroad for tax purposes. He found a business he can excell at – promoting tennis.

Karl XII of Sweden

King Karl XII is another famous Swede born under the sign of Gemini, who, like Borg, experienced early phenomenal success, and whose downfall has also been attributed to overstretching his resources.

Karl XII's chart shows six planets in the Ninth House, the House of travel and foreign affairs. Karl XII established Sweden as a seventeenth-century world power, creating an empire encompassing Scandinavia and Russia, and stretching as far south as Turkey. Once crowned king he never returned to live in the country of his birth, only visiting Sweden between campaigns.

Following the death of his father, Karl XI, he succeeded to the throne in 1697 when 15 years old. Denmark, Poland and Russia signed an alliance treaty to unite against Sweden and take advantage of the vulnerability of a nation with so youthful a king. Karl XII responded swiftly, however, leading his army to Denmark and forcing the Danes into a humiliating peace. His army of 8000 men then engaged in conflict with the Russian army, which numbered 50,000 soldiers. At a historic battle at Narva (by the Estonian border) in 1700 Karl XII's army, against overwhelming odds, defeated the Russians.

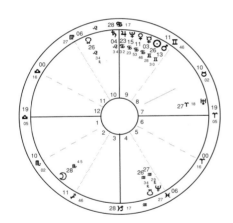

Asc	19 05 Lib	
MC	28 17 Cnc	
Sun	26 28 Gem	9
Moon	28 45 Sco	2
Mercury	03 46 Cnc	9
Venus	11 53 Cnc	9
Mars	13 30 Gem	9
Jupiter	23 32 Cnc	9
Saturn	04 34 Leo	10
Uranus	27 18 Ari	7
Neptune	27 29 Aqr R	4
Pluto	15 23 Cnc	9

Karl XII 17 June 1682 14:05 Stockholm Sweden (Source: JA)

Karl then travelled to Poland and dethroned the disloyal Augustus II. At the age of 20, the same age as Björn Borg when we won his first Wimbledon championship, Karl XII ruled the largest empire in Europe. And just as Borg was the undefeated champion for a further five years, so was Karl XII an undefeated king for the same period.

In 1707 Karl XII was once more engaged in conflict with Russia, almost capturing Peter the Great at Grodno. Following several more victories, his army was finally defeated when the promise of assistance from an army of Cossacks failed to materialize. Karl XII fled to Turkey, where he was imprisoned. He escaped and made his way through Hungary and Germany in 16 days.

Undaunted, in 1716 he rallied his army to attack Norway, and formulated an elaborate scheme of making terms with Russia by surrendering the Baltic states, then conquering Norway, and advancing to Scotland. In Scotland, with the aid of the Jacobite faction, he was to reinstate the House of Stuart on the throne.

He succeeded in purchasing peace with the Tsar, and attacked Norway. During a siege at Halden he was slain by a musket-shot from the Norwegian fortress. He was 36 years old. Björn Borg was also 36 when his financial empire collapsed around him and he left Sweden. Permanently, says Borg.

Historians record that Karl XII was a remarkably versatile monarch: an accomplished mathematician and musician, a linguist and a strategist. But like Borg and Maxwell, Karl XII is an example of a man who overstretched his extraordinary resources. He was brave to the point of recklessness, determined to the point of obstinacy. He endured heat and cold, fatigue and hunger, and shared the same conditions as his men: he was always at the forefront of battle. He is recorded as having an unassailable good temper – always cheerful, yet capable and shrewd in counsel.

Today Karl XII is a hero among Sweden's youth and the populist nationalist movements in Sweden. However, his lofty ambitions proved disastrous for his country. Twenty years of overseas campaigns and expensive wars left Sweden in financial ruin, and the country's brief moment as a world empire passed very rapidly into the history books.

Sweden, Monte Carlo, Fleet Street – heroes do not come cheap.

Xaviera Hollander

The Happy Hooker was published in 1972, when Xaviera Hollander was 29, the year of her Saturn return, marking the beginning of a new career. In this, her autobiography, she describes her rise from independent New York call girl to entrepreneur par excellence, running a prostitution business of unprecedented scale. Her success, she claims, was largely due to only employing girls who, like herself, 'enjoyed the work'.

Her love of sex, she maintains, was a primary motivation in choosing her vocation, transforming what began as a hobby into a lucrative career. Mars in Aries in the Tenth House indicates investing energy, even sexual energy, into one's career. She describes frequent altercations with the law – 'the risks of the business', she maintains. She spent time in prison: the four planets in the Twelfth House further indicate her 'netherworld' realm of activities – socially condemned, ignored, persecuted, yet always there.

Xaviera Hollander is described as a brilliant linguist with a command of seven languages – a Gemini attribute emphasized by the Sun's conjunction with a Gemini Ascendant. The Sun–Saturn conjunction signifies difficulty, restriction and discipline; her career has involved blackmail, bribes and pay-offs, police raids and high expenses. Jupiter, Venus and Pluto in the Second House suggest a love of money, comfort and physical gratification – a true sensualist.

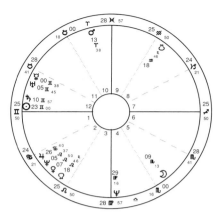

Asc	25 50 Gem	
MC	28 57 PSc	
Sun	23 00 Gem	12
Moon	09 13 Sco	5
Mercury	00 38 Gem	12
Venus	07 50 Leo	2
Mars	13 38 Ari	10
Jupiter	26 40 Cnc	2
Saturn	16 57 Gem	12
Uranus	05 45 Gem	12
Neptune	29 16 Vir	4
Pluto	05 37 Leo	2

Xaviera Hollander 15 June 1943 06:14 Soerabaja Java Indonesia (Source: ADB)

Four planets in Gemini and a Gemini Ascendant are a strong indication of a career involving writing and the communication of ideas, as well as a broad area of interests. In her books Xaviera Hollander expresses her appreciation of ballet, opera and the arts.

Geminis' intellectual curiosity leads to the pursuit of new experiences in order to learn, understand and gain knowledge. Geminis are on a restless quest for knowledge. Xaviera Hollander describes an exhaustive range of sexual activities for some of the most exclusive clients in the world, some extremely bizarre, and although some experiences she cared not to repeat, she said she was always prepared to try anything once.

The success of her book ensured her a new career as a writer, and her later books became the subject matter for Hollywood films.

John Kennedy

Another Gemini famed for a varied sex life is John F Kennedy, whose sexual exploits became, after his death, more publicized than his political activities.

During his period as President his affairs were taboo as far as the media were concerned, but in the licentious decade of the 1970s reports surfaced regarding his amorous escapades. Former lovers who sold their stories to disreputable newspapers claimed that JFK's main attraction was not his sexual prowess, but his sense of fun and good humour. The biographers of Marilyn Monroe note similar comments from her lovers. The Gemini actress

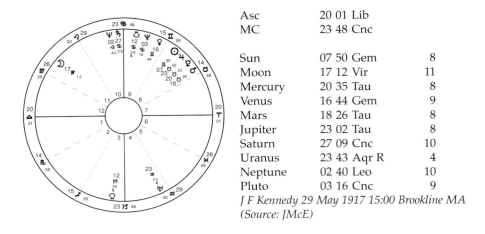

Asc	20 01 Lib	
MC	23 48 Cnc	
Sun	07 50 Gem	8
Moon	17 12 Vir	11
Mercury	20 35 Tau	8
Venus	16 44 Gem	9
Mars	18 26 Tau	8
Jupiter	23 02 Tau	8
Saturn	27 09 Cnc	10
Uranus	23 43 Aqr R	4
Neptune	02 40 Leo	10
Pluto	03 16 Cnc	9

J F Kennedy 29 May 1917 15:00 Brookline MA
(Source: JMcE)

was herself romantically linked to President Kennedy, and died two years after singing 'Happy Birthday Mr President' in New York's Times Square in 1962.

Marriage to Jacqueline Bouvier was not a hindrance to his affairs; though JFK remained emotionally aloof from his involvements, once remarking, 'I'm not the tragic lover type.' Kennedy also famously said: 'What the last administration (Eisenhower, see Libra) did for gold, this one's going to do for sex.'

Kennedy holds the record for the fastest rate of delivery of a public speech, when he was timed at 327 words a minute in 1961. He was a smooth talker as well as a fast talker, and an unusually frank politician who readily admitted his mistakes. He took full responsibility for the 1962 Bay of Pigs fiasco and the Cuban crisis, and was a President with the ability to adapt readily to any given situation. Despite back problems and Addison's disease, Kennedy led an active life – swimming, sailing and outdoor sports, in addition to his celebrated indoor ones.

Former US President Bill Clinton claims that Kennedy was his inspiration, yet why is so much of Kennedy's life and death still shrouded in mystery compared to the 'open book' life of Bill Clinton? As we noted in Bill Clinton's chart (see Leo), important personal planets are placed in the First House of prominence and exposure. Like Clinton, Kennedy's rising sign was Libra. (Also Tony Blair, Vladimir Putin and many other political leaders.) In Kennedy's chart, Mars, Moon and Jupiter are all in the Eighth House, which relates to sex, death and mystery. In Hindu astrology, Mars in the Eighth House is interpreted as violent death

In Dallas, Texas, in November 1963, he was killed by an assassin's bullet. Now, four decades later, the myths and mysteries around the life and death of JFK remain as powerful and compelling as ever.

Other prominent Geminis: Yuri Andropov, George Bush, Joan Collins, Sir Arthur Conan Doyle, Bob Dylan, Sir Anthony Eden, Douglas Fairbanks, Che Guevara, Bob Hope, Henry Kissinger, Marilyn Monroe, Sir Laurence Olivier. Peter the Great, the Marquis de Sade, Jean-Paul Sartre, Queen Victoria, John Wesley, Mary Whitehouse, W B Yeats.

Libra

22 September – 21 October
Ruling planet: Venus
Element: Air
Quality: Cardinal
Symbol: The Scales

Librans are excellent allies in legal contests; they have an uncanny knack of seeing an issue from the position of the opposition. The scales symbol is sometimes said to mean that Librans can never make up their minds about anything, but it is incorrect to describe Librans as indecisive. The methodical reasoning side of Libra likes to weigh an issue on the pair of scales, assessing and evaluating all sides with care before making a commitment.

Librans take decisions seriously, carefully considering the consequences of the choice they are about to make. They have a strong sense of moral order, and live in trepidation of the consequences of a hasty or ill-judged decision.

If they can get away with it, Librans will put off making a decision as long as possible; Librans are ruled by Venus, which opts for the course of least resistance. They like to keep things comfortable and harmonious. However, in times of crisis Librans are most adept at decisive action – Gandhi and Mrs Thatcher, for example. President Carter, on the other hand, had to pay the price of ill-conceived decisiveness – the attempted rescue of US hostages in Iran where two helicopters collided, and the mission was ignominiously aborted.

Once the decision is made, Librans carry it through to the end. Hence the Libran hesitancy to decide: a decision carries with it responsibility, and the acceptance of all its consequences. Librans do not walk away from the consequences but, being an Air sign, instead assimilate them.

Librans might procrastinate. But Librans always decide.

This ability to think oneself into the place of the adversary bodes well for the traditional Libran role of diplomat. As the great harmonizers of life Librans prize fair play and justice and will go to lengthy extremes to ensure it. This attribute is exemplified again in the lives of Mahatma Gandhi, John Lennon and Bob Geldof.

Librans mediate. Bringing two parties together and enabling a transaction satisfactory to both sides is as natural to Librans as adhering to the sanctity of 'fair play'.

The Venus side of Librans appreciates comfort, beauty and harmonious living. It also means that Librans are incurable romantics who invariably function best when in partnership with another.

In the lives of Libran leaders, in politics and in business, one finds wistful stories of romance and heartbreak. Gandhi's 'child marriage' resulted later in a life-time of denying romance. Eisenhower discovered love on the eve of entering a political career, and was prepared to give up politics, but after coercion from the President, sacrificed love in favour of duty. Lee Iacocca refers in his books to the lifelong devotion between him and his wife, and his heartbreak over her untimely death. Alfred Nobel, having devoted his youth to science and invention, in his forties fell in love for the first time with a flower-shop girl 20 years his junior. The romance was never consummated but Nobel continued writing love letters to her until the end of his life.

More recent champions of peace, such as Librans John Lennon and Bob Geldof, have also been closely associated with their respective partners, Yoko Ono and Paula Yates. Libra is the polarity of Aries: where Aries is focused on the 'self', Libra focuses on 'the other' and Libran activities emphasize partnerships.

The Libran preoccupation with harmony is most evident in social situations. When Librans go into their 'social role' routine, with the plastic smile and kind words, it can be difficult to penetrate the mask and know what is really going on. What are Librans really thinking behind the smile and the handshake and the exchange of courtesies? Have we made a good impression, or do they respond to everyone like this?

Fire signs, and perhaps Scorpio, will attempt to provoke a reaction through antagonism, but the only hint of annoyance will be a slight, subtle hardening of the upturned corners of the Libran's smiling lips.

Libra is a Cardinal sign, which indicates that for all their love of harmony, graceful living and their abhorrence of conflict, when Librans get a good idea, they are capable and adamant when putting it into motion.

Libra as Leader

Librans have a strong sense of social order and the status quo; having reached the top, they tend to become detached, maintaining a level of formality. This does not mean that Librans suddenly assume a dictatorial role: far from it – concern for fair play and a convivial working environment remain paramount. But if you take your latest globe-stopping, world-shattering project up to the Libran's tastefully arranged executive suite on the top floor, do not expect a spontaneous outburst of enthusiasm. The scenario will be played along the lines of: 'Yes. We shall consider it. We shall discuss it in full at the Board meeting. We'll get back to you.'

The Libran chairperson is reluctant to use the first person singular, identifying their role so undividedly with the company as a whole that 'we' encompasses the Board, the managing director (usually a belligerent type who does the dirty work and blood-letting that Librans cannot bear to be party to) and the company identity. The 'we' is a good way of avoiding commitment, so that when 'we' get back to you, 'we' can say, 'We've considered the project carefully. We have weighed up the positive and the negative, and we feel that by the end of the year we can let you know one way or the other.'

If you want quick decisions from Libran leaders, arrange a company crisis. They go into action with a vengeance, and, without the luxury of 'time to consider all the possibilities', can achieve miracles. Librans are the reluctant leaders – the burden of decision-making is to them a heavy one. Librans may excel as strong-willed MDs because there is a Chairman who bears the ultimate responsibility. 'Ultimate responsibility' is enough to send most Librans back to their loved ones. An interesting example of a Libran 'we' leader forced to take up the first person singular, and with positive results, is Lee 'I am Chairman of Chrysler Corporation America' Iacocca.

Libra as Manager

Librans are born strategists, and when conflicts erupt, they leap into action as negotiators. Libran managers are adept team coordinators, and enjoy sorting out problems with diplomacy and style.

They are tact personified and can quote chapter and verse of company regulations: when in doubt Libran managers go by the book. In the case of severe staff altercations Libran managers will summon all parties, and after listening to a heated exchange, will say: 'Well, I'm glad we had that little talk. I'm sure we've cleared the air now, haven't we?' – then it's back to work.

A certain Libran manager in the entertainment industry insists that during intense work periods the entire department – usually numbering about 20 – goes out at lunchtime to play soccer for half an hour. This, he says, demonstrates the principles of team work – and gets rid of aggressions that have built up under pressure (particularly, one suspects, any aggression directed at him).

When it comes to promotions, bribes will not win the day with Libran managers. They appreciate sociable and well-behaved people, but rewards are based entirely on merit.

Libra as Employee

Librans take work very seriously and they make it a point of honour to fulfil obligations. They often underestimate their own abilities, and more often than not are ready for promotion long before they themselves think so. Librans need firm but discreet pushing.

Librans are sociable people and it is always a good idea to place them as close as possible to the front of the office, where they will be seen first by any incoming visitors or spies from the top floor. Librans always make a good impression, are well versed in social graces, and know how to say, 'Hello, how are you,' without being offensive or condescending. Nor will Librans sulk, weep or have tantrums in public.

Librans will go to great lengths to avoid a confrontation and will use their social and verbal skills to get their views across, rather than brute force (like Aries or Sagittarius, for example) or anger and emotional scenes (such as Scorpio or Cancerians). However, they are often excellent debaters with aspirations to political or legal careers, which means that Libran employees are very popular choices as the line of communication between colleagues and the different levels of management.

A Profile of the Libra Manager

The Office

There will be a photograph of the wife/husband/partner on the desk and a few meaningful tokens of the loved one discreetly on view. In extreme cases you may find Valentine's Day cards in March, but although Librans have romantic inclinations, they do have some measure of taste and discretion. Evidence of their romantic life may be limited to a vase of flowers – something Librans are also likely to buy for themselves, to satisfy their love of beauty.

Now that you are inside, check out the symmetrical arrangement. If you sit in the Libran's own comfortable yet tastefully designed office chair, you will note opposite two guest chairs, with sufficient space in between so that the Libran can look at one and then the other. After allowing the two guests to present their points of view, the Libran manager can suggest that Mr A is right in some ways, and Ms B correct in others. Can't we come to a compromise?

The furnishings are tasteful, discreet and, apart from planning charts and area maps, at least one wall is kept for decorative purposes, graced with thematic works of art – Japanese prints perhaps, or Samuel Palmer etchings. There will be facilities for making real coffee. Libran managers do not make an issue of it, but to them instant coffee is an abomination, and they will only drink it under duress. Tea-drinking Librans are sticklers for the ritual of traditional afternoon tea-time, requiring a proper bone china teaset.

Any hint of ugliness can be traumatic for a Libran. This means that not only is the office a place of pride and beauty, but also it requires exacting standards of dress code and behaviour for visitors. Sloppy and slovenly dressers, be warned! You may not be openly chastised by your Libran colleague (Librans do not confront), but you may soon find yourself the subject of unkind office gossip.

The Company Car

Lee Iacocca, Libran manager par excellence, claimed he was part of the team that designed the perfect car: 'We wanted to develop a car that you could drive to the country club on Friday night, to the drag strip on Saturday, and to church on Sunday.' He described it as 'feline in nature'. Originally called the Cougar, then the Torino, and finally the Mustang, it began to run off the production lines in 1964. According to the ad agency, 'it had the excitement of wide open spaces and was American as all-hell,' and its huge success, says Iacocca, was due to the fact that it looked expensive but was reasonably priced. Librans appreciate a good deal.

Nearly 40 years later affordable 'fantasy-fulfilment' compromise cars are being produced by the Japanese – a country attributed to the sign of Libra, as it happens. A sporty looking Mazda, the surrogate 4-seater Porsche-look-alike Toyota, or the latest up-market Honda, are cars with strong Libran appeal. Just the kind of automobile to park outside the winebar on Friday night, drive down to the coast on Saturday, and to take to the local fleamarket on Sunday.

The Business Lunch

It may take a while before you end up going somewhere. These sorts of decision cannot be rushed. Will it be a discreetly elegant place with a refined, even romantic, ambience, or would the gypsy violinist who sometimes plays there be too passionately over the top? Maybe my guest will misconstrue my choice and think I am making sexual overtures...

What about Bertorelli's, the Italian place renowned for its Tuscan specialities? Or the Japanese sushi bar, or...

Gracious living and gracious eating are the hallmarks of Librans, who will go to considerable lengths to ensure that the place is right, and that, if the business meeting is intended to be productive, the ambience is conducive to the transaction.

The Libra Business Venture

Librans favour enterprises with aesthetic qualities, or that are stimulating for the mind: design, layout, occupations related to the arts, publishing, film, or music. Legal and political careers appeal to the Libran sense of justice and the love of a good debate. Librans are 'team people' who enjoy the social aspects of working within a company. The independent Libran career usually involves much social interaction: public relations, consultancy firms or advisory councils. Librans delight in being consulted. It is the nearest thing to flirting that they can indulge in without endangering their love life.

The Libra Natal Chart

Anita Roddick

An innate feeling for beauty, harmony and a strong sense of social justice characterize the Libran personality. They are the attributes that are seen in Body Shop, in both the organization and in any of the 800 retail outlets around the world. They are also strongly apparent in the natal chart of Body Shop founder, Anita Roddick.

Anita Roddick opened the first Body Shop in Brighton in 1976. Today Body Shop is a multinational empire represented in over 40 countries, with 2000 employees and a turnover of about £350 million per annum. Consequently Roddick is one of Great Britain's wealthiest businesswomen and was once the country's most successful businesswoman. In the 1990s the Body Shop image began to fade and shares fell, but new strategies and a general facelift are bringing Body Shop in tune with the twenty-first century. Roddick claims that all her business strategies are based on intuition – not leaving events to chance, but arriving at decisions spontaneously following a series of events and considerations that independently may not seem at all significant.

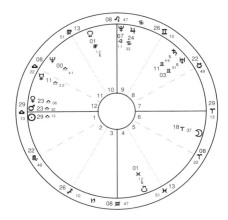

Sun	29 13 Lib
Moon	18 37 Ari
Mercury	11 32 Lib
Venus	23 06 Lib
Mars	23 32 Lib
Jupiter	24 33 Cnc
Saturn	11 49 Gem R
Uranus	03 51 Gem R
Neptune	00 41 Lib
Pluto	07 11 Leo

Anita Roddick 23 Oct 1942 Littlehampton UK (Time unknown)

If that 'go with it' spontaneity sounds more like Aries than Libra (Librans, remember, can spend time agonizing over which restaurant to go for lunch), Anita Roddick's chart is a significant contrast between Sun, Mercury, Venus, Mars and Neptune all in Libra, in opposition to Moon in Aries. Where Moon is about instinctive drives and 'gut-feelings', Aries is the celebration of such feelings as 'all mine – and I'll do it no matter what anyone says!'

The chart is a Solar Chart, cast at sunrise for lack of an official accurate time of birth, but even without the Rising Sign and House placements, it is a revealing and powerful chart. The Aries Moon polarizing all that Libran energy suggests a personality who takes her own strongly felt convictions and is able to integrate them into the sphere of social action.

'Those working in the business world are interested only in profit,' says Anita Roddick. 'They don't realize that there are other goals as important or more important. They don't understand the effects a company has for society, the environment or its employees.' She describes the company as a protest movement against the cosmetic industry. 'The traditional cosmetic industry is a form of racism exploiting women's anxieties. We sell products people need without deceiving them into believing they can work miracles.'

Anita Roddick's strong personal convictions extend to her management style and the ideology behind the company. 'We hire people for more than just a job,' she says. 'We are trying to create a sense of community in the stores themselves. This is easier said than done when you have 2000 people in the workplace, which we have at our International Headquarters in Littlehampton. To create a sense of community, we bring in all different age groups: parents and grandkids and kids can all work together in The Body Shop.'

The head office community includes a child development centre attached to the workplace, offers paternity and maternity leave, and includes a project called the Love Program. This may sound like the Libran idea of a dating agency; in fact it is an initiative which allows any member of Body Shop staff to use £100 a year on any skill that has nothing to do with the business, 'whether it's studying fear of spiders or tightrope walking or whatever.' Body Shop also runs a community volunteer programme, where each department participates. So many activities in one place, says Anita Roddick, makes headquarters a creative place; there is very much a carnival atmosphere.

The company's Mission Statement opens with: '(we) dedicate our business to the pursuit of social and environmental change.' 'Why should a skin and hair care company get involved in political activism anyway?' asks Anita Roddick. 'As an international businesswoman, political awareness and activism must be woven into the fabric of business – to do otherwise is to be not merely an ostrich, but criminally irresponsible.' Her first sense of moral outrage came at the age of ten, she says, when she began reading about the Holocaust. She began her career teaching, then travelled, finally taking a job at the United Nations in Geneva, working in the women's rights division of the International Labour Organization.

'The Body Shop and I have always been closely identified in the public mind. Undoubtedly, because it is impossible to separate the company values from my own personal values, and the issues that I care passionately about – social responsibility, respect for human rights, the environment and animal protection, and an absolute belief in community trade.'

In *Business As Unusual* (2000) she writes: 'Spirituality in business is not about religious ideas but rooted in the concrete action of people whose sense of caring stands beyond themselves.' Business leaders should shift their emphasis to the human spirit, argues Anita Roddick, and suggests that a good way of running a business is to view it as not just a job 'but as an honourable livelihood, where you can, by using your imagination, develop the human spirit'. She concludes: 'I believe in businesses where you engage in creative thinking, and where you form some of your deepest relationships. If it isn't about the production of the human spirit, we are in big trouble.'

Lee Iacocca

Iacocca, who became the hero of American management in the 1980s, maintained that he never had aspirations of leading a company. He was quite content to work as the behind-the-scenes strategist. His claims are borne out by his natal chart: Sun and Mercury in Libra; a Virgo Ascendant, the sign of the backroom analyst; and Moon in Taurus, giving him an instinctive knack of getting down to basics.

He devoted his working life to the Ford automobile company in Detroit, fully aware of the company's dynastic structure. A Ford heir would always run Ford. Iacocca, son of an Italian immigrant, rose to the position of President under the chairmanship of the company founder's grandson, Henry Ford II, who fired Iacocca in 1978. Iacocca, 55 years old, was out of a job.

After several months recovering from the shock – according to his memoirs, Iacocca's only shortcoming at Ford was working too hard – he was offered a job at Chrysler. On the same day that he was named as the company's new President, the Chrysler Corporation reported the biggest quarterly loss in its history. In *Iacocca – an Autobiography*, published in 1984, Iacocca describes the setbacks and crises over a three-year period which almost finished Chrysler, through to the stage when the company's fortunes reversed. Chrysler made profits, not losses, was cited as a model automobile plant and Lee Iacocca was hailed a national hero.

What was Iacocca's management make-up? Shrewd judgement, intellectual analysis and compromise (Libra), precision analysis and fault detecting (Virgo) and an instinctive realism (Taurus). In addition there are three planets in the Second House, which relates to money issues, including Saturn, which means money is hard work and is something to be taken seriously.

In his autobiography and his follow-up book, *Talking Straight* (1988), Iacocca emphasizes communications, strategy and people. 'Business operations can be reduced to three words: people, product and profits. People come first. Unless you've got a good team you can't do much with the other two.' At Ford Iacocca instigated a quarterly review system, asking key people certain questions: What are your objectives for the next 90 days? What are your plans, your priorities, your hopes? How do you intend to achieve them? This system makes employees accountable to themselves, makes each manager consider his own goals, and is an effective way to remind people not to lose sight of their dreams. And dreams and aspirations – for all the pragmatic indications of Iacocca's chart – are a strong component of his astrological chart. Venus and Neptune are conjunct in the Twelfth House – the house of empathy, dreams and visions.

In his various leadership roles, Iacocca has each manager meet with their superior to review the past quarter's achievements, and to outline the goals for the next three months. Then they are put down in writing. 'Putting your thoughts on paper forces you to get down to specifics,' he writes. 'It's harder to deceive yourself – or anybody else.' The system ensures that talent does not get passed over; nor do time-wasters have a chance to hide away. But most important is that quarterly reviews make the manager and the boss talk to each other.

With both Sun and Mercury in Libra, Iacocca shows Libran talent for negotiation, fair play, listening to the other side, and compromise. 'A good manager needs to listen at least as much as he talks. Too many people fail to realize that real communication goes in both directions.' According to Iacocca: 'A major reason capable people fail to advance is that they don't work well with their colleagues.' Over and over Iacocca refers to the importance of diplomacy and tact – people who do not get along with people, no matter how bright, hard-working or creative they may be, have no place in the Iacocca world of management.

Asc	13 48 Vir	
MC	11 08 Gem	
Sun	21 41 Lib	2
Moon	20 11 Tau	9
Mercury	14 05 Lib	2
Venus	08 43 Vir	12
Mars	28 40 Aqr	6
Jupiter	16 39 Sgr	4
Saturn	03 31 Sco	2
Uranus	18 18 Psc R	7
Neptune	22 07 Leo	12
Pluto	13 33 Cnc R	10

Lee Iacocca 15 Oct 1924 17:00 Le Highton PA (Source: AA)

'Why have I succeeded?' asks Iacocca of himself, admitting that he has by-passed managers more clever and more knowledgeable about the automobile industry. 'Because I'm tough? You don't succeed very long by kicking people around. You've got to know how to talk to them, plain and simple... management is nothing more than motivating other people. The only way you can motivate other people is to communicate with them.'

Iacocca reveals his Libran style of diplomacy when having to deal with Chrysler's 'uninformed and uninterested' board of directors. 'When I became Chairman I moved in on the Board members very gradually. I wasn't crazy enough to point my finger at a group that had just hired me and tell them: "It's your fault." But once or twice I did ask the Board, as politely as I could: "How did management ever get their plans past such a distinguished group of businessmen?"' Iacocca fired 33 of 35 vice-presidents over a three-year period.

Iacocca's priority at Chrysler was to curb the animosity between head office and the dealers, and establish good relations between them. 'Dealing with customers takes knowledge, time and patience – if salespeople don't have that they should look for another line of work.' He describes a good manager as someone who can bring all the information together, set up a timetable and act.

Another innovation based on the Iacocca concept of 'fair play' was when, against fierce opposition, he invited a union official to sit on the board of directors – the first time a major US corporation board had had a labour representative.

'My management style has always been pretty conservative. Whenever I've taken risks it's been after satisfying myself that the research and the market studies supported my instincts. I may act on intuition – but only if my hunches are supported by the facts.'

He describes himself as 'a very private person', and in spite of the offers has no intention of running for public office.

Why was Iacocca's book a bestseller? Does it offer sound management advice? Does Iacocca reveal the key to success? The magic recipe? How to turn failure into triumph? Or is it a collection of clichés and truisms?

What Iacocca provides is a good story. Virtue, hard work and reason triumph over 'a mad despot', which was Iacocca's description of Henry Ford II. Iacocca was the voice of reason against the injustice of tyranny.

But what if Iacocca had lost and Chrysler sunk? Chrysler's survival was solely dependent on a Congress loan. Chrysler got the loan by just a few votes – it could easily have gone the other way. History is written by the winners.

The largely self-penned *Iacocca – an Autobiography* (co-writer Willam Novak) legend adds fuel to the great myth that we are in control of our own destiny, that we can shape order from the chaos that surrounds us, that justice will prevail. But beyond the myth lie the fates. They are the three Norns of Nordic legend, who spin out our frail human destiny on their spinning wheels, as blind as the Libran motif of justice. Libra herself carries a sword in one hand and a pair of scales in the other. Her eyes are blindfolded.

Vladimir Putin

Vladimir Putin, a virtually unknown security chief, was appointed Russian Prime Minister by President Boris Yeltsin on 8 September 1999. In his inauguration speech he vowed to wipe out the rebels of Chechnya. He swore he would stop terrorists shortly after Russia launched its Chechen war in September 1999. Putin was appointed President in March 2000, and although he made attempts to Westernize a crumbling economy, it was his stand against Chechen separatists that boosted his career. In early 2004 his presidential rating stood at an unprecedented 54 per cent.

In October 2002 Putin's stand on the Chechen crisis took a dire turn for the worse: about 800 Moscow theatre-goers were held hostage by Chechen separatists. For Russian President Vladimir Putin it was a 'worst possible scenario'. For three days the world media focused on how Putin would handle the crisis. One hundred and twenty civilians died, mainly from gas used by the Russian special forces, yet Putin emerged – once again – a hero.

For many in the West Putin's popularity may be somewhat difficult to fathom. The poker-faced ex-KGB spy is considered to be a pragmatist, and has demonstrated that he is aware of the scale of the problems facing Russian society and the Russian economy. He seems adamant about fighting corruption. His origins are humble; born to factory workers in St Petersburg (then Leningrad), Putin grew up in a communal apartment shared by several families. Yet to the outsider, the impression given by Putin is remarkably similar to that of British Prime Minister, Tony Blair. Who is the real Vladimir Putin? Who is the person behind the facade?

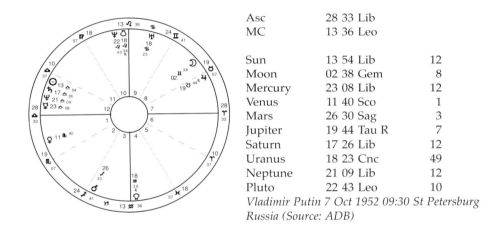

Asc	28 33 Lib	
MC	13 36 Leo	
Sun	13 54 Lib	12
Moon	02 38 Gem	8
Mercury	23 08 Lib	12
Venus	11 40 Sco	1
Mars	26 30 Sag	3
Jupiter	19 44 Tau R	7
Saturn	17 26 Lib	12
Uranus	18 23 Cnc	49
Neptune	21 09 Lib	12
Pluto	22 43 Leo	10

Vladimir Putin 7 Oct 1952 09:30 St Petersburg Russia (Source: ADB)

Blair and Putin are roughly the same age, and both their Sun-signs are ruled by Venus (Taurus and Libra, respectively). Astrologically, however, what is most revealing for both personalities is the strong Twelfth House (see the chart of Tony Blair, given under Taurus, for a more detailed analysis). The Twelfth House is the House of secrets, the hidden agenda, and hidden insecurities. It is a House well-suited to the master spy and the stage actor; Twelfth House predominance is found in the charts of performers ranging from Madonna Ciccione to Orson Welles and Mata Hari. Sun, Mercury, Neptune and Saturn are placed in the Twelfth House of Putin's chart.

Putin's organizing and analytical skills are undeniable. He may lack the rhetorical gifts of Tony Blair, but there is a chilling similarity to the television broadcasts that unified their respective nations: Putin's 'Forgive us!' following the Moscow theatre siege, and Blair's 'Princess of Hearts' eulogy after the death of Princess Diana.

Putin graduated from university in 1975 with a degree in civil law, then spent 15 years as a KGB agent, mainly based in East Germany. US intelligence observers claim Putin was assigned to industrial espionage missions, primarily to infiltrate IBM, the computer corporation. In 1990 he returned to St Petersburg, and as deputy mayor became involved with Western business people and investors in a more official capacity.

Details of Putin's biography are sketchy, yet the consensus is that he is intelligent and astute. He was quick to earn the trust of his superiors and be entrusted with highly sensitive assignments. His success in politics is attributed to his psychological acuteness, and an ability to manipulate behind the scenes. In 1996 he was recruited by the Kremlin, and became head of the FSB (Federal Security Bureau), a successor to the KGB.

Like Blair in his early years as Prime Minister, Putin finds most popularity among young people, the urban population and the educated. His reputation for toughness and resourcefulness was enhanced following the Moscow theatre siege. His handling of the siege and the Chechen issue at large, and his declaration for 'justice at all costs', has earned him the epithet of 'iron man'.

Margaret Thatcher

A Libra–Scorpio combination intensifies the Libran quest for 'justice at all costs', as is exemplified in the charts of Mahatma Gandhi and Margaret Thatcher, two Sun in Libra natives with a Scorpio Ascendant. Margaret Thatcher's favourite expression, 'There is no alternative...', suggests that alternatives were at least considered before they were rejected. This is Libra. The ruthlessness with which a course of action is pursued (alternatives having been rejected) is Scorpio. Once a decision is made, then it is 'to the death'. Rather like the 'harsh medicine' to be swallowed by the British population in order to stimulate an ailing economy.

The Soviet Defence Military journal *Red Star* described Margaret Thatcher in January 1976 as 'the Iron Lady attempting to revive the Cold War'. This was in reply to Margaret Thatcher's speech in which she claimed: 'The Russians are bent on world dominance... the Russians put guns before butter.'

On 31 January 1976, speaking to her constituents in Finchley, she said: 'Ladies and gentlemen, I stand before you tonight in my green chiffon evening gown, my face softly made up, my fair hair gently waved... the Iron Lady of the Western world. Me? A Cold War warrior? Well, yes – if that is how they wish to interpret my defence of values and freedoms fundamental to our way of life.'

Librans are reputedly indecisive but there was little question of hesitation when Margaret Thatcher retaliated against the Argentinian junta to reclaim Britain's furthest outpost, the Falkland Islands. When it came to Britain, and any injustices against Britain, Margaret Thatcher was resolute. A resolve so adamant that compromise was not a consideration, even regarding the European Common Market. By the 1990s it was a resolve that even the Conservative Party viewed as outdated, and after more than a decade as Britain's 'Iron Lady', Margaret Thatcher was forced to step aside.

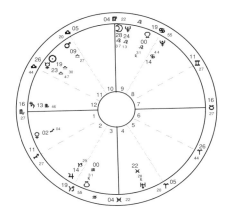

Asc	16 27 Sco	
MC	04 22 Vir	
Sun	19 30 Lib	11
Moon	28 37 Leo	9
Mercury	23 47 Lib	11
Venus	02 04 Sgr	1
Mars	09 27 Lib	11
Jupiter	14 29 Cap	2
Saturn	13 46 Sco	12
Uranus	22 28 Psc R	4
Neptune	24 13 Leo	9
Pluto	14 44 Cnc	8

Margaret Thatcher 13 Oct 1925 09:00 Grantham UK (Source: JK)

In addition to the Libra–Scorpio combination, the former Prime Minister's chart includes Moon in Leo, the sign of the monarch. It is interesting that the British press made much of her so-called attempts to 'out-queen the Queen'. Neptune rules dreams, visions and illusions (as well as delusions) and it is in conjunct to the Leo Moon, in the Ninth House – the House of expansion. Some astrologers might argue that Margaret Thatcher considered herself to be of the stuff of which monarchs are made.

Mahatma Gandhi

Gandhi, who spent a lifetime advocating peace and non-violent revolution, was killed by an assassin's bullet in 1948. Through his efforts his goal was realized: the independence of India.

He married according to Hindu custom at the age of 13, went to England to study law at 18, and in 1893, aged 23, arrived in South Africa, where he worked as a lawyer for 21 years, becoming a leader of the South African Indian community. He was 37 when he took the Hindu vow of *brahma-charya* – a pledge of celibacy which was to allow him to pursue political and religious goals, freed from the entanglements of personal relationships. His role as political and religious leader began in his mid-forties, after his return to India in 1915. He rejected all Western influences, choosing a simple village life. He adopted the spinning wheel as a symbol of tradition and self-sufficiency, and encouraged villagers to spin and weave cloth instead of buying imported fabrics.

His political philosophy was based on the Hindu concept of *ahimsa* – a philosophy of dynamic harmlessness. In a series of confrontations with the occupying British forces Gandhi organized mass demonstrations of passive resistance. In spite of provocation from the British, including the massacre of unarmed civilians in Amritsar, Gandhi remained adamant. Violence was to be opposed only by passive resistance.

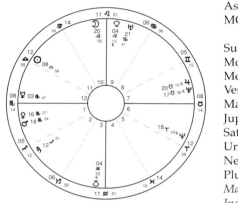

Asc	08 14 Sco	
MC	11 21 Leo	
Sun	08 56 Lib	11
Moon	20 16 Leo	10
Mercury	03 47 Sco	12
Venus	16 27 Sco	1
Mars	18 24 Sco	1
Jupiter	20 10 Tau R	7
Saturn	12 21 Sgr	2
Uranus	21 41 Cnc	9
Neptune	18 24 Ari R	6
Pluto	17 39 Tau R	7

Mahatma Gandhi 2 Oct 1869 07:33 Porbandar India (Source: JK)

He was gaoled on several occasions, and each time began a hunger strike. The status of Gandhi, the 'Mahatma', was so influential throughout the sub-continent that the British authorities were forced to acquiesce. In 1947 India was granted independence.

Gandhi's life exemplifies the Libran qualities of achievement through non-aggressive means, demonstrating that conflicts can be won without arms and violence. Gandhi's aim in his provocative programme of passive resistance was to force the British authorities to open up negotiations. Disagreements can be resolved by people talking to each other, he reasoned, without taking to arms.

After a lifetime of campaigning for peace, and in the midst of negotiations attempting to resolve differences between Hindus and Muslims, Gandhi was shot by a Hindu extremist.

Libra is the sign of peace and reconciliation, which is so strongly expressed in Gandhi's life and actions. Yet his chart is strongly affected by Scorpio. In addition to a Scorpio Ascendant, Gandhi's chart shows three personal planets in Scorpio – Mercury, Venus and Mars. These Scorpio influences suggest an intensity and strength of will, as well as the passion with which he was devoted to the cause of *ahimsa* – the philosophy of non-violent action. In contrast to Libra, Scorpio confronts adversity head-on, and this combination of Libran diplomacy and Scorpio perseverance is foremost in Gandhi's chart.

In addition, the tight conjunction of Mars and Venus in the First House brings these two contrasting qualities to prominence: Venus, which rules Libra, as the agent of harmony and compromise; and Mars, which rules Scorpio, as the agent of conflict and battle.

Dwight Eisenhower

Decision-making is the millstone around every Libran's neck, and Eisenhower almost lost out on D-Day by hesitating in a crucial dilemma. In June 1944, while the Allied forces waited to launch an assault on the German army, weather conditions deteriorated rapidly. Finally he decided: 'No matter what the weather we have to go ahead. Waiting any longer could be even more dangerous. Let's move it!'

According to another Libran strategist, Lee Iacocca, the same lesson applies in corporate life. There is a certain point when a leader must decide. That is why risk-taking is essential. A leader takes a chance and corrects any mistakes along the way. Eisenhower's chart reveals seven Air planets – four of them in Libra, including the Moon. The Ascending sign is Virgo – the sign of the analyst.

Eisenhower was chief military assistant to General MacArthur in the Philippines, and in 1942 assumed command of the Allied forces for the amphibious assault on French North Africa. He had had no former experience of high

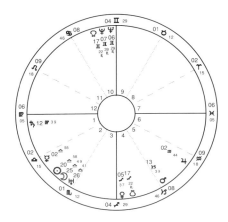

Asc	06 05 Vir	
MC	04 29 Gem	
Sun	20 58 Lib	2
Moon	25 49 Lib	2
Mercury	02 55 Lib	2
Venus	05 37 Sgr	4
Mars	13 39 Cap	5
Jupiter	02 44 Aqr	5
Saturn	12 39 Vir	1
Uranus	26 41 Lib	2
Neptune	06 29 Gem R	10
Pluto	07 39 Gem R	10

Dwight Eisenhower 14 Oct 1890 03:00 Denison TX (Source: JK)

command – but his reputation for perception and assimilation, and his ability to turn strategic military theory into practical action, ensured a meteoric rise.

Colleagues described his genius for smoothly coordinating the activities of an Allied staff, which, according to many, was his most valuable contribution to the war effort. After the success of the North African campaign, he became supreme commander for the 1944 cross-channel invasion at Dunkerque. There, despite adverse weather, he went ahead.

Historians describe his acute appreciation of the psychology of the US forces, as well as that of the enemy. For Librans, decision-making is a thorough process whereby one must see oneself as the opposition in order to understand an issue from both sides. However, Eisenhower's reticence and reluctance to push on beyond the Elbe and occupy Berlin – together with the hasty dismantling of the Anglo-American armies – resulted in Soviet control of Eastern Europe.

General Eisenhower was made supreme commander of the NATO land forces (established 1950), and the popularity he gained in Europe led him to the US presidential nomination and election in the 1952 ballot. He was re-elected for a second term in 1956. In spite of his political inexperience Eisenhower was a popular President, mainly due to his Libran qualities: 'sincerity, integrity and a flair for conciliation'.

Alfred Nobel

Nobel invented dynamite in 1866. He also invented blasting-jelly and several kinds of smokeless powder. He set up a factory in Bofors, Sweden, experimenting with steel armour-plating and establishing one of the world's major arms manufacturing industries. He bequeathed his enormous fortune to awarding annual prizes in the fields of physics, chemistry, medicine, economics, literature and peace. He stipulated that they were to be awarded to individuals who had done most for the well-being of mankind in their particular fields. The Nobel Prize was to make Sweden renowned throughout the world. The prizes are presented to their recipients by the Swedish king in Stockholm each December. His contemporaries referred to Nobel as 'the man no one knew': he avoided publicity and self-promotion of any kind.

In his youth, Nobel's ambition was to be a writer. He wrote poetry and drama, and his early play *Nemesis* was a desperate tirade against the eternal injustice in this world and the next. His close friend and the executor of his will, Ragnar Sohlman, described Nobel as 'a wind-driven swallow flying from one subject to another'. He loved to explore the possibilities of language one day, then conduct experiments with cicadas in a laboratory the next. He was a man obsessed with discovery, spending up to 18 hours a day in his laboratory, straining his already delicate health. He was generous to the needy, and regarded as considerate and compassionate by his employees, although he remained impersonal and aloof.

Nobel was greatly interested in the peace movement – to a friend he confided

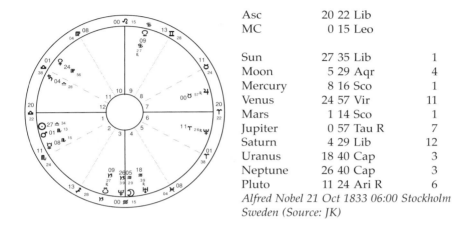

Asc	20 22 Lib	
MC	0 15 Leo	
Sun	27 35 Lib	1
Moon	5 29 Aqr	4
Mercury	8 16 Sco	1
Venus	24 57 Vir	11
Mars	1 14 Sco	1
Jupiter	0 57 Tau R	7
Saturn	4 29 Lib	12
Uranus	18 40 Cap	3
Neptune	26 40 Cap	3
Pluto	11 24 Ari R	6

Alfred Nobel 21 Oct 1833 06:00 Stockholm Sweden (Source: JK)

that his 'invention of destruction and devastation was so terrible that it would bring about world peace far more effectively than all the peace congresses'.

Just as Mahatma Gandhi took a vow of celibacy, Nobel remained a bachelor, maintaining that marriage would distract him. But at 43 he fell in love with a 20-year-old girl whom he met in a flower shop. In the 218 letters he wrote to Sophie Hess over the remaining 20 years of his life, he extolled her beauty, her youth, and her love of pleasure. It was a confused and desperate love story, and in his old age Nobel declined into depression, proclaiming contempt for mankind. In his final will he wrote that man was doomed to annihilation. By creating his fund he hoped to gain understanding for his life's work, and he wanted to reward those who contributed something new in the future with the same humanitarian motive as himself.

Nobel's chart, with Libran Sun, Saturn and Ascendant, embodies the Libran values of peace, fair play and romance, values which seem so at odds with the man who invented dynamite, and in contrast to a man who would descend into dark misanthropy. But the combination of Moon (square Jupiter, Mars and Midheaven) together with Uranus in Aquarius, suggest the detachment and originality of the creative inventor – of a personality where intellectual prowess would lead to personal isolation.

Other prominent Librans: John le Carré, Jimmy Carter, Alistair Crowley, Sara Ferguson, Marshal Foch, Bob Geldof, Graham Greene, Thor Heyerdahl, Heinrich Himmler, Buster Keaton, John Lennon, Martin Luther, Arthur Miller, Horatio Nelson, Friedrich Nietzsche, Eugene O'Neill, Jacques Tati, Oscar Wilde.

Aquarius

21 January – 19 February
Ruling planet: Uranus
Element: Air
Quality: Fixed
Symbol: The Water-bearer

An astrologer once summed up Aquarian attributes for the benefit of Russian President, Boris Yeltsin. Aquarians are humanitarian, believe in the brotherhood of mankind, are averse to routine, and experience periods of intense activity followed by periods of lethargy. President Yeltsin concurred.

Aquarians are idealists, often with many talents but little ambition when it comes to the established view of material success. They work best with 'causes' or 'ideas'; Aquarians live in a curious world of ideals and abstracts, and would like to impose their very sensible world vision upon us all.

However, the world consists of many individuals, and individuals are troublemakers. It is these egocentric individuals who have sabotaged the magnificent Aquarian ideals for a sensible world.

Although Aquarians favour groups, associations, communal living and a broad spectrum of friends, they are strongly individualistic types themselves, who frequently gain the reputation for being eccentric, odd or just plain peculiar. As Air signs Aquarians are reasoning people, but as a Uranian Air sign, Aquarian reasoning is original, sometimes provocative, sometimes outrageous.

Aquarians are scientific by nature, and even if they have never studied nuclear physics or biochemistry, they have an insatiable hunger for knowledge, and a strong yearning to find out what makes things tick. For Aquarians the world is a laboratory of objects and subjects awaiting dissection. The Aquarian's favourite subject is the human being.

Aquarians are endlessly amused by the follies of human beings, and may tend toward a self-congratulatory pose that suggests aloofness, in the knowledge that they are sensible and reasonable while everyone else is a bit 'off'. Aquarians derive hours of intellectual stimulation by assessing and quantifying just what it is about individuals that makes them less sensible and less reasonable than themselves. Some turn to astrology, which for Aquarians is a respected system for qualifying aspects of human behaviour and the human personality. Others turn to group therapy sessions.

Even a conversation with a single Aquarian (unusual in itself as Aquarians move about in groups) resembles a group therapy session, where during the course of the discussion you gradually come to realize you are being assessed. Providing you do not get too emotional or passionate about any given subject you might pass the Aquarian 'sensible human being' seal of approval. If not, Aquarians will help you attain the status of 'sensible human' by recommending the right books, films and television programmes.

Aquarians are not too clever for their own good, but they just might be too clever for everyone else's. They can excel in any chosen field, but frequently they decline to choose. They need motivation, and the motivations need to be universal. For Aquarians a business enterprise is a form of scientific experiment. As a gathering of different personalities is a form of experiment in the variety of human responses in a given situation, a business enterprise provides a first class opportunity for observing causes and effects.

Aquarians are innovators: inventive, original, bursting with new ideas, and itching to break social conventions. They have little concern for material success, and business ventures are either of an intellectually stimulating nature, or serve a higher cause – whether it is an ideology or some scheme to help a disadvantaged group or the community at large. Many Aquarians become academics, protected from reality, and free in their pursuit of knowledge.

Aquarians seem detached – even the Aquarian in love creates an idealized world of romance. For the most part Aquarians regard a dispassionate exterior as a case of mind over matter – the triumph of the 'higher self' over the 'lower self'.

Aquarians do not get angry: they are too knowledgeable and sensible to lose control and expose the weaker or darker side of the human condition. Nor do they hate anyone. Scratch a Fire sign, or a Water sign, and all sorts of prejudices and irrational passions rise to the surface. Aquarians will not hate, and when they come across 'an interesting case' which offends their sensibilities, they embark upon a campaign of reform. After all, why should only Aquarians be imbued with good will and concern for the welfare of all? Even the most irrational of human specimens can be reformed.

Aquarius as Leader

'Leader' does not sit well with Aquarians, who see themselves more as team co-ordinators. Aquarian leaders are humanitarians who see all people as equal, and who make sure they thrust 'equality' on to everyone else.

Office routine is scheduled around 'assessment sessions' at which department teams 'share experiences' and evaluate each other without ever losing their tempers. This at least is the Aquarian ideal.

Aquarians may be up to date on all the latest management techniques, and are always deeply concerned for the welfare of both staff and clientele. Their deep-rooted concerns, however, sometimes backfire, as their genuine conviction that they know what is best for others may ruffle the fur of colleagues and customers. Preoccupied by the ideal of universal welfare, they may forget people are quite capable of looking after themselves. However, Aquarians mean well.

Aquarius as Manager

The symbol of Aquarius is the sign of the water-bearer, and Aquarian managers disperse knowledge and wisdom in the manner of a water-bearer spilling the contents of his vessel before those who gather around him. Those who are thirsty are appreciative, those who are not get wet. Aquarian managers can solve any problem and apply reason to the most difficult situation. What they lack in diplomacy they make up for in solutions. And they will insist that you heed their advice.

Aquarian managers go through periods of frantic activity, after which their energy may suddenly dissipate. At such times the loyal employee may provide a new idea, or some mental stimulation in the form of a staff crisis. Aquarians enjoy a good staff crisis. Only the disloyal employee would ask: 'What's wrong?' – nothing goes wrong with an Aquarian.

Aquarian managers are familiar with their staff, acutely knowledgeable about them, yet keep a distance, reluctant to become too personally involved with 'team-mates'. Interviews with Aquarian managers are highly stimulating – they are unprejudiced, with little taste for power-game playing. The impression is of individuals genuinely interested in other people. Aquarian managers appreciate lively minds and stimulating conversationalists.

Aquarius as Employee

When the rest of the staff turns against a tyrannical boss, or an incompetent receptionist, Aquarians will leap to their defence, praising their good qualities and excusing the bad. Aquarian employees are unprejudiced, talk to everyone, and get on with everyone, from the chairperson to the cleaner.

Bright and alert Aquarians may soon come to the conclusion that the so-called superiors are not all that superior, and take things into their own hands, re-organizing filing systems, work schedules, meetings, and the like. If any injustices or discrepancies are detected on the Aquarians' floor, they are likely to arrange instant trade union solidarity.

Aquarian employees are quick to learn, hungry for knowledge, and loathe boredom. Aquarians finding themselves in a position that is no longer stimulating take one of two options: they either head for the door, or take the next job up – within a month they will have what they want.

A Profile of the Aquarian Manager

The Office

Aquarians favour open-plan – they can 'share experiences' that way, and inject a community spirit and sense of humanity into the proceedings of business at the same time. If they have an office, the door is left open, the plate-glass panel uncovered, and a host of empty chairs beckon the visiting guest. The Aquarian manager's chair will be the same as everyone else's – the 'big chair' status symbols of the Aries and Leo managers are mere frippery to Aquarian executives, who like to meet even subordinates on equal terms.

The Aquarian love of innovation will find expression elsewhere, however – an electronically-operated filing system perhaps, or a telephone system that can lock into intercontinental satellite communications, or maybe a lead-wire that extends to their own satellite dish just outside the office window.

A lot of the furnishings (hi-tech, eccentric or just plain bizarre) will have been constructed personally, along with some of the electronic gadgets. Aquarians love inventing things. This includes timetables, work schedules, filing systems – all of which are imbued with genuine Aquarian originality, capable of driving Earth-sign colleagues to despair.

The Company Car

British inventor Clive Sinclair launched the Sinclair Electric Car in the 1980s. It failed on the market and ruined him financially. The main problem was the very limited market: golf players and a few Aquarians. The Sinclair would appeal to the Aquarian love of the eccentric, the electric and the technologically new. Revolution is a keen interest for the Aquarian mind, and revolutionizing the transport industry, together with the environmental issue of avoiding pollution, makes electric cars an attractive proposition.

Since the Sinclair's launch and subsequent 'sinking' in the mid-1980s, electric cars have developed into viable, albeit expensive, alternatives. Come the day when electric cars are the norm, and company executives plug into sockets rather than petrol pumps, Aquarian managers will opt for the latest eccentricity.

Aquarians pay little heed to the company car as status symbol, nor do they need the company car to sublimate or express sexuality, success or power. The Aquarian vehicle (if the Aquarian drives at all) must signify a highly developed state of mind – either hi-tech or weird. Beware of Aquarians in high places. They may insist the entire company drive electric scooters.

The Business Lunch

The Aquarian love of eccentricity certainly extends to restaurants, the rule being the more offbeat the better. Clients and guests should refrain from expressing shock, surprise or concern as they are led into a curious establishment with exotic-looking motifs decorating the walls, as this only fuels Aquarian mirth while they revel in being the social iconoclast once more.

Your business lunch may be held in 'an all proceeds to Live Aid' café, or the latest hi-tech up-market designer in-crowd wine bar, mixing sushi and tacos on the same menu, with wine imported daily from its own vineyards in Transylvania. Even if your office is in a highly-conventional suburb, Aquarian hosts will find some offbeat place. The bowling alley cafeteria perhaps.

Aquarians prefer 'sessions' to one-to-one business lunches, and in the name of equality and freedom of expression, will invite their entire department to join the lunchtime session, assuming a chairing role in between gulps of coffee from paper cups.

The most favoured point of assembly for the Aquarian managers of any large enough company is the staff canteen, which they imbue with a spirit of solidarity and camaraderie, usually against the wishes of the canteen staff. They have probably insisted that the kitchen serve veggie-burgers to save the Brazilian rainforests and the ozone layer.

Otherwise, think Aquarians, let's take the department down to the local shish-kebab bar and show a bit of Third World solidarity.

The Aquarian Business Venture

A community leisure or sports centre is an admirable Aquarian enterprise. Aquarians favour collective undertakings – money-making is not a priority, so long as a lot of people are gathered together in one place and having a good time and, of course, are doing good works for humanity.

Many Aquarians involve themselves with academic pursuits where the unreasonableness of real life does not intervene too often: they feel comfortable as electronic engineers, scientists and inventors.

Aquarians will take an ordinary business and make it different: Boris Yeltsin took up Communism as a career and turned it into free enterprise; Reagan took up acting, and turned it into politics; Sven-Göran Eriksson began as a player, but realized his real talent was in coaching.

Aquarian publishers specialize in pop-up books or electronic talking books; Aquarian travel agencies organize trips for reincarnated Egyptian high priestesses to the Great Pyramid; Aquarian management consultants specialize in successful management through group therapy sessions.

As for traditional Aquarian business enterprises...

A traditional Aquarian? What's that?

The Aquarius Natal Chart

Oprah Winfrey

Psychologist Abraham Maslow describes a special kind of personality, the 'self-actualizer' – the person who overcomes great adversity to finally fulfil their creative potentials. Oprah Winfrey is one such personality. Against all odds she has become one of the best known and highest paid entertainers with her TV talk show, business and publishing ventures, and an acting career on the side.

Born illegitimate and virtually abandoned in the Deep South, she was raised first by her grandmother on a farm, then moved about between her mother and various relatives. Oprah's harrowing biography reveals that she was raped at nine and endured five years of sexual abuse, leading to adolescent rebellion and lifelong insecurity. She gave birth to a baby boy when she was just 14. Born two months prematurely, the baby died after two weeks.

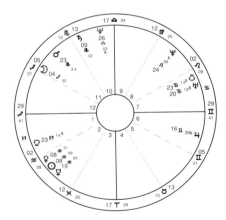

Asc	29 41 Sag	
MC	17 24 Lib	
Sun	08 59 Aqr	2
Moon	04 32 Sag	11
Mercury	19 09 Aqr	2
Venus	08 51 Aqr	2
Mars	23 34 Sco	11
Jupiter	16 39 Gem R	6
Saturn	09 02 Sco	10
Uranus	20 18 Cnc R	7
Neptune	26 03 Lib R	10
Pluto	24 09 Leo R	8

Oprah Winfrey 29 Jan 1954 04:30 Koscuisko MS (Source: ADB)

Yet Oprah went on to win two beauty titles while studying at college and by the age of 19 she was a CBS news journalist. She left college to become the first female and the first black newscaster in Nashville, earning $15,000 a year. She moved into her own show in Baltimore, 'People Are Talking', in 1977. 'The Oprah Winfrey Show' was first televised in September 1986 and she soon established herself as one of the most popular hosts in American TV. By 2000, her fortune was estimated at $415 million, making her one of the United States' richest women.

What comes across in Oprah Winfrey's talk shows is that she seems to be interested in everything and everyone. Any subject relating to self-improvement is fascinating and any person prepared to take steps towards taking control of their life is granted their 15 minutes of television. Looking at Oprah Winfrey's life this is not hard to understand; analyzing her natal chart, even less so.

Oprah Winfrey embodies the Aquarian love of knowledge, and the need to discover one's identity through the study of other people – all kinds of people, without prejudice or discrimination. The Sagittarian Ascendant, greatly strengthened by Moon in Sagittarius, suggests optimism in the face of adversity. Many successful sports competitors have the Sagittarian Ascendant–Moon.

The Sagittarian Ruler is Jupiter, and for Oprah Winfrey Jupiter is placed in the Sixth House, the House of social obligations, duties and sense of community. (Many nurses have this placing.) Oprah Winfrey has had to deal with many issues relating to personal relationships and intimacy. But Aquarians are generally adept at seeing the 'big picture' – whether that's the local community, or humanity in general, or global environmental issues. The fact that both Mars and Moon are in the Eleventh House (the Aquarian House) only strengthens these universal convictions. However, the Libra MC (Midheaven) indicates success in personal relationships later in life rather than earlier, and this seems the case in Oprah Winfrey's life. She became engaged to PR executive Stedman Graham in 1992, although the couple first met in 1986. Aquarians are not sticklers for convention, and often are in no hurry to get married. The couple arrange scheduled time together at any one of her homes – a 25-room condo in Chicago, an 85-acre ranch in Telluride, Colorado, an island retreat near Miami, or her 160-acre Indiana ranch.

She and Stedman Graham began teaching classes in the 'Dynamics of Leadership' in 1999. In April 2000, Oprah released her new magazine, *O*, in partnership with the Hearst Corporation, which together with her book-club has made her a real presence on the US publishing scene. Talented Aquarians are multi-talented and Oprah Winfrey is no exception; she made her screen debut in Steven Spielberg's film *The Color Purple* in 1988, for which she was nominated for an Academy Award.

Sven-Göran Eriksson

If relationships came late in Winfrey's life, they come like bolts of lightning in the life of English soccer team manager, Sven-Göran Eriksson.

After an undistinguished career as a right back for a Swedish second division soccer team in the 1970s, Eriksson was appointed coach for a third division team which he succeeded in quickly moving up the ladder. He became a sought-after first division coach, led his team to a Swedish championship, and subsequently took up an appointment in Portugal. From 1984 to 2000 he consolidated his coaching career in Italy. In October 2000 he was appointed to manage England.

Sports writer Sean Tyler commented: 'I like what I've seen of Eriksson and think he's the best manager England could have, but the poor man's doomed...

What has he let himself in for?' Overcoming considerable resistance, 'Svennis' quickly gained popularity, especially after leading England to an unprecedented 5–1 victory over arch-rivals, Germany. It was a match few England supporters expected them to win, but such an outstanding victory secured Eriksson's reputation and validated his 'strange Swedish approach to leadership'.

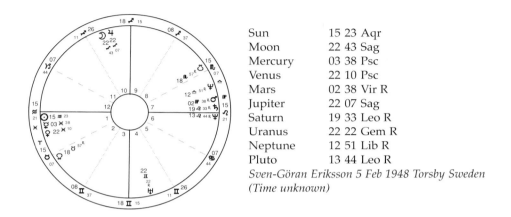

Sun	15 23 Aqr
Moon	22 43 Sag
Mercury	03 38 Psc
Venus	22 10 Psc
Mars	02 38 Vir R
Jupiter	22 07 Sag
Saturn	19 33 Leo R
Uranus	22 22 Gem R
Neptune	12 51 Lib R
Pluto	13 44 Leo R

Sven-Göran Eriksson 5 Feb 1948 Torsby Sweden (Time unknown)

In their book, *Leadership the Sven-Göran Eriksson Way*, Julian Birkenshaw and Stuart Crainer analyze the success of Sven-Göran's management style, a style which 'brilliantly exemplifies a new leadership which defies conventional and historical stereotypes of how leaders think and behave'. They compare his approach to the Swedish management model – it is polite, non-assertive and founded on the principle 'that you should believe in and respect the ability of every individual who works for you'.

Eriksson may not have succeeded in taking the English soccer team to the World Cup Final in 2002, but he gave them a good shot at it, and most importantly, injected a new spirit of self-confidence into a morally deflated group of players. How did he achieve it? To the surprise of UK sports analysts, he kept the same players, but succeeded in changing their attitudes. Instead of eleven skilful individuals playing their own game on the field, he made them into a team, integrating individual skills into a single cohesive unit.

Comparisons have been made between Sven-Göran Eriksson and another celebrated international business leader, Percy Barnevik, former CEO for ABB, a multinational engineering company. Both leaders foster teamwork, non-hierarchical management and consensus, and encourage dialogue and input from all members of the group. They both advocate a strong sense of team identity and corporate culture, and, of course, they are both Swedish. And guess what? They are both Aquarians. Swedish leadership style or Aquarian leadership style? Mundane astrologers would argue both: Sweden is ruled by the Sign of Aquarius.

What more can the chart of Sven-Göran Eriksson tell us about his approach to leadership? Without an accurate time of birth we can only evaluate the positions of planets in signs, but they tell us a good deal. Moon and Jupiter conjunct in Sagittarius are often found in the charts of sports competitors, and instinctive 'survivors'. Otherwise Aquarius and Virgo dominate – analysis, strategy, communication; a 'softly softly' approach with a minimum of grandstanding and raised voices. A leadership style that works best quietly and efficiently behind the scenes. Eriksson's chart indicates control, teamwork, a keen analytical mind with a remarkable insight into personality and strategic problem-solving. There is only one placing in his chart that indicates a lack of order and control, namely Venus in Pisces. Venus rules relationships and Pisces is the watery sign of feelings, passion and impulsive behaviour. Think Liza Minelli and Elizabeth Taylor – two personalities with Sun and Venus in Pisces.

'The strongest psyche in the world of sports – finally cracked by a woman!' So ran one of the milder newspaper headlines at the height of the 'Svennis–Ulrika affair' in 2002. Eriksson maintained his cool Aquarius/Virgo façade as the UK media had a field day: the brilliant strategist who could take England to the World Cup was suddenly the centre of a tug-of-war between passionate Italian fiancée Nancy, and cool Swedish man-eater, Ulrika (b. Stockholm 16.8.1967).

Just as astrological counselling could have helped former US President Bill Clinton avoid the pitfalls of power, so could Eriksson, perhaps, have maintained his otherwise unblemished reputation – not through astrological predictions, but simply through the insights astrology has to offer in understanding character traits. In the final analysis an understanding of character is an understanding of destiny; as the Greek philosophers taught two and a half thousand years ago, character is fate.

Ronald Reagan

One leader who did take astrological counselling seriously is former US President Ronald Reagan. His time of birth is a closely kept secret between himself and his astrologer – some astrologers suggest a Sagittarius Ascendant, others claim Scorpio. Reagan's reticence on this point, in contrast to his frankness regarding other areas of his life, public and private, may have been inspired by Mao Tse Tung's secrecy on the same issue. The Chinese have long believed that the knowledge of an emperor's time of birth outside the immediate imperial court could have devastating effects in the hands of the enemy.

Following Jimmy Carter's revelations about seeing flying saucers, US Presidents are discreet concerning matters of the occult, so just how influenced Reagan was by Joan Quigley, the White House astrologer, and her sessions with Nancy Reagan is a matter of speculation.

Joan Quigley gained fame following her prediction that Reagan's life was in danger in 1981 – prior to the assassination attempt that nearly cost him his life. In her book *What Does Joan Say?* (1991) Joan Quigley claims that she selected the particular dates and times most beneficial for certain presidential activities – journeys, press conferences and official engagements. In her assessment of astrology as applied to matters of state, she maintains that some moments are 'fateful', over which the astrologer has no jurisdiction, while others are moments of 'free will' which the astrologer can orchestrate to the benefit of the client – in her case the US President.

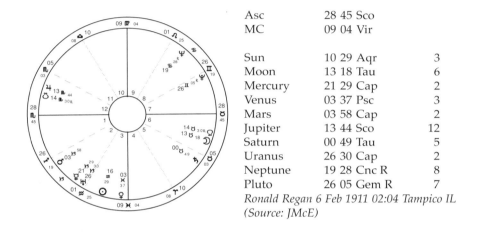

Asc	28 45 Sco	
MC	09 04 Vir	
Sun	10 29 Aqr	3
Moon	13 18 Tau	6
Mercury	21 29 Cap	2
Venus	03 37 Psc	3
Mars	03 58 Cap	2
Jupiter	13 44 Sco	12
Saturn	00 49 Tau	5
Uranus	26 30 Cap	2
Neptune	19 28 Cnc R	8
Pluto	26 05 Gem R	7

Ronald Regan 6 Feb 1911 02:04 Tampico IL (Source: JMcE)

Many Aquarians are attracted to astrology, as it provides a system for categorizing human types; it allows a scientific probing into just what makes people tick. Just as Geminis might take a clock to pieces to put it back together again, so Aquarians like to do the same with people. Reagan's memoirs concerning the early talks with Soviet leader Gorbachev emphasize the personal rapport established between the two men. 'Here was a man I could talk to... that I could communicate with...' etc. Indeed, his recollections are preoccupied with 'the great work being done on behalf of humanity in working toward disarmament and world peace', and the personal chemistry between himself and the Soviet leader. And this only a year after the President's dire warnings of the Soviet 'empire of evil'.

Reagan embraced many different careers in his lifetime – as radio announcer, sports commentator, actor, union leader, Governor and President. He was not exceptional in any one field, but succeeded in many. His political career was marked by periods of intense activity interspersed with prolonged periods of languor – a President who was so laid-back, suggested some of his critics, as to be horizontal.

A decade later, similar criticism was to be levelled at another Aquarian world leader, Comrade Yeltsin.

Boris Yeltsin

A Russian television programme portraying Russia's first freely elected President in a thousand years begins with Boris Yeltsin sitting in a park and talking with an astrologer about the characteristics of his Aquarian Sun-sign. 'A humanitarian, a man of the people,' she suggests. Yeltsin smiles and nods. 'Hates routine,' she continues. Yeltsin nods vigorously. 'Da!' he replies. 'Periods of intense activity followed by periods of apathy and lethargy,' she suggests cautiously. Yeltsin hesitates and nods wistfully. 'An idealist. But stubborn.' Yeltsin smiles again and nods approvingly.

Who knows? Perhaps Boris Yeltsin is genuinely interested in astrology. Many Aquarians are. Aquarian Ronald Reagan had Joan Quigley on the White House payroll. Is Boris Yeltsin, like Reagan, a man so fascinated by destiny that he involves himself with its orchestration?

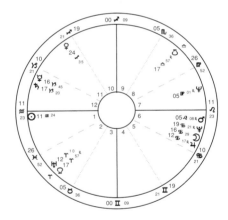

Sun	11 24 Aqr
Moon	16 29 Cnc
Mercury	16 45 Cap
Venus	24 35 Sgr
Mars	05 08 Leo R
Jupiter	12 17 Cnc R
Saturn	17 20 Cap
Uranus	12 10 Ari
Neptune	05 01 Vir R
Pluto	19 21 Cnc R

Boris Yeltsin 1 Feb 1931 Sverdlovsk Russia
(Time unknown)

The eldest son of a peasant family, Yeltsin grew up in Sverdlovsk in the Urals, the mountains which traditionally divide East and West. He worked as a construction engineer, became involved in local politics and rose to the position of Sverdlovsk Communist Party leader. He made a name for himself as a reformer, declining to take advantage of Party member benefits. Soon after Gorbachev came to power, Yeltsin was summoned to Moscow to take charge of a campaign to clean up corruption and begin reforms inside the party.

Yeltsin became an increasingly unpopular figure in Moscow as far as the Party was concerned. Once more he refused the standard Party privileges, including the elite Party member accommodation. Until the aftermath of the November 1991 attempted *coup d'état* Yeltsin lived with his wife in a standard Moscow worker's apartment, even rejecting Party member shops, with his wife joining the food queues along with the many thousands of other Moscow *cheloviks*.

In the late 1980s his reform campaign was brought to an abrupt halt and he was sacked by the KGB. In true Russian tradition Yeltsin took to the bottle, but even when taken into the 'drying out' programme he refused special Party clinics, choosing the treatment available to any other Moscow worker.

Many Aquarians have a highly developed intellect, expressing themselves in abstracts and ideals which most people find difficult to follow. This Aquarian mode of communication makes politics a difficult career for Aquarians, as speaking directly and accessibly to the people is a basic prerequisite. Significantly, in the charts of both Reagan and Yeltsin, two politicians renowned for their ability to speak to 'the people', Mercury is in Capricorn – an Earth sign, where communication is down-to-earth, direct and uncomplicated. For both Yeltsin and Reagan, their strength lay in the presentation of complex abstractions (Reagan's Star Wars defence programme, Yeltsin's economic reforms and conversion to market economy) in a language that can be readily grasped by the electorate.

Yet idealism is always at the forefront. Reagan's talks with Gorbachev in the quest for world peace, and Yeltsin's claim in 1992 that Russia could take its place in a world economy alongside Japan, Germany and the US, providing the people were free to work and profit from their labour, each exemplify this. Like Reagan, Yeltsin has no military background, which makes him a rarity in Russian politics.

Political commentators ask was Yeltsin a genuine decentralist? Or a new Russian tsar? A democrat or a dictator? Aquarius is a fixed sign; there is a dictatorial side to the most intellectual of Aquarians, because they perceive the world in terms of abstracts, like 'the people', 'humanity', 'the common good', rather than the individual. For Aquarians, the needs of the individual must be sacrificed for the greater good of the collective.

In keeping with his Aquarian profile Yeltsin, in his role as Russian President, was a multi-faceted personality, playing tennis and volleyball, favouring youth and intelligence over age and experience, sleeping only three or four hours a night, and, according to his wife, oscillating between periods of intense activity and passive indolence. Just like the astrologer claimed in the interview.

Aquarians are rebels and revolutionaries. Yeltsin is on record as the first Party member to deny Party privileges. When he saw he could go no further within the Party itself, he quit, and against all odds set up in opposition. His term of office was an erratic one: as well as health problems and drinking, he was involved in outrageous media spectacles – conducting a German military band while under the influence, and being caught by TV cameras in a flirtatious moment with a female interpreter.

'It is always the people, humanity, that can save us,' Yeltsin claimed. There was little doubting his conviction. The problem for Yeltsin was that 'humanity' in his new Russia consisted of lots of individual people. And individuals are trouble. On the eve of the new millennium, ravaged by drink and in poor health, he resigned, surprising observers both inside and outside Russia by insisting his office be filled by a young and unknown former KGB spy, Vladimir Putin.

Thomas Alva Edison

The traditional view of an Aquarian is the eccentric scientist, the crackpot inventor, content in an ivory-tower world of mental abstraction and eternal youth. Thomas Edison was just such a character; at his death in 1931 he had patented 1300 inventions.

The son of a timber-dealer with little formal education, he began experimenting with telegraphic devices at the age of 10. At 12 he began working as a newspaper vendor for the railways, and at 15 he had a job as a telegraph operator. In 1868, aged 21, Edison patented his first invention – the stock ticker. Then, beginning with inventions to improve the telegraphic system, Edison commenced a lifetime of creating gadgets. In 1871, the year of his Jupiter return, he set up a plant in Newark, manufacturing telegraphic devices for Western Union.

However, the pressures of business and management distracted Edison from what he loved doing, so in 1876, at the age of 29 (his Saturn return), he gave up the factory and founded a research laboratory in Menlo Park, New Jersey. Here he developed the carbon microphone necessary for the articulating telephone device invented by Alexander Graham Bell that same year. Then came the phonograph and the electric light bulb.

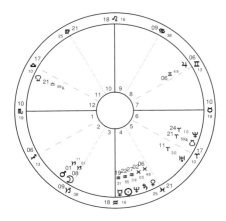

Asc	10 19 Sco	
MC	18 16 Leo	
Sun	22 55 Aqr	4
Moon	08 01 Cap	2
Mercury	19 31 Aqr	4
Venus	06 48 Psc	4
Mars	01 11 Cap	2
Jupiter	06 49 Gem	8
Saturn	02 05 Psc	4
Uranus	11 30 Ari	5
Neptune	27 39 Aqr	4
Pluto	24 10 Ari	6

Thomas Edison 11 Feb 1847 23:33 Milan OH
(Source: JK)

The British Parliamentary Committee of 1878 set up to investigate the potential of Edison's light bulb reported that it was 'good enough for our transatlantic friends... but unworthy of the attention of practical or scientific men'. The Edison Company expanded in 1887 and two years later Edison unveiled the

Kinetophonograph – the forerunner of the present-day moving picture projector. He was 42 years old, and experiencing the mid-life crisis often precipitated by the Uranus opposition. However, just as Saturn returns are kinder to Capricorns – Saturn ruling Capricorn – so is the Uranus opposition more amenable to Aquarians, Uranus being the sign's ruling planet.

In 1893 Edison opened the world's first film studio, and on 23 April 1896, he unveiled the Edison Vitascope, which projected film on to a screen: when this was added to the developments made by French inventors, the Lumière brothers and Georges Méliès, the motion picture industry was born.

In 1909, Edison, now in his sixties, united some of the early motion picture companies to form the Motion Picture Patents Company, but in 1917 it ran into problems with the US anti-trust laws and was dissolved. Edison, aged 70, quit the movie business. However, he did not stop inventing, and continued to patent new inventions up to his death in 1931, at the age of 84 (the Uranus return). The ruling planet of Aquarius takes 84 years to complete one cycle.

Edison invented the machinery that enabled the development of moving pictures, but using the technology as a revolutionary new form of popular entertainment was largely the work of two other original and inventive Aquarian personalities, D W Griffith in the US, and Sergei Eisenstein in the Soviet Union.

D W Griffith

Realizing the potential of the cinema as a form of mass entertainment – a means by which to convey popular stories to a worldwide public – Griffith and Eisenstein between them laid down the basics of film form. They were born within a solar degree of each other, and both died in 1948 in disfavour and obscurity, having between them, through the medium of motion pictures, changed the face of world history.

Griffith's career began as a travelling stage actor, his meagre income supplemented by odd jobs as he attempted to establish himself as a writer. He was 32 when he sold his first play and moved to New York, where he tried to get work at the newly-formed film studios, including the Edison Company. He acted and wrote scripts, mainly for the Biograph studios, and in 1908 directed his first film. By 1913 he was production chief and general director at Biograph, and when he left to set up his own film company he had already directed an astounding total of 450 films.

Griffith was the first film-maker to use changing camera angles, moving camera, parallel development and crosscutting, dramatic lighting and editing as narrative devices. Even the close-up was an innovation developed by Griffith.

In 1915 his film *The Birth of a Nation,* a re-enactment of the American civil war, three hours long and the most elaborate film up till that time, split the feelings of public and critics alike, who were on the one hand overwhelmed by the technological achievement, and on the other enraged by what was referred to as 'a flagrant incitement to racial antagonism'.

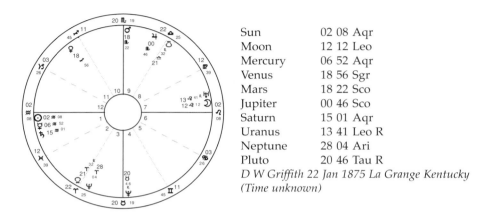

Sun	02 08 Aqr
Moon	12 12 Leo
Mercury	06 52 Aqr
Venus	18 56 Sgr
Mars	18 22 Sco
Jupiter	00 46 Sco
Saturn	15 01 Aqr
Uranus	13 41 Leo R
Neptune	28 04 Ari
Pluto	20 46 Tau R

*D W Griffith 22 Jan 1875 La Grange Kentucky
(Time unknown)*

In 1919 Griffith joined forces with Charlie Chaplin, Douglas Fairbanks and Mary Pickford in the formation of Universal Artists. His subsequent films continued to lose money and by the late 1920s he had lost his creative independence. In 1926 he wrote an article proclaiming that sound and talking pictures would never happen. The following year the first talking picture was released in Hollywood and the silent era was over.

Griffith's career declined rapidly, and although he received an honorary Academy Award in 1935, he spent his remaining years in hotel rooms. He died of a cerebral haemorrhage, aged 73, embittered, impoverished and forgotten.

Sergei Eisenstein

At his father's wishes, Eisenstein trained as a civil engineer in Petrograd (now St Petersburg), while harbouring a secret passion for the theatre. During the 1917 revolution he sold sketches to the newspapers of the dramatic scenes taking place around the city. He served briefly in the army, then formed an amateur theatre group. He developed an interest in oriental languages and later claimed the *kanji* picture-words of written Japanese inspired his theories of film montage. He wrote and produced several plays before directing his first film, *Strike*, in 1925. Lenin, realizing the propaganda value of film, supported the struggling Soviet film industry, and Eisenstein was commissioned to make a film commemorating the 1905 revolution. The result was *Battleship Potemkin*, one of the most influential films of all time. Even more than Griffith, Eisenstein was not concerned with a single protagonist, but with the collective. His subsequent films became more experimental and bold, and although these were highly praised abroad, Soviet cultural officials eventually curtailed his film productions.

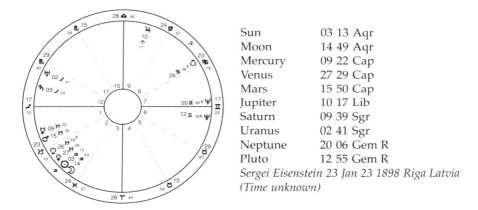

Sun	03 13 Aqr
Moon	14 49 Aqr
Mercury	09 22 Cap
Venus	27 29 Cap
Mars	15 50 Cap
Jupiter	10 17 Lib
Saturn	09 39 Sgr
Uranus	02 41 Sgr
Neptune	20 06 Gem R
Pluto	12 55 Gem R

Sergei Eisenstein 23 Jan 23 1898 Riga Latvia
(Time unknown)

In 1930 Eisenstein travelled to America seeking work from US film studios, but no projects materialized. He began a film in Mexico, *Que Viva Mexico*, but production, financial and political problems prevented him completing the project (a version was finally completed in the Soviet Union in 1979, 47 years after the project's inception, and 31 years after Eisenstein's death).

Eisenstein's remaining years in the Soviet Union were dogged by political strife and condemnation. He completed two more films, but was mainly involved with teaching and writing, and he remains today one of the world's foremost film theorists. He died of a heart attack in 1948, aged 50.

Other prominent Aquarians: Francis Bacon, Charles Darwin, Angela Davis, Galileo Galilei, Germaine Greer, Abraham Lincoln, Charles Lindbergh, General MacArthur, John McEnroe, W A Mozart, Olof Palme, Jackson Pollock, Mary Quant, Vanessa Redgrave. F D Roosevelt, August Strindberg, Jules Verne.

Water Signs

Cancer

George W Bush
Prince William
Richard Branson
Jan Carlzon
J D Rockefeller

Scorpio

Bill Gates
Ted Turner
Jack Welch
Prince Charles
Indira Gandhi
Billy Graham

Pisces

Steve Jobs
Ivar Kreuger
Rupert Murdoch
David Puttnam
Rudolph Steiner
Mikhail Gorbachev

Cancer

21 June – 21 July
Ruling planet: Moon
Element: Water
Quality: Cardinal
Symbol: The Crab

Like the Moon which rules this sign, there is a subtle quality to Cancer. Cancer does not move directly toward a chosen goal, preferring to approach in discreet sideways movements that only the trained eye can detect. Check out your Cancer colleagues at the next company conference buffet. You can bet they would love that last crabmeat vol-au-vent, but instead will skirt around the sausage rolls for a bit, then at an unsuspected moment – gone. The vol-au-vent plate is empty, and Cancer is content.

Cancerians avoid direct confrontations, and are as evasive with themselves as they are with other people. Evasion is a protective measure, linked with that well-publicized Cancerian sensitivity; they carry their past with them, their childhood, and memories of all the wrongs they have experienced. They do not want to get hurt again. They approach people in the same way that they cope with their ambitions: cautiously, warily, waiting until the 'feel' is right – until the Cancerian instincts say it's OK. Then they move in, take a grip and hold fast.

There is a feline quality to Cancerians. A cat is endearing, and evokes images of gentleness and domesticity, or a nap on a soft rug in front of an open fire. But at night the cat is a predatory creature, merciless with its victims – the captured prey's suffering is prolonged as the cat pursues its game of torment. A cat is a creature of instinct – domestic it may be, but a cat cannot be tamed.

Cancerians are also creatures of instinct – relying on feelings and intuition when making decisions. When Cancerians get hold of something, whether it is an idea, a relationship, a job, or a designer jacket at a bargain price, they will not let go. Cancerians rarely give the impression of being ambitious, but the self-contained, self-protective and repressed side of the Cancerian personality is an excellent breeding-ground for resentment, and whenever Cancerians hear of a close friend's success, a little piece of them dies.

Cancerians stick to old habits, which is admirable when the old ways are good ways – but Cancerians who get in a rut end up staying in it until forced into major upheaval. For this reason Cancerians are cautious about committing themselves to people or vocations; for the uninitiated a Cancerian commitment can be an overwhelming experience.

Cancerians are home-loving, family-orientated, and have a strong sense of the past. They are creative, and abundantly so if left to their own devices, but with a tendency to lose themselves in daydreams. Like the crab, Cancerians have a tough shell and a soft centre: they are subject to lunar rhythms, carry their home around with them, and, in the case of threat, hide away safely in their shell, with sideways glances into the harsh world outside.

The Cancerian writer Hermann Hesse described the human condition as a constant yearning for home: 'All we have to guide us is our homesickness, though we never know where home is... '. This is why Cancerians have such sad eyes.

They have excellent memories, however, with uncanny recall of minute details from the past, and an encyclopedic knowledge of their chosen subject of interest. Forgetting and forgiving does not appeal much to Cancerians. They hold on to memories of any unintentional offence you may have caused, and just when you thought it was gone and forgotten, they will drag it out in clear and sharp detail.

Cancerians are traditionalists and conservatives in the true sense of the word – they like to keep things. They just cannot bear to part with anything. The Cancerian home is filled with old jars, old pairs of slippers, worn-out clothes, and miscellaneous packaging materials. You just never know when these things might come in handy.

Cancerians enjoy looking after people, but they enjoy being looked after even more – they're always seeking security. Cancerians worry a lot – particularly if they think someone is after their job, or their office, or their parking space.

Cancer as Leader

Cancerian leaders create a close-knit unit, transforming a company into a surrogate family. Either you are an esteemed member of the family, stamped with the Cancerian leader's seal of approval, or you are not. As a family member you will be looked after, nurtured, encouraged and duly rewarded. If you are not in favour you may as well give up now and get a job at the local brewery.

Cancerian decisions are based on feelings rather than a well-reasoned and objective line of argument. When the accountants asked Richard Branson, 'Why an airline?', he replied, 'Because it feels right!' And that is about as straight an answer as you will get from a Cancer boss.

There is an evasive side to Cancerian bosses – if you want a straight answer to a given question you should probably ask their spouse. The higher Cancerians get the more aloof they become. This is due to the Cancer resentment of other people's successes and consequently the assumption that everyone else is resenting theirs.

Generally Cancerian heads of companies are wary of risk-taking and quick success, preferring application, resolve, hard work and a close watch on needless extravagances, such as paper clips and tea-breaks.

Cancer as Manager

Cancerians are the caring managers – the managers who look after their teams, nurturing them, and defending them from any hostilities emanating from the executive suite. But just as a child can be smothered with love, subordinates under the Cancerian manager's wing may soon find their own wings clipped. Caring managers do not care for those who wander from the roost, nor those who have lofty ambitions. Handing a notice of resignation to a Cancerian manager is a delicate matter requiring tact, resolve and an ability to deal with intensely emotional and tearful scenes.

For those seeking interesting experiences, try a conversation with your Cancerian manager at three o'clock on a Friday afternoon. You can explain something for five minutes, catch them looking through the window with a blank gaze, say their name, once, then again. They turn slowly, look up at you with sorrow-laden eyes, and say: 'Uh?' Then, slightly irritated (which they pick up at once), you explain all over again. They reply, 'Well, of course. I know that.'

Cancerians appreciate a peaceful working environment, close to nature: a proximity to water is conducive to an even working tempo. An aggressive urban environment exhausts Cancerians, and by mid-afternoon they will have crept off to a quiet place for a nap. Cancerians like to nap.

Cancer as Employee

Many successful salespeople are born under this sign, falling into the categories of 'hard' and 'soft', but each prospering in their own way. 'Hard' Cancerians are go-getters who like money and writing out orders; after each call they will go straight into a café and count up the profits, then proceed post-haste to the next account to see if they can do better.

'Soft' Cancerian salespeople have deep sad eyes and are relaxed, very relaxed. One such Cancer salesman was going through his samples one after the other for an especially hard buyer. After an hour he had gone through everything and not made a single sale. He closed up his bag and sighed (Cancerians sigh regardless). The buyer touched the salesman's shoulder and said, 'Look. Tell you what. The last one you showed me. I'll take ten.' The Cancerian salesman took out his pad and pen, and wrote the order. 'Just out of interest', he asked, 'what made you change your mind?' 'Well,' said the buyer, 'your eyes. They're so sad. I thought you were going to cry.' This is a true story and the Cancerian salesman went on to become director of a large and successful advertising agency.

In an office environment moody Cancerians can drive people crazy. Service-orientated Cancerians are nearly always admirable employees, however, and never create a fuss about making tea for six unexpected visitors.

A Profile of the Cancer Manager

The Office

This is probably the cosiest office in the entire building. It is the place where the company cat comes to take it easy after a busy night's mousing. There is not much new stuff in here – the desk and chair have a well-worn look, and the visitor's chair is large and comfortable, just to make the guest feel at home.

As you look around, you notice a curious assortment of artefacts adorning shelves. Some are relevant to the Cancerian's job, others make no sense at all. For Cancerians each relic is a memory.

There are lots of cupboards and cabinets with combination locks. Lots of places to hide things away. Old jars, files, newspapers, magazines and journals, matchboxes from a dozen different restaurants. Nothing gets thrown out – they never know when any of these things might come in handy.

Be careful not to violate the Cancer office. You can do what you like at an Arian's or a Sagittarian's place – they have nothing to hide – but the Cancerian office is sanctified and prying eyes are not welcome.

The photograph on the desk might be the wife, husband, or might be mother. It is probably mother. There is a pair of shoes by the door. Cancerian colleagues change into slippers when they come into the office and tend to stay there for the day – you can count on Cancerians being 'in' at least, unlike Geminis and Sagittarians.

If they are not answering the telephone it is because they do not want to be disturbed. Three possibilities. Firstly, the task with which they are engaged is of so demanding a nature as to require total concentration. Secondly, the Cancerian is in a desperately overwrought mood. After a few moment's reflection, and a little time to 'pull themselves together', they will be fine and the telephone will be back on the hook. The third possibility is that after a decent home-cooked lunch, they have decided to join the company cat on the blanket in the office corner for a short nap.

The Company Car

Last year's car! How does that work? It's like this. When all the other executives are upgrading every second year, the Cancerian managers say: 'She's running fine. I'll upgrade next time round.' And Cancerians, being the creatures of habit they are, quite properly stay with the same vehicle year after year (see 'The Dreadful Alternative' below...).

Many Cancerians, respected and established business executives included, call their cars 'she', treat them like pets and give them names like Jessie, Bessie or Toots. They transform the standard-issue company car into an extension of their home, with sockets for water heaters, shaving apparatus and photographs of the family. Within a very short space of time the Cancerian company car resembles a Greek taxi, complete with pictures of spouse and kids, and a St Christopher medallion on the dashboard.

The Dreadful Alternative, or why Cancerians should not be encouraged to change cars: a Cancerian publicity director was once persuaded, reluctantly, to upgrade. A brand new Ford Scorpio. On his way home he ploughed straight into a lamppost, and wrote the car off. He was uninjured. His excuse for this extraordinary behaviour? 'I must have been day-dreaming. I don't remember a thing!' This is a true and cautionary tale directed to any MD who insists on a Cancerian executive upgrading.

The Business Lunch

Getting Cancerians to leave the office is not easy: given the choice, they would prefer to eat at home. But as this is a business appointment, they will make one of two choices – the in-house canteen (at least the place is familiar, and Cancerians will have the same table, by the window with a view of at least one tree), or Mama Rosa's.

Mama Rosa's is a quiet, intimate place with a reputation for the best Italian seafood pasta. The main attraction for Cancerians is Mama Rosa herself, a benign, generously bosomed matriarch, who decides what you are having for lunch before you have even seen the menu. She has a family of 15 sons, and she knows just what young men like for their dinner. No arguments.

When Cancerians are not busy looking after clients, there is nothing they appreciate more than being looked after themselves, and a restaurant ruled by an all-powerful matron figure, who takes care of all the decision-making, has strong Cancerian appeal. Besides, with the peripheral details taken care of (right down to the bottle of house Chianti) Cancerians can concentrate on other things – like the contract.

Cancerians decide on the terms of the agreement, and no matter how much you harangue, these quietly-spoken, dewy-eyed managers will not budge. Not only will you sign the contract, but you will pick up the tab. 'Oops. Left my wallet at home,' say Cancerians, with a helpless smile. That is the third time this week.

The Cancer Business Venture

Cancerians feel at home in the service and people industries: catering, restaurants, airline companies, charter holiday companies, health centres, pre-natal clinics and account management.

Cancerians are sensitive, artistic types with a keen interest in history and their family past, and often develop careers in the arts. In publishing, Cancerians choose books on cooking, child-rearing and gardening. In films, they opt more for introspective, self-analytical, brooding psychological dramas. Sylvester Stallone is a Cancerian. So is Ingmar Bergman.

The Cancer Natal Chart

George W Bush

In our astrological analysis of former US President Bill Clinton (Leo), we considered the perceptions of the USA in the post-2001 period, compared to the Clinton years, 1993–2001. Cancer and Leo are the two signs most strongly related to family. Under Clinton, the outward perception of the US was outgoing and extrovert, whereas under George W Bush, a more inward-looking and introvert perception has predominated. For the Bush administration – even prior to the events of 11 September 2002 – the US corresponds to an all-embracing American tribe that must focus on internal issues, taking care of the 'family' whilst harbouring strong reservations about the outside world.

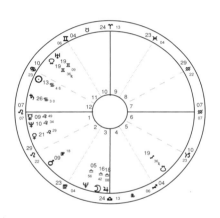

Asc	07 07 Leo	
MC	24 13 Ari	
Sun	13 46 Cnc	12
Moon	16 42 Lib	3
Mercury	09 49 Leo	1
Venus	21 29 Leo	1
Mars	09 18 Vir	2
Jupiter	18 08 Lib	3
Saturn	26 30 Cnc	12
Uranus	19 09 Gem	11
Neptune	05 56 Lib	3
Pluto	10 34 Leo	1

George W Bush 6 July 1946 07:26 New Haven CT (Source: ADB)

The role of George W Bush in the Bush family is also of interest; Cancer is the sign most strongly associated with the home and the family. Yet where the Kennedy dynasty burned bright and brief for a few years of the 1960s, the Bush dynasty, whatever it lacks in glamour, it makes up for with continuity. The family's presence in US politics began in the late 1970s when George Walker Herbert Bush (b. June 1924) became head of the CIA, then 41st President 1989–93. George W is the first man since John Quincy Adams (US President 1825–29) to follow his father into the White House. George W's brother Jeb was elected the Governor of Florida in 1998, and re-elected in November 2002.

The Bush family is perhaps a less conspicuous dynasty than the Kennedys of the 1960s, but a dynasty nonetheless, complete with influential and powerful matriarch, Barbara Bush. And mother is always a strong influence in any young Cancerian man's life.

Before politics, George W had a career as a Texas oil millionaire, then baseball team owner. He was elected the governor of Texas in 1998.

Initially George W was considered a political lightweight who had stumbled into the presidential role after the closely contested election with Democrat candidate, Al Gore. Yet after the September 11 terrorist attacks he emerged as a media personality who could unify a traumatized nation. Here his conservatism and overt nationalism were in tune with the media and the electorate, and America underwent a surge of patriotism unparalleled since the 1950s.

Political commentators describe his style as conservative, with his policies based on the principles of limited government, personal responsibility, strong families and local control. The White House website describes Bush as pursuing the same common-sense approach and bi-partisan spirit that he employed in Texas. His 'bold initiatives ensure that America's prosperity has a purpose'. He is improving public (state) schools by strengthening local control and insisting on accountability; reducing taxes on all taxpayers; strengthening the military, and 'ushering in the responsibility era in America'. His opponents claim it is a return to an age of self-interest, an America in which the divisions between the rich and the poor will continue to widen.

What does the natal chart of George W Bush indicate, apart from the Cancerian attributes of home, family and conservatism? The Leo Ascendant, combined with Venus, Mercury and Pluto in the First House, suggests a personality secure in the role of performer and orator, and a capacity to manage the media, the stage and the political arena. Sun in the Twelfth House indicates the hidden and obscured side of the personality that is also represented in the charts of Tony Blair and Vladimir Putin. The Saturn–Sun–Twelfth House combination suggests a more Nixon-like approach to leadership than that of Kennedy or Clinton: the deeply felt responsibilities, hidden insecurities and self-doubts, drinking problems and uncertain self-esteem.

Moon in Libra indicates emotional fulfilment through a relationship. According to the popular press and to Bush himself, his wife Laura has been a strong influence, arousing his interest in social issues, religion and the Bible, and helping him deal with those Twelfth-House issues listed above. His problems with alcohol ceased in 1986, just after his 40th birthday, when he decided to stop drinking for good. Perhaps it is through the influence of his wife that he has learned to take hold of self-discipline, and to come to terms with his life in public service. He expressed the relaxed and domestic image of the Cancerian in an interview when he said: 'I want the folks to see me sitting in the same kind of seat they sit in, eating the same popcorn, peeing in the same urinal.' Or was that statement just inspired by down-to-earth Texan machismo?

Prior to his election, Bush Jr was considered a lightweight by many political commentators, and likely to be more dependent on White House advisors than any predecessor. The relaxed Cancerian approach may have helped to give this impression, but the strong Pluto, Mercury conjunct Ascendant in the First House suggests another image. It is a conjunction that indicates strong feelings and determination, an intensity of purpose, and – if provoked – a propensity for retribution. It is this image that has emerged following the 11 September attack, and the subsequent actions of the US forces in Afghanistan and Iraq.

Prince William

The natal chart of Prince William could possibly be the one with which the general public will be most familiar. Predictive astrologers and magazine columnists already speculate on the personal life of the Prince, his prospects of assuming the throne, attributes of personality and idolization by members of the opposite sex. Our purpose here is to consider what astrology can tell us about the managerial qualities of the Prince. When Prince William assumes the throne what kind of leadership style will he manifest? How will he deal with the pressures that a ruler in a democratic monarchy must face? And how will he manage the very specific challenges that the British media has bestowed upon their monarchs and other members of the Royal Family?

The similarities between Prince William and his late mother, Princess Diana, both in terms of appearance and character, are self-evident; significantly, Princess Diana was also a Cancerian with Sagittarius as her Rising Sign.

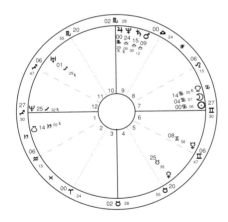

Asc	27 30 Sgr	
MC	02 28 Sco	
Sun	00 06 Cnc	7
Moon	04 57 Cnc	7
Mercury	08 58 Gem	6
Venus	25 39 Tau	5
Mars	09 12 Lib	9
Jupiter	00 29 Sco R	9
Saturn	15 38 Lib	9
Uranus	01 29 Sgr R	11
Neptune	25 32 Sgr R	12
Pluto	24 09 Lib	9

Prince William 2 June 1982 21:03 London
(Source: AA)

Cancerians prefer an indirect approach to leadership to a direct one, through suggestions, indications and subtle manoeuvring. Princess Diana was most prominent and most powerful when lacking any official position, through her masterful use of behind-the-scenes stage management, and indirect control and subtle seduction of the media. The traditional, direct and authoritarian approach of Queen Elizabeth II in media-management was no match for Diana's skills.

Given his background there is little doubting the influence of his mother in how Prince William comes to manage both the media and his future role as Prince of

Wales, and some day, King. Moon conjunct Sun in Cancer in the Seventh House (relationships) suggests a deep and complex emotional bond with his mother; she is an ever-present influence which can be overwhelming, even smothering.

Asked how he coped with media attention, Prince William, then 18, replied: 'I don't like the attention. I feel uncomfortable with it...' He added: 'I have particularly appreciated being left alone at Eton...' Whether attempts at stringent media controls from the Palace succeed into the Prince's later years may depend on the strong Sagittarian side of his personality: the Sagittarius Ascendant, and Mars, Jupiter, Saturn and Pluto all in the Sagittarian Ninth House.

In contrast to the withdrawn and sensitive Cancerian attributes, the strong Sagittarian side can lead to blunt and direct communication, which may provoke or may inspire. How will the media respond to the Prince's communication style? With Mercury in Gemini in the Sixth House (a quick mercurial mind orientated to the needs of the community), combined with the experiences of his formative years, the Prince should prove skilful in adapting to the fickle demands of the media.

Sagittarius Rising, and Mars and Jupiter in the Ninth House, favour the outdoor life, sport and nature. It is these aspects of Prince William's personality that are expressed in his enthusiastic accounts of sojourns in the Belize jungle, in Africa, in southern Chile, a survival course with the Welsh Guards, and even working as a labourer on an English farm. Likewise the Prince's predilection for team sports – water polo, football and rugby.

In September 2001, Prince William began a four-year art history course at St Andrews University in Scotland. St Andrews 'felt right...' he explained, and the strong Fire–Water combination in the chart indicates a potential leader who responds to instinctive feelings, rather than logic; a personality strongly attached to the past and with a passion for the future, but who requires grounding in the present. His expressed wish to work with environmental issues, perhaps inspired by Venus in Taurus, may be just what such strong feelings require to be brought down to earth.

Richard Branson

In the 1980s, Virgin UK, already a multi-company mega-corporation, entered the risk-filled business of movie production. In *1984,* Virgin's film version of George Orwell's novel , the company would utilize its diverse marketing possibilities: film, video, music, book sales, product placement.

In the 1990s, Virgin Airlines seemed to be fulfilling an Orwellian new-world prophecy – an Oceanic state incorporating the United States, Great Britain and Australasia. Even into the twenty-first century, Richard Branson may claim the Virgin vision is global – in fact, it is tribal. It began as a tribe of esoteric music devotees, grew to a tribe outside the established order, united by common interests in popular culture, eventually extending to a tribe of Orwellian proportions – an Oceania uniting the English speaking peoples of the world, with air travel, music, books and movies.

'Our companies are part of a family rather than a hierarchy. They are empowered to run their own affairs, yet other companies help one another ... we are a community, with shared ideas, values, interests and goals.' So runs the Virgin 'mission statement'. And now Virgin is laying the foundations for a new tribe: the Virgin consumers, a people united by their choice of services and commodities – travel, finance, soft drinks, music, mobile phones, holidays, cars, wines, publishing, even bridal wear (very Cancerian!).

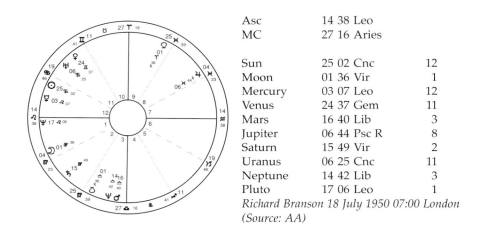

Asc	14 38 Leo	
MC	27 16 Aries	
Sun	25 02 Cnc	12
Moon	01 36 Vir	1
Mercury	03 07 Leo	12
Venus	24 37 Gem	11
Mars	16 40 Lib	3
Jupiter	06 44 Psc R	8
Saturn	15 49 Vir	2
Uranus	06 25 Cnc	11
Neptune	14 42 Lib	3
Pluto	17 06 Leo	1

Richard Branson 18 July 1950 07:00 London
(Source: AA)

As we have explored in the charts of US President George W Bush, and Prince William, the future Prince of Wales, Cancerians are associated with the family, the home and nurturing the interests of 'their own people'; the feelings of the tribe, or the family, run strong in Cancerians.

This is also manifest in the leadership style of Richard Branson. 'What ties all these businesses together,' says Branson, 'are the values of our brand and the attitude of our people.'

Being in charge of over 200 companies worldwide, employing over 25,000 people and with total revenues around the world exceeding £3 billion in 2000, does not just come from being a sensitive, world-shy and withdrawn astrology-textbook Cancerian. With Leo Rising and Moon and Pluto in the First House (image), Branson's chart suggests a personality comfortable in the public gaze, and comfortable with decision-making on a grand scale.

One strong Cancerian attribute is worth noting, however. Cancer is ruled by the Moon, and in contrast to the brash and upstaging Sun-ruled Leo, is secretive, hidden and subtle. Sun-dominated magnates see their name in lights: Woolworth

Stores, Sinclair Electronics, Amstrad, IKEA. Richard Branson, who originally considered calling his discount record business 'Slipped Disc', turned instinctively within and used his Virgo Moon sign – as one might expect of Moon-ruled Cancer – to coin the name Virgin. But if Cancer is shy and shuns the limelight, a Leo Ascendant wants to be centre-stage. Branson has a public image to maintain and continues with his Howard Hughes-style transatlantic flights (see Capricorn) and record-breaking attempts, in boats, planes and balloons.

In 1992 Branson sold off the record business in order to focus on Virgin Airlines. It was a difficult time for Branson, who according to colleagues 'was genuinely hurt' by the 1990s spate of rumours and criticisms thrown at both him and his companies. Aged 42, a time astrologers refer to as the Uranus opposition – a time in life that heralds unforeseen changes, disruptions and transformation – Branson was in the throes of a mid-life crisis. Said one friend, 'You have to understand that Richard takes things at face value.'

The humble origin of Branson's Virgin empire was when, still in his teens, he advertised cut-price records to help finance an ailing student magazine. This made him Britain's first underprice record retailer. He opened a shop above a shoe shop in London's West End in 1971 (aged 21); now there are over 100 Virgin record shops, including Megastores, in Europe, Australia and Japan.

When Mike Oldfield's *Tubular Bells* had been turned down by every major record company, Richard Branson released it under the Virgin Record label. It stayed on the bestseller lists for a decade, helping to finance Virgin's expansion. He went on to produce a host of acts, including the Sex Pistols in 1978, and in the 1980s went into film production – the film of Orwell's *1984* (released in 1984), *Electric Dreams* and others, tying in record, video and book deals in Virgin media package deals.

Cancerians are described as emotional, moody and sensitive, but armoured with a hard shell in order to conceal their vulnerability. Film producer Simon Perry describes Branson as 'slightly extravagant, kind of mercurial, a rather appealing character because he is very unexpected. But he doesn't appear to have a solid, personal, heartfelt opinion about anything... he has no real passion. He's desperately shy, terrified of being caught out.' If this description sounds familiar it is because it has been levelled at Tony Blair, Vladimir Putin and many others with Sun (and/or other planets) in the Twelfth House.

'I don't want people telling me what to do...' he once said. 'I like my company to have the feel of being small and intimate.' The UK company employs about 2000 people located in a variety of old buildings around London – Branson doesn't consider high-rise office blocks as conducive to a good working ambience. There is no Virgin HO or towering Virgin corporation building.

Informality is integral to the Branson style of business – a relaxed environment with the emphasis on comfort. Branson himself never wears a suit – usually jeans and sweaters. He arranges company holidays for company people only and sees the enterprise as 'one big happy family'. He relies on intuition. He claims 'If you sit down with accountants and look at profit and loss projections they'll manage to come up with all sorts of reasons why something won't work. If you've got a gut feel about something then trial and error can produce the best results. The only way to learn is to give it a try.' His approach to the airline company, began, as with the record company, with discounting and cheap prices, aiming for the youth market.

'Big airlines are clumsy,' says Branson. Keeping small allowed for fast innovations; Virgin provide extra legroom, a limousine service (borrowed from SAS), hand-held in-flight video entertainment and neck massage! Service – the Cancerian attribute of 'looking after the customer' has been Virgin's priority. Originally a budget airline, Virgin's Business Class has been voted 'best business airline' by *Business Traveller* magazine and it is support from the full-price fare passenger that distinguishes Branson's airline strategy from that of the ill-fated Laker Airlines.

By 2000 Branson's new enterprise, Virgin Cola, was bigger than Pepsi in Europe. To enter the US market Richard Branson drove a tank up to the Coke sign in Times Square and fired at it to launch his challenge. This is the flamboyance of the Ascendant Leo, the strategy of the Virgo Moon, and the tribal family-orientation of the Sun in Cancer. 'I never went into business solely to make money', says Richard Branson. It is not craving for money, but an instinctive drive to extend the family. The Virgin family gets bigger and bigger. 'It all comes down to people', Branson told *Forbes* magazine. 'Nothing else even comes close.' Each month he writes an informal handwritten letter, distributed to all 5000 Virgin employees. He invites them to write or call with their problems, ideas and visions. Richard Branson's vision? One big happy Virgin family.

Jan Carlzon

Just as Branson's strategy with Virgin Atlantic has been 'looking after the customer', so the youthful chairman of SAS, Jan Carlzon, applied a similar strategy to transform that company from a loss-making, bureaucratic state airline to a profit-making customer-orientated airline with a reputation for personalized service. Jan Carlzon became President of SAS Airlines in 1981, the year it made an $8 million loss. The following year SAS turned in a gross profit of $71 million.

Success has been attributed to Carlzon's philosophy of 'looking after the customer'. Carlzon reversed the company hierarchy so that the main priority was meeting the customer's needs at each point of contact with the organization. He emphasized the importance of the frontline people, those who have direct contact with the customer.

In his book *Tear Down the Pyramids* (*Riv Pyramiderna!*, Bonniers, 1985), Carlzon outlines his strategy for successful management. The old system, he maintained, consisted of an administration directing the frontline service, in turn catering to the customer. At SAS Carlzon claimed to have reversed the perspective and placed the customer at the top, served by the service front line, in turn served by 'support troops' who were provided with strategic leadership. Carlzon described how at the age of 32 he was appointed managing director of a market-leading package holiday company and applied himself to the role of 'boss'. 'You get a new voice, you begin to act in a new way, you play a role to which you believe you have been nominated. You begin to live up to the expectations you think have been bestowed upon you. I began bossing!'

Cancer types like to look after people and take care of things, but they like to hold on to things too: once their pincers have locked on to something they will not let go. They are not gifted delegators. Carlzon describes the process he went through of clinging on to preconceived roles of 'boss' and 'employee', of trying to manage everything himself. By the time he was appointed at SAS in 1981 experience had taught him a new management philosophy – that the manager has to 'let go'. He encouraged the formation of teams working as integral units, by-passing the bureaucracy of administration, allowing employees to take on-the-spot decisions, and extending responsibilities in all areas. The aim was simple: to provide customer service and ensure customer satisfaction.

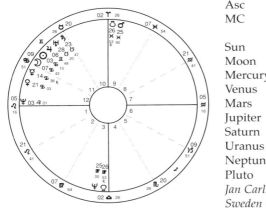

Asc	05 16 Leo	
MC	02 26 Ari	
Sun	03 13 Cnc	11
Moon	07 43 Cnc	11
Mercury	14 38 Cnc R	12
Venus	21 03 Cnc	12
Mars	25 50 Psc	9
Jupiter	06 49 Gem	11
Saturn	23 47 Tau	11
Uranus	28 20 Tau	11
Neptune	25 00 Vir	3
Pluto	03 01 Leo	12

Jan Carlzon 25 June 1941 05:45 Nykoping Sweden (Source: JA)

Carlzon extended the SAS services beyond the mere freighting of passengers from one place to another by setting up a hotel chain and hotel arrangements, and even a limousine service which picked up and returned passengers to their doorstep at a cost lower than a taxi. It was an application of the Swedish socialist model of cradle-to-grave 'taking care of people' with an important difference. The SAS service came wrapped in blue uniforms and a friendly smile rather than white coats and a hypodermic syringe.

Like Branson, Carlzon was a media 'star' – youthful, innovative and, above all, informal. Also like Branson (and George Bush Jr), Carlzon's chart features a Leo Ascendant in conjunct with Pluto. For Carlzon it meant transforming a bureaucratic and sterile SAS image to a customer and service-orientated airline.

He begins his book with an epigraph that could have been lifted from an astrology book describing the Cancer Sun-sign: 'Most important is that a person knows and feels they are needed.'

J D Rockefeller

John Davidson Rockefeller began his working life in 1857, aged 18, as a clerk at a commission house. He then moved to take up a clerical job with a small oil refinery at Cleveland, Ohio.

This was the beginning of a career in oil, which, three decades later, with the advent of the automobile industry, would become one of the most valuable commodities in the world. J D Rockefeller founded the Standard Oil Company with his younger brother William and by 1875 had secured control of the US oil trade. It marked the beginning of a dynasty of unprecedented privately earned wealth. Rockefeller gave over $500 million in aid grants to medical research. Other charities included universities and Baptist churches. He founded the Rockefeller Foundation in 1913 'to promote the wellbeing of mankind'.

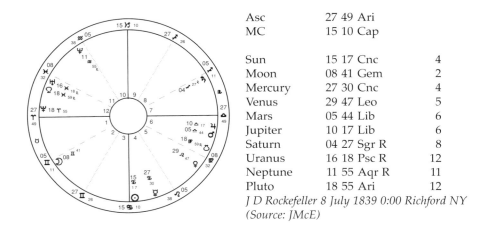

Asc	27 49 Ari	
MC	15 10 Cap	
Sun	15 17 Cnc	4
Moon	08 41 Gem	2
Mercury	27 30 Cnc	4
Venus	29 47 Leo	5
Mars	05 44 Lib	6
Jupiter	10 17 Lib	6
Saturn	04 27 Sgr R	8
Uranus	16 18 Psc R	12
Neptune	11 55 Aqr R	11
Pluto	18 55 Ari	12

J D Rockefeller 8 July 1839 0:00 Richford NY
(Source: JMcE)

The sign of Cancer represents family issues and historical continuity, and the name of Rockefeller is synonymous with three generations of philanthropy. John Davidson died in 1937; his son John Davidson Rockefeller II (1874–1960) became chairman of the Rockefeller Institute of Medical Research in 1906. In turn his son John Davidson III became chairman of the Rockefeller Foundation in 1952. The second son, Nelson Rockefeller, pursued a career in politics and spent three terms as New York Governor in the 1950s and 1960s. Like his grandfather he has Sun in Cancer, then Libra Ascendant, and Moon in Scorpio in the First House. The Moon in the First House indicates that family ties are part of the image on public display.

Other prominent Cancerians: Ingmar Bergman, Carl Bildt, Marc Chagall, Jean Cocteau, Bill Cosby, Princess Diana, Gerald Ford, Giuseppe Garibaldi, Ernest Hemingway, Hermann Hesse, Sir Edmund Hillary, Franz Kafka, Rose Kennedy, Herbert Marcuse, George Orwell, Georges Pompidou, Marcel Proust, Esther Rantzen, Diana Rigg, Ringo Starr, Natalie Wood.

Scorpio

22 October – 21 November
Ruling planets: Mars and Pluto
Element: Water
Quality: Fixed
Symbol: The Scorpion

Scorpios have a reputation for cruelty and vindictiveness, which appeals to the Scorpian ego no end. However, Scorpios, like the other Water signs, are 'service-orientated' and are adept at looking after people, particularly people in crisis. There is no crisis too big for Scorpios – the bigger the better, providing it is not their own. In an intense personal crisis (and all Scorpio crises are intense) there is an unfortunate side to the Scorpio personality which says: 'If I'm going down I'll take a few people with me.' Consequently, one should be wary of accepting a lift home with a Scorpio whose company has just gone bankrupt, or who has just been made redundant.

However, there is another side to the well-publicized sting in the Scorpio tail, apart from pain and death. Desert folk, going back to the ancient Egyptians, extract the scorpion's poison for medical purposes, and Scorpio is as much the sign of the healer as the tormentor. Often the two are inextricably linked – healing through purging; Mahatma Gandhi and Margaret Thatcher, both with Scorpio Ascendant, spoke of 'harsh medicine' to cure their ailing countries (see Libra).

The Mars side of Scorpio indicates energy, determination, resolve, fearlessness, tactlessness, even recklessness – attributes comparable to the Mars-ruled Aries. Pluto, however, the ruler of the underworld, suggests certain hidden qualities. The 'dark forces' traditionally associated with Scorpio are not necessarily always dark (although Scorpionic jealousy, anger, vindictiveness and rage are fairly dark) but also transformatory and healing.

For those who feel they have been harshly treated by Scorpios, it may be some small consolation to know that it is not nearly as harshly as Scorpios treat themselves. Scorpios are personalities at war with themselves – making ruthless demands upon both flesh and spirit.

The Strange Case of Dr Jekyll and Mr Hyde, by Scorpio writer R L Stevenson, has been taken as a description of split personality or schizophrenia, but on a deeper level it is about a man coming to terms with his latent evil. Scorpios need to go through darkness to get to light – if life is too comfortable, they devise a 'trial' to purge themselves of any 'shortcomings' in a form of self-inflicted surgery without anaesthetic (see Scorpio Business Ventures). Many Scorpio torments are readily assuaged by a taste of salt and a swift tequila.

There is a mystical side to Scorpios and, significantly, R L Stevenson claimed that the Jekyll and Hyde story came to him in a sequence of dreams, in ready-written chapters. The Scorpio personality is driven by more than material gain, constantly seeking values and meanings beneath the surface of ideas, people and events. Consequently few Scorpios are interested in ambition or success for its own sake. Once a task is undertaken, it must be completed thoroughly. Whereas Fire-sign people leap eagerly from promotion to promotion, Scorpios decline, preferring to have exhausted utterly the current post: thoroughness rather than ambition. Similarly Scorpios like to know who and what they are dealing with, and, again, the key word here is thorough.

Scorpios have a magnetic quality, inciting suspicion and scrutiny from others, inspiring comments like: 'What it is it with that guy?' or: 'What's up with her?' Scorpios prefer a few close friends to a broad circle of acquaintances, demanding and returning abject loyalty. Scorpios are either loved or hated; or (more frequently) loved and hated; no one is indifferent to a Scorpio.

The Scorpio sex symbol has a cold yet compelling quality – Grace Kelly and Alain Delon are two names that come to mind. Scorpios themselves are either sex-obsessed, consulting the *Sex Maniac's Diary* for the daily position, or obsessively prudish, writing off to the BBC or Board of Censors if a naked breast is displayed on a black and white art-house movie imported from Denmark.

Scorpios are brooding, persistent, resentful, stubborn, suspicious, and strong-willed. Scorpios make hard work of play and 'play' of hard work. For them, work is a mission. Whatever they want to achieve they usually will. A Scorpio enterprise must contain some spiritual or transformatory dimension, a sense of purpose and movement towards a goal, rather than mere self-gratification. Few Scorpio leaders or heads of companies have their names on the tops of buildings. This is for one of two reasons: they are not interested in careers of self-glorification, or they have made so many enemies they have not a hope in hell of ever making it to the top under their own name.

Even the Prince of Wales, who has all the prerequisites for being one of Britain's most relaxed individuals – abundant wealth, lots of property, and an army of security guards to defend his privacy so he can do more or less anything he wants – does not relax. He is a crusader, taking his role as a mission, in contrast to many other European monarchs and crown princes who buy fast cars and have a good time. Scorpios do not have a good time. Scorpios have an intense time.

Scorpio as Leader

'Just because I'm paranoid doesn't mean they're not out to get me,' says the distrustful Scorpio leader, who having got that far, watches their back.

Scandinavia's once most influential media baron, Scorpio Jan Stenbeck (b. 14 November 1942), described his 'attack and win' corporate strategy in a radio programme in 1997, five years before his death in 2002. Stenbeck compared his companies to the nomadic tribes of the Mongolian steppes – always travelling, always changing and adapting to new situations. 'The nomads are hunters,' he said, 'that strike quickly and take the enemy by surprise' This was the corporate policy of Stenbeck's London and Stockholm based MTG Group: to identify a weakness in the market, attack quickly and ruthlessly, and become market leaders before the competition had a chance to realize the opportunities lost.

Stenbeck's vast media empire comprises newspapers (including *Metro*, the free newspaper available in many European and US capital cities), television and radio stations, mobile telephones and more. Many of these companies have been described by financial analysts as 'unscrupulous and unprincipled', yet for all of Jan Stenbeck's perilous risk-taking, they have remained highly profitable. Stenbeck himself prized the 'bad-boy' reputation. 'It only makes us stronger,' he said. A biography of Jan Stenbeck published in 2002 describes his companies as a 'mafia-like' network that demands 100 per cent loyalty of its subordinates and tolerates no intrusion from outsiders.

Scorpios are not the most sociable of creatures, and Scorpio bosses are often lone wolf leaders inspiring devoted but subservient alliegance. Literary examples include Holmes, the penetrating investigator who having once accepted a case, resolves it, aided by the more affable and sociable (Taurean) Dr Watson. The good doctor always insists on a hearty breakfast, but once Holmes is on a case, food and sensual pleasure of any kind is a bothersome intrusion. And in moments of boredom, it is 'Pass me the slipper Watson!' – the dreaded cocaine that may momentarily assuage the Scorpio's torment.

Scorpio leaders are constantly seeking possibilities, and having once decided on a course of action, are relentless. Scorpios enjoy the strategy and scheming of marketing campaigns: these lead to the most satisfying prospect of all – the 'kill'.

Scorpio as Manager

It is not always easy to know when to disturb a Scorpio manager. They tend to give nothing away, and you need to know them very well before you learn to read their moods – and the danger signs that warn you to keep away. Scorpio managers know every dark and hidden secret of subordinates, upper level management, and all their competitors. An interview with a prospective employee is referred to by Scorpio managers, with a smile, as 'the third degree'. Particularly incriminating information will only be used in very special cases – requiring blackmail, extortion and other means of non-violent coercion.

Be wary of ill chosen words with Scorpio manager, or thoughtlessly optimistic target figures, for Scorpios will hold you to them. Beware the ill-timed joke – Scorpios will glare into your eyes and say in a soft yet grave voice, ''Just what do you mean by that?' Hardened globe-trotting trouble-shooters go to pieces.

Scorpio John Cleese wrote a book entitled *Families and How to Survive Them*, which could easily have been *Companies and How to Survive Them*. He then devoted his efforts to producing management videos. The Cleese alter ego, Basil Fawlty, is a case-study of depressed Scorpio middle management.

Basil Fawlty lives in paranoid fear of upper management (Sybil), finding an outlet for his suppressed anger in lower management (Polly), and even more in staff (Manuel), and, inadvertently, the clientele. When Basil Fawlty organizes the fire-drill, for example, it is with a Scorpionic insistence on sticking to a pre-determined schedule, even if it means hotel occupants perish because of it. When

Fawlty fails to provide a client with a Waldorf Salad ('Sorry. We're out of Waldorfs'), an apology is not enough – he produces a fictitious letter of apology from the (absent) cook, and dramatizes a fictitious punishment to said (still absent) cook, behind the closed kitchen doors. Sorry is not enough for the erring Scorpio – they will torture themselves with remorse.

Balanced Scorpio managers, however, are staunch allies who will defend loyal staff team members to the end – team leaders who maintain a distance between themselves and colleagues, yet when the situation demands, can inspire the kind of commitment to a task they demand of themselves.

A Taurus marketing director with a reputation of demolishing five telephones and three secretaries per week, telephoned the Scorpio head of a distribution firm. He sought advice regarding the print run of a particular publication.

Scorpio: You've got a nerve.
Taurus: I just need a figure...
Scorpio: I'm not your sales manager. How should I know how many copies?
Taurus: An approximation...
Scorpio: Do your own damned work!

The Scorpio slammed the phone down, walked across to a visiting agent with a severe and intense look on his face – then broke into a broad grin: 'That's the trouble with Charlie, you know. He can't take stress.' I was the visiting agent, and this is a true story.

Scorpio as Employee

The Scorpio employee is devoted, hard-working, and will not tolerate fools. Pity the employer or manager unable to command a Scorpio's respect. Scorpios thrive on achievement – they set themselves to a task with purpose and resolve, and will not rest until it is done, and done properly. Scorpio has no patience with the trivial – they consider employment as 'The Work'.

However, Scorpio employees who are not happy, either with the work, or with immediate superiors, have the power to transform a restful and tranquil ambience into an inferno of Dante-esque proportions. Not that they will shout or show signs of losing their temper – just the opposite.

Incompetent manager: Everything all right is it?
Discontent Scorpio employee: Fine, fine – just fine.
(*Meanwhile, thinks to self:* Right! First the car tyres, then the sugar in the petrol tank. I can do the coffee percolator tomorrow!)

You can tell if things are going badly – Scorpio employees seethe. Though not usually prone to violence nothing antagonizes Scorpio more than a foolish person exercising authority.

A Scorpio junior manager of a major UK publishing house was so annoyed by a company driver that he turned and punched the fellow square on the nose, staining the courtyard crimson. He became a marketing director at the age of 29, and went on to his own publishing firm, one of the largest independent publishers in the UK. This is a true story.

If a manager needs help in envisaging a prospective Scorpio employee, consider the relationship between agent 'licensed to kill' James Bond (Scorpio) and his anxious superior, M (Virgo).

A Profile of the Scorpio Manager

The Office

Lighting is subdued and there may be a stuffed Moose head on the wall. Unlike the average office, the atmosphere is mystic, eccentric and reminiscent of an old castle. The desk lamp will be of the swivel variety that can be turned immediately toward the eyes of the visitor in the single guest chair – just in case they have difficulty answering certain questions. The guest chair may well conceal a whoopee cushion.

The unusual wallpaper design that resembles a pattern of random splattered sepia stains as if from coffee cups hurled against the wall, is in fact stains from coffee cups hurled against the wall. An enterprising Gemini will no doubt patent the design and make a fortune, appealing at once to the Scorpio appreciation of the eccentric, while at the same concealing further ill-judged moments of loss of temper.

Otherwise the walls may be decorated with Tibetan Buddhist motifs, or perhaps paintings of the Hindu destroyer-goddess Kali. In the bottom drawer of the very large mahogany desk can be found a container of salt and a bottle of tequila (or vodka might be substituted). In extreme cases there will also be a packet of razor blades.

The Company Car

Ford launched a vehicle in the 1980s in an attempt to secure the elusive market of executives eligible for a company car born between late October and late November. Success has been limited. In the first place, Scorpios are quite secretive and do not like to advertise being a Scorpio. In the second place, Scorpio managers do not care that much what they drive – chances are they are content with the car they inherited from a deceased uncle.

More status-conscious Scorpio managers prefer a vehicle with a dangerous reputation, preferably in black or midnight blue, with tyre-shredding devices a desirable option. Check the side of the car for 'notches': they most likely denote pedestrian crossing victims. The Scorpio manager who has 'arrived' drives a Jaguar – a predatory vehicle in the classical mould.

The Business Lunch

Scorpio hosts may select a place recommended in the current year's edition of the *Sex Maniacs Diary*. Scorpios appreciate low key lighting and an unobtrusive setting. American-style restaurants where fresh-faced large-toothed Californians announce brashly at the table 'Hi, I'm Bill', do not impress Scorpio clients, who demand good taste, discretion and decorum.

Scorpios tend to favour places with stuffed animal heads on the wall and establishments where you can choose your own live fish or an amphibious creature swimming about in a tank and have it despatched in the manner of your choice (preferably at the table). This is one of the few occasions on which you will see the Scorpio face beam in pleasure.

Whereas Arians, also ruled by Mars, order hot curries as an invitation to a contest of endurance, Scorpio hosts are likely to order hot curries as an overt gesture of inflicting discomfort. Scorpios themselves, impervious to pain, look on with contained relish.

At an impeccably-timed moment Scorpio hosts may remove a pen from the pocket, and present a contract. 'Shall we sign that deal now?' the Scorpio host will say. 'Or shall I have your canary liquidized?' You'll probably sign.

The Scorpio Business Venture

Scorpios make excellent surgeons as they are rarely afraid of blood, and enjoy cutting things open, removing the bad bits and patching up the good. For this reason, non-surgeon Scorpios are often to be found as editors for film companies. The film editor fulfils the same role on a 'story' as the surgeon on a body – taking out the bad, examining the good, ensuring they are healthy, and putting back what is left, in order to make sure everything is whole and healed. For the same reason, you will find many Scorpio editors working for publishing companies and newspapers. Just check out how many red pens the Scorpio editor gets through.

An enterprise that involves investigation, exploration and research appeals to the penetrating Scorpio mind. Occult literature, security, surveillance and private investigations, are favoured Scorpio pursuits. So is dentistry – they do not mind inflicting pain.

Scorpios are rarely ambitious for wealth for its own sake, only power. However, in the pursuit of power Scorpios usually only succeed when realizing a spiritual dimension to their vocation. In positions of moderate power Scorpio prefers the possibility to influence or torment a select few rather than an anonymous mass. Similarly Scorpio will cultivate one or two close business liaisons, and get to know them thoroughly. This, they find, is preferable to superficial acquaintances with many people.

The Scorpio Natal Chart

Bill Gates

'Resistance is futile. You will be assimilated.' This was a T-shirt slogan of the 1990s, originally from a Star Trek movie, but deftly applied to Microsoft's corporate strategy. Between the legal battles and global marketing of Windows, Explorer and a range of PC software, for a while it seemed that the company founded by Bill Gates in 1976 would indeed take over the world.

Today William H. Gates is listed as chairman and chief software architect of Microsoft Corporation, and, according to *Forbes* magazine, is the richest man in the world. In 2002 Microsoft was employing more than 40,000 people in 60 countries, and had revenues of over $25 billion.

Does the natal chart of Bill Gates tell us he is destined to be the richest man on the planet? In *Accidental Empires* (1995), author Robert Cringley argues that the success of Microsoft, Bill Gates and the 'computer nerds' who ran Silicon Valley was down to good luck – a few individuals being in the right place at the right time. In classical times luck went by the name of Fortuna. In one hand she held a cornucopia, the horn of plenty; in the other, a scythe. Fortuna could give you everything, or cut you down with a single sweep of the scythe. In today's business world we avoid terms like good and bad luck, and talk instead of 'best possible' and 'worst possible' scenarios. The terminology will adapt to each new age and culture, but the unpredictable vagaries of fate are with us in every epoch. The planetary cycles provide us with images of possible scenarios, but the sharp-focused details of the big picture are available only after the event.

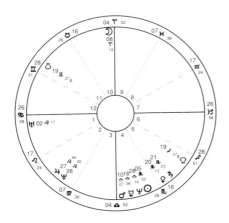

Asc	26 58 Cnc	
MC	04 52 Ari	
Sun	05 02 Sco	4
Moon	08 14 Ari	10
Mercury	16 36 Lib	4
Venus	20 13 Sco	5
Mars	10 07 Lib	4
Jupiter	27 46 Leo	2
Saturn	21 35 Sco	5
Uranus	02 17 Leo	1
Neptune	28 14 Lib	4
Pluto	28 20 Leo	2

*Bill Gates 28 Oct 1955 22:00 PST Seattle WA
(Source: ADB)*

165

For example, Bill Gates' chart reveals Jupiter conjunct Pluto in the Second House. Jupiter represents wealth, good fortune and expansion; Pluto represents change, transformation and upheaval; and the Second House is the House of money, property and material well-being. This does not tell us Bill Gates is destined to be the richest person in the world, but combined with other factors, indicates he could be financially well-off.

Apart from the earthy Second House, the chart is dominated by Water and Fire: Sun in Scorpio, Cancer Ascendant and Moon in Aries. The Moon (which rules Cancer) is in conjunction to the Midheaven, which represents the focus of individual will to overcome any obstacle in order to fulfil a chosen goal. In the early 1980s 'a computer in every home' seemed unimaginable; today it is much closer to reality.

In *Business @ the Speed of Thought* (1999), Bill Gates outlines a new vision: how computer and Internet technology will change corporate structure, business strategies and the way we define production and commerce.

Gates' books, *Business @ the Speed of Thought* and *The Road Ahead* (1995), reveal little about leadership strategies and management style. You have to get the inside story from people inside the company. Have they been assimilated? They wear the same company 'casual' dress style, and every event (trade fair, conference, business seminar) is a sales opportunity; an opportunity to demonstrate unflagging company loyalty. If you are part of the Microsoft organization, you are committed 100 per cent – 'either you're with us or against us', commented one European-based Microsoft sales person.

It is a level of commitment and tribal loyalty reminiscent of media mogul Jan Stenbeck's description of the Mongolian nomads. Mobility combined with an astute eye for weaknesses in the enemy camp: the swift attack, the plunder and the sharing of the spoils of victory. It was the strategy that enabled Bill Gates to capture the computer market from IBM in 1981; it is the strategy Microsoft pursues in the dominance of the Internet, the games market, and biotechnology.

Ted Turner

'If I only had a little humility, I would be perfect', said Ted Turner of himself. The founder of CNN started his empire with his father's bankrupt billboard company, became a sports entrepreneur in the 1960s, and with the purchase of an ailing television station, revolutionized the television industry.

Ted Turner is not known for his humility. He grew up in Atlanta, was expelled from Brown University but developed a passion for the classics. He has assumed the role of a contemporary Odysseus battling against the major problems of our age, wrote one biographer. At a conservationist speech in 2001 Turner claimed that 'CNN forced me to really hone myself on global and national issues… CNN is a national and international news service and has to deal with the most important, pressing issues.' These he listed as:

1. The Cold War and subsequent nuclear arsenal
2. The population explosion
3. Global warming and the environment

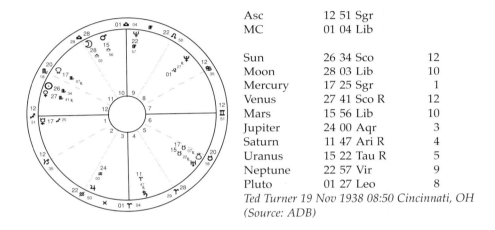

Asc	12 51 Sgr	
MC	01 04 Lib	
Sun	26 34 Sco	12
Moon	28 03 Lib	10
Mercury	17 25 Sgr	1
Venus	27 41 Sco R	12
Mars	15 56 Lib	10
Jupiter	24 00 Aqr	3
Saturn	11 47 Ari R	4
Uranus	15 22 Tau R	5
Neptune	22 57 Vir	9
Pluto	01 27 Leo	8

Ted Turner 19 Nov 1938 08:50 Cincinnati, OH
(Source: ADB)

At present the major threat, according to Turner, is the nuclear arsenal – a catastrophe waiting to happen. He describes such a catastrophe in graphic terms.

Scorpios are the masters of the 'worst possible scenario' and Ted Turner is no exception; with Sagittarius Rising and Mercury in the First House, he is not likely to keep quiet about it. The 'Terrible Ted' reputation is not based on his penchant for doom, as much as his forthright statements on just about everything.

Yet it is through his risk-taking and business acumen that he is most renowned. Turner created four cable stations when cable television was in its infancy: WTBS Superstation, CNN (Cable Network News), Headline News, and TNT (Turner Network Television). In 1986, he purchased MGM for $1 billion, and created a scandal by having the extensive library of black-and-white movie classics digitally 'colored'.

The other side of Ted Turner is the philanthropist. He was named *Time's* Man of the Year in 1991 for his work in international relations, and at a press conference in 1997, he donated $1 billion to the United Nations, the largest single philanthropic contribution in history. 'What good is wealth sitting in the bank?' he said in an interview with CNN's Larry King. 'The more good I do, the more money has come in', he added. 'You have to learn to give.'

After two marriages he married Jane Fonda in 1991, a combination that led to a strong media profile; both with strong ego and commitment to causes, and both with a reputation for speaking out of turn. (The 'Mouth of the South' is another Turner epithet.) Jane Fonda's reputation began with her anti-Vietnam war protests in the 1960s; Ted Turner's continues into the twenty-first century with his public jokes about the Pope, birth control and the commandment against adultery being outdated. She is Sagittarius, he has Sagittarius Rising.

Their media profile as a 'power-pair' is appropriate; Turner's natal chart shows Moon and Mars in Libra in the Tenth House – relationship as status, as power, and as representing the mutual benefits of a well-honed business contract. In 2000, they separated, and the pre-nuptial arrangement meant Turner retained his nine substantial ranches, including vast estates in Montana and New Mexico, notably a 578,000-acre ranch spreading over New Mexico and Colorado.

Jack Welch

The corporate leader perhaps most representative of the Scorpio 'surgeon's-knife' approach to successful business is Jack Welch. In his 20 years as General Electric's CEO he became renowned for his ruthlessly competitive business style and two celebrated maxims: 'Be number 1 or 2 in your business or get out,' and 'Change before you have to.'

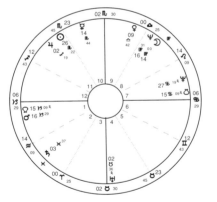

Asc	6 29 Cap	
MC	2 30 Sco	
Sun	26 22 Sco	11
Moon	14 00 Vir	8
Mercury	14 44 Sco	10
Venus	09 42 Lib	9
Mars	16 29 Cap	1
Jupiter	02 19 Sgr	11
Saturn	03 37 Psc	2
Uranus	02 36 Tau R	4
Neptune	16 31 Vir	8
Pluto	27 19 Cnc R	7

Jack Welch 19 Nov 1935 10:30 Peabody MA
(Source: AA)

He joined General Electric Company in 1960 and was elected Vice-President in 1972 and Vice- Chairman in 1979. In 1981 he became the eighth Chairman and CEO in the company's 117-year history.

The Jack Welch 'select and concentrate' management style transformed an ailing GE into an unrivalled global business group. Soon after his appointment as CEO in 1981, Jack Welch sold off GE's TV and VCR manufacturing divisions, while acquiring NBC, one of the three US networks. These and other drastic 'acts of surgery' led to mass lay-offs and a good deal of harsh criticism outside and inside the company. But during the 20 years up to 2000, GE more than quadrupled sales and expanded net profit six-fold. When he retired in July 2001 he had a record of returning more value to shareholders than Bill Gates – an increase of more than 3000 per cent.

In his best-selling autobiography, *Jack: Straight From the Gut* (2001), Welch defines the secret of successful leadership as an ongoing commitment to change. His management slogans have become business school standard: 'Number One Number Two Strategy' based on the 'be 1 or 2 or get out' maxim, and 'Work-Out', the Jack Welch euphemism for initiating change throughout the whole organization.

In an interview in 2002 Jack Welch defined leadership as a mix of chemistry and passion. 'It's caring more than the next guy. It's connecting. It's getting in the skin of those you work with, getting each employee to understand where you're going and what you're doing. Even in the smallest operation, when I had one employee, I was living in his skin so that he felt it and he cared about what he was doing more than anything else, and he knew I cared about him and could make him something special. That's what leadership is all about.'

Jack Welch describes his 'cruel to be kind' approach as the essence of corporate survival. When the US airline Pan Am was in economic difficulty GE was offered the Intercontinental hotel chain. 'You shouldn't be selling the hotels. You should be selling the airline,' advised Welch. Their problem, said Welch, was that they hung on to a bad business for some legacy reason. They couldn't get beyond Pan Am as an airline company. Any corporate leader has an obligation 'not to be doing yesterday's stuff'.

A good employee, he says, depends on the values in the company. 'At GE, integrity is a core value. We assume everybody has integrity; that's the ticket to the game. And we assume everybody makes their commitments.' Each employee was rated on the Four Es: Energy Level, Energize (how a person inspires others), Edge ('the ability to make the calls'), Execution ('Get it done. Don't talk about it. Just deliver the goods.')

Success has its price, however, and the personal tribulations of Jack Welch provide the morality tales any committed leader must confront. Jack Welch went through two divorces and two heart attacks, and said that, as a parent to his four children he was 'the ultimate workaholic'.

His natal chart tells the same story. Capricorn Rising and Moon in Virgo indicate a focus on work, career, and a slow and steady rise to the top. Mars in Capricorn in the First House suggests a 'do what must be done' approach, and no attempt to conceal it (nothing is hidden in the First House). 'Leadership is about caring more than anybody else,' he writes.

There is one more astrological configuration of note in Jack Welch's chart: Saturn in the Second House. It is the placement that indicates more than any other that money is a serious business. No matter how much wealth is accumulated, it will always mean hard work. It is also a placement that represents a burden of responsibility that we find manifest in another Scorpio subject, Prince Charles.

Prince Charles

Royal family charts are favourites among astrologers and public alike, as we search vainly for clues suggesting Destiny. What we find are horoscopes as applicable to a future rag-and-bone man as to a future king. As an example, an unsubstantiated but oft-cited case of 'time twins' concerns King George III of Great Britain and an iron merchant, who were both born in London at the same time on 4 June 1738. They were married on the same day, the merchant took over his father's business on the same day that George was crowned king, they had the same number of children, both men suffered mental illness and both died on the same day, 29 January 1820. Although this particular case is conveniently estranged by history, authentic case-studies of time twins with documented parallel lives have been published in reputable psychology journals.

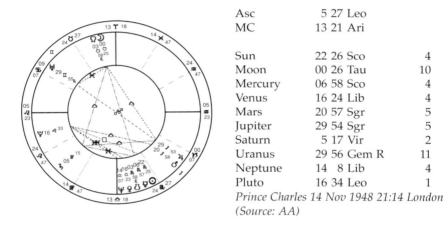

Asc	5 27 Leo	
MC	13 21 Ari	
Sun	22 26 Sco	4
Moon	00 26 Tau	10
Mercury	06 58 Sco	4
Venus	16 24 Lib	4
Mars	20 57 Sgr	5
Jupiter	29 54 Sgr	5
Saturn	5 17 Vir	2
Uranus	29 56 Gem R	11
Neptune	14 8 Lib	4
Pluto	16 34 Leo	1

Prince Charles 14 Nov 1948 21:14 London
(Source: AA)

In the case of Prince Charles we see a prominent Fourth House: the Sun, Mercury, Venus and Neptune all in the House of family, home and domestic issues. The implication is the taking over of the 'family business'. Saturn in the Second House indicates that money is taken seriously. In the case of Prince Charles his Second House issues have involved raising money for charity; most of his working hours are concerned with raising money for communities, regional projects and unemployed young people. A Second House Saturn means money does not signify 'good times' – money means hard work. It can also indicate a resistance, even fear, of matters relating to the Second House. In addition to money, the Second House concerns property and possessions, even sensual pleasure.

The main structure of the chart, however, concerns the Scorpio Sun, a Leo Ascendant and Moon in Taurus in the Tenth House. The Moon in an Earth sign and an Earth House suggests a personality with an intuitive ability to get down to basics, to respond to problems with practical and plausible solutions.

The Scorpio side of Prince Charles is identifiable in the 'all or nothing' attitude with which he broaches issues, whether it is saving Britain from modernist architecture, or advocating alternative medicine. After a term at the exclusive Timbertop school in Victoria, Australia (while still in his teens), he described the burden of royalty as not having to be as good as anyone else, but having to be better, as 'one' is always in the public eye. Regardless of his personal feelings he must never be content with being merely competent but must always excel, whether at playing polo, holding a debate, or dancing Scottish reels.

The Prince now has two sons, offspring to ensure the continuity of the 'family business', but the question is, when will the Prince of Wales become King? In 1995 Princess Diana in a television interview described Charles as incapable of overcoming his 'limitations' to take on the role. But limitations can be a strength: the British monarchy needs to adapt if it is to survive with the kind of popular support other European constitutional monarchies have achieved. Prince Charles' 'limitations' – the human foibles of mere mortals – may have weakened the credibility of the House of Windsor, but they have also brought the monarchy closer to the people. Perhaps it is the healing powers of Scorpio that are needed to return the monarchy to a position of cultural and national significance. Whatever the weaknesses of members of the Royal Family, they should not be confused with the institution of the monarchy.

In 2006, Saturn will enter Charles' Second House, intensifying the issues of discipline, responsibility and hard work in affairs of money, wealth and property already indicated by Saturn's natal placement in that House. The following year his second Saturn return will increase this focus still further.

If and when Prince Charles should assume the throne, the chart reveals a personality who considers his duties with serious intent.

Indira Gandhi

Another head of state who took over the 'family business', continuing the family dynasty, was Indira Gandhi. As in the chart of Prince Charles, here is another prominent Fourth House: Sun and Mercury suggesting 'family business', family roots, and the continuation of a blood line. Both Indira Gandhi's father and son were Prime Ministers of India. Also, like Prince Charles, we see a Leo Ascendant, a symbolic ascending to the 'throne', suggesting a life of prominence.

In 1965 Mrs Indira Gandhi, daughter of former Prime Minister Jawaharial Nehru, became Prime Minister. Her first years were politically precarious, confronting opposition from within the ranks and terrorism from outside.

In 1971 she won a landslide majority and began a programme of major socialist reforms. Government crises, devastation following the 1971 monsoon, and the subsequent food crisis led to increased opposition. She faced allegations of dictatorial government.

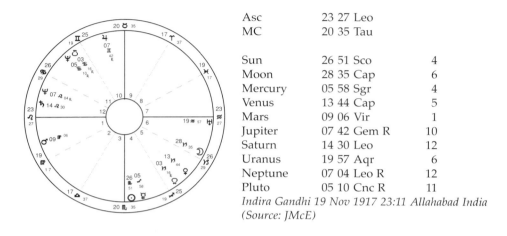

Asc	23 27 Leo	
MC	20 35 Tau	
Sun	26 51 Sco	4
Moon	28 35 Cap	6
Mercury	05 58 Sgr	4
Venus	13 44 Cap	5
Mars	09 06 Vir	1
Jupiter	07 42 Gem R	10
Saturn	14 30 Leo	12
Uranus	19 57 Aqr	6
Neptune	07 04 Leo R	12
Pluto	05 10 Cnc R	11

Indira Gandhi 19 Nov 1917 23:11 Allahabad India
(Source: JMcE)

Her election victory of 1975 was declared null and void by the Allahabad High Court and Mrs Gandhi was barred from office for six years. Shortly after, a state of emergency was declared.

Indira Gandhi's political popularity had suffered with her compulsory sterilization campaign, and support of Soviet aid. The personality cult around Mrs Gandhi was still strong, but she was put on trial nonetheless, facing charges of violation of parliamentary privileges. In December 1978 she was sent to prison.

In July 1979 the government collapsed and, following another general election in January 1980, Mrs Gandhi was re-elected with an overwhelming two-thirds majority. Political analysts described Indira Gandhi's triumph as being entirely due to the personality cult surrounding her. Her Congress Party had no policies as such, nor any strategy for tackling India's pressing problems of population growth, poverty and illiteracy.

She pursued India's so-called 'non-alignment' policy. The Soviet Union invaded Afghanistan in December 1979, and in January 1980, just after Mrs Gandhi returned to power, the United Nations voted to condemn the act. India did not take part in the vote. Later that year her son, Sanjay Gandhi, who had been groomed as his mother's successor, was killed in a plane crash.

During the 1980s the Sikh separatist movement gathered momentum, and Mrs Gandhi's government was threatened with full-scale rebellion. On 31 October 1984 Indira Gandhi was assassinated by two Sikh members of her personal bodyguard. The ensuing riots claimed more than 3000 lives.

Her second son, Rajiv, a trained commercial pilot without a political background, took over the role of Prime Minister. He promised a strong programme of communal reconciliation and economic reform. Five years later Rajiv Gandhi was himself assassinated when a young woman presented him with flowers at a political meeting. The concealed bomb killed the assassin, Gandhi and several other guests. Despite pressure from the Congress Party on Rajiv Gandhi's Italian-born widow to assume a political role and continue the Gandhi dynasty, she declined.

Indira Gandhi ruled with an iron hand: 'The problems of India require drastic measures,' she had remarked. But Scorpio is not strong will alone. It represents an intensity of spirit that may be destructive or may be spiritual. 'India is a land of contradictions,' wrote Indira Gandhi, 'but basically isn't every developed human being so? Can one even know a human being fully? How so a country? India's seeming lack of sophistication is the result of centuries of spiritual evolution: the wisdom of countless saints mingled with experience of vast political upheavals.'

In a book entitled *Eternal India* (1980), which she wrote during her term in prison, she concludes with an Indian verse that is as relevant to India as to her own life, and to the mystical side of Scorpio:

> *From the unreal lead me to the real*
> *From darkness lead me to light*
> *From death lead me to Eternal Life.*
> (Brihadaranyaka Upanishad)

Billy Graham

Billy Graham is a Christian crusader – an American evangelist who began revivalist campaigns before 'Born Again' Christianity became a media cliché'. A major theme of his sermons and writings is the need to be reborn, to accept the faith and become a new person.

His Christian rallies and crusades, held in the United States in the 1950s, attracted thousands of believers and non-believers alike. He organized world tours, and by the late 1950s Billy Graham was an enterprise on a global scale. He held rallies in Britain: in Haringey, north London, in 1954, and in Glasgow in 1955. He filled football stadia in Australian cities in the 1960s.

His books, *Peace with God* (1954), *Mission Accomplished* (1956) and, later, *How to be Born Again* (1977), describe how the origin of sin is seen as the Fall. The cause of the Fall was, according to the Gospel of St John, which Graham quotes, 'the lust of the flesh and the lust of the eyes.' Like Indira Gandhi, he claims: 'Man is a contradiction. On the one side hatred, depravity and sin; on the other side kindness, compassion and love.'

At the height of Billy Graham's US popularity, Burt Lancaster (Scorpio) starred in the film *Elmer Gantry* (Richard Brooks, 1960) as an impassioned revivalist preacher. The film satirized the Billy Graham style of revivalism, but conveyed the power of 'a man with a mission' and his ability to sway crowds. Scorpios make you feel guilty with a passion.

Billy Graham has Sun, Mercury and Venus in Scorpio, and Aries Ascendant, the sign of the crusader. The spiritual side of Scorpio concerns fulfilment through confrontation with 'darkness'. In order to be redeemed a soul must first endure hell. Graham's sermons have a terrifying quality, but the message is redemption. Scorpio Jim Jones persuaded an entire commune to follow him in death in a Central–American collective. Charles Manson (Sun and three planets in Scorpio), who led a cult responsible for the ritual murder of Sharon Tate and her household in the 1960s, is also a Scorpio.

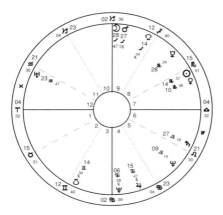

Asc	04 32 Ari	
MC	02 39 Cap	
Sun	14 37 Sco	7
Moon	28 47 Sgr	9
Mercury	28 24 Sco	8
Venus	10 36 Sco	7
Mars	27 18 Sgr	9
Jupiter	15 47 Cnc R	4
Saturn	27 18 Leo	6
Uranus	23 47 Aqr	12
Neptune	09 19 Leo	5
Pluto	06 28 Cnc R	4

Billy Graham 7 Nov 1918 16:30 Charlotte NC (Source: JK)

Martin Luther, a Scorpio born in Eisleben on 10 November 1483, has succeeded in filling cool Scandinavian souls with burning guilt for over 500 years – leaving only alcohol and hard work to assuage the torments of sin.

Other prominent Scorpios: James Boswell, Richard Burton, Albert Camus, James Cook, Marie Curie, Alain Delon, Fyodor Dostoevsky, Erasmus, Art Garfunkel, Katherine Hepburn, Chiang Kai-Shek, John Keats, Grace Kelly, Robert Kennedy, Burt Lancaster, Vivian Leigh, Roy Lichtenstein, Martin Luther, Marie-Antoinette, Field Marshal Montgomery, Mike Nichols, Pablo Picasso, Sir Walter Raleigh, Theodore Roosevelt, Martin Scorsese, Paul Simon, Robert Louis Stevenson, Dylan Thomas, Leon Trotsky, Ivan Turgenev, Jan Vermeer, Lucchino Visconti, Kurt Vonnegut, Evelyn Waugh.

Pisces

20 February – 20 March
Ruling planets: Jupiter andNeptune
Element: Water
Quality: Mutable
Symbol: The Fishes

Pisceans are considered kind, sympathetic and receptive; also vague, imprecise, careless, and secretive. These are the romantic dreamers of the zodiac who allow things to get on top of them, find they cannot cope, and go off somewhere to find religion or study ballet. All the Water signs are emotional signs, and Pisces most of all; Cancer sighs, Scorpio seethes, Pisces weeps.

Imaginative rather than practical, Pisceans are not well equipped to contend with the real-life issues of income tax returns, operating manuals, budgets and deadlines. Pisces is the sign of the dreamer: the dreams may be those of the visionary, the artist and the writer, or idle and time-wasting fantasies, fuelled by wine bottles and television soap operas.

Many Pisceans are drawn into film, theatre, music and the arts, either to realize their dreams and visions, or to live in otherwise fabricated make-believe worlds. Compassionate, over-sensitive, romantic, unambitious – many Piscean salespeople stay 'on the road', not through lack of managerial ability, but because they like a drifter's lifestyle: the anonymous hotel room, the prospect of a new place and new faces the next day, the feeling of not being tied down or burdened with responsibilities.

Pisces is a dual sign represented by two fishes swimming in opposite directions, one tied to the other. This symbolizes the two sides of the Pisces personality: one side which wants material wealth and public acclaim, the other side drawn to 'an open sea' of things unknown and mystical – the spiritual side of life.

Pisces' ruling planet, Neptune, is the god of oceans, and if and when Pisceans drown under a heap of unfinished office papers, or under the emotions of a love affair out of control, they can be seen struggling in the symbolic waters, choking wretches with outstretched hands: 'Help me – I'm going under for the third time.'

Pisceans like to be consumed by things: whether it is work, religion, love, or a television series, they become absorbed in order to withdraw into another world – an alternative 'unreality' to the one in which they live.

Pisceans are often convinced that they inevitably drift in and out of occupations, relationships, and places, unsure about their direction in life – though in fact they are as much in control as anyone else. They leave decisions to 'destiny' ('Let fate decide!'), but as the German romantic poet Novalis wrote: 'Character is destiny.'

The film *Patty Hearst* (1988) about the Pisces Hearst heiress (W R Hearst, see Taurus) who was kidnapped by terrorists, 'brainwashed' and who finally joined the group who kidnapped her in their bank raids and terrorist exploits, was a box-office disaster. Paul Schrader, the writer/director, said later: 'In making this film I have broken the cardinal rule of the cinema.' He had made a film about a passive protagonist. As far as Patty Hearst was concerned, passive though she may appear to the outside world, her 'involvement' was the means by which she could explore the darker side of her own personality.

The cinema, both as a holy temple of screen entertainment and as an industry, is a benign hiding-place for Pisceans who have trouble coping with reality. Ex-Beatle George Harrison found a niche setting up Handmade Films, which has produced most of the Monty Python films and a string of other British comedies. The story of British producer David Puttnam, who describes film as 'an art form which can unite mankind', is outlined here.

Pisces, the last sign of the zodiac, perceives issues as global; when Arians speak it is as 'I, the individual'; for Pisceans, it is 'I, a small part of universal humanity.' Piscean British Prime Minister Neville Chamberlain declared 'world peace' in 1938; the Piscean ex-Soviet leader Mikhail Gorbachev in 1984 prophesied the end of the Cold War and offered the hope of world peace with an alliance between the superpowers. Fifty years earlier, a Piscean psychic named Edgar Cayce foretold that by the end of the millennium the US and the USSR would unite as allies to become 'the hope of world peace'.

Born in Kentucky on 18 March 1877, (Sun in Pisces, Leo Ascendant, Taurus Moon, and three Eighth House planets including Saturn), Edgar Cayce was described as an unusual child who talked regularly to invisible playmates, and conversed with 'presences'. He would pass on their advice on treating ailments and injuries, which proved uncannily accurate. He discovered psychic powers accidentally at the age of 24 (in 1901) when he lost his voice. After a year of speaking in a whisper he consulted a hypnotist, and under hypnosis worked out his own cure. He subsequently (and reluctantly) became a diagnostician, but only under hypnosis. His readings became more detailed, extending to fields outside medicine. At the instigation of a philosopher named Lammers, Cayce began his 'life readings' in 1923. In the first year he made 2,500 such readings describing the building of the pyramids, the society of Atlantis, forthcoming earthquakes, catastrophes, and the 1929 Wall Street crash.

Cayce's readings occurred under trance, hence his name 'the Sleeping Prophet', and due to his strict Protestant upbringing, he refused to accept the readings of his trances concerning world religions, past civilizations, and those utterances in direct contradiction to his fundamentalist understanding of the Bible. He recounted people's past lives in minute detail, though in his conscious state he could never accept the idea of reincarnation.

In spite of offers of large sums of money to do readings he refused and rejected efforts to commercialize his 'gift'. Cayce gave up his photography business and devoted himself full-time to readings. He was publicized during the war years as 'the miracle man of Virginia Beach' and was inundated with requests, which he obliged in spite of his failing health. He died on 3 January 1945, aged 67, leaving behind a total of 14,246 readings covering virtually every field of human thought and enterprise.

Pisces as Leader

The mere heading reads like a contradiction in terms, yet the names of Kreuger, Murdoch and Gorbachev reveal that Pisceans indeed may be leaders, and with quite special qualities. Piscean leaders see themselves responding to a higher calling – offering up their own identity for the sake of the corporation, or the public, or a country, or the world at large.

In addition, behind every Piscean boss is a Leo spouse. Or Capricorn. Or Aries. When Piscean Desi Arnaz took over a major television studio in the 1950s, dominant Leo Lucille Ball was behind him all the way. Gorbachev's rise through the ranks of the Soviet Politburo was guided and steered by his ambitious Capricorn wife, Raisa (her memoirs, *Reminiscences and Reflections*, published in 1991, reveal to just what extent this was the case).

Piscean leaders make a brave show of authority – that they are boss and everything is under control. But, beneath the surface, uncertainty waits.

Pisces as Manager

Piscean managers are understanding, sympathetic, indecisive and easily manipulated. Pisceans put off difficult decisions: unresolved small problems may soon become crises. In times of urgent decision-making, Piscean managers favour the 'let's just wait and see what happens' approach. The other favoured Piscean axiom is 'to go with the flow'. Sometimes it even works.

An interview with a Piscean manager may leave the interviewee confused: Pisceans are vague when expressing what they want, and expect people to intuitively understand what they mean. Piscean managers like to appear as though in control, but scratch the surface and you find chaos. It is an endearing chaos, however, and Pisceans have a knack of charming folk. Employees are seduced by and feel sympathetic towards well-meaning Piscean managers; they do their best to help them out during times of hardship and difficulty – which are constant.

Well-intentioned, well-liked, and lost in fantasies about their secretaries, Piscean managers, at the height of their mid-life crises, may declare: 'There must be more to life than an office and weekly pay cheque!' They might just embark on a whole new lifestyle.

Pisces as Employee

In the hands of the right manager Piscean employees are a godsend. For the right boss Pisceans are capable of anything. Piscean Roger Daltry, one-time lead singer with The Who, embarked on an acting career with Ken Russell as his director. 'If he wrote the scene,' said Roger, 'I'd die for that man!' That's devotion. That's Pisces. No hours of overtime are too long, no task too demanding, no reward too small – if the Piscean employees love the boss.

Once involved in a task Pisceans soon become engrossed. If not involved in a task they are still engrossed: the body may be present but the mind is somewhere far away in fairyland. Pisceans daydream. If you have something important to say to Pisces employees, make sure you have their undivided attention. When you give instructions, make the Pisceans write them down. Conversations with a Piscean have a dream-like and surreal quality at the best of times. But see what happens in the 'I'm sorry, you're redundant' scenario:

Boss:	I'm sorry. You're fired.
Pisces:	I'm sorry?
Boss:	No, I'm sorry. Thank you and goodbye.
Pisces:	*(Rising slowly, packing bag.)* No, really. It's my fault – I'm sorry.
Boss:	No. I'm sorry. It's the cut-backs. Nothing we can do. Sorry.
Pisces:	No, really. I'm quite sure it must be my fault. I'm very sorry. *(Reaches into pocket and takes out some banknotes.)* Can I make a contribution? You know, so other people don't get fired?

Someone has unkindly suggested that the only time a Piscean gets enthusiastic is when the company is handing out redundancy notices: 'Hey. Over here. I'm a Pisces. Sacrifice me.'

A Profile of the Piscean Manager

The Office

This office has a cosy, almost bordello-like atmosphere, with subdued lighting, sensual and romantic prints on the wall, a thick carpet, and a well-stocked bar.

As you enter, your charming and affable Piscean host/hostess will offer you a drink, invite you to an easy chair, and suggest, 'Now, tell me your troubles.' At which, you, as the guest, will explain that the department is facing a major crisis, staff cut-backs need to be made, and budget problems faced. 'Tell me about it!,' the Piscean leader will reply with a shrug, rolling their eyes to the heavens, and will then proceed to explain that if you think you have troubles, wait till you hear this... And you will leave defeated.

If the office belongs to a male Piscean, on the desk is a photograph of a stylish and ambitious-looking woman – if the Piscean is upwardly mobile and heading for the executive suite, she will probably have pointed teeth.

Some Pisceans go for technical gadgets in a big way, but like to have secret hiding-places for them. They are also day-time soap opera addicts, so there will probably be a TV hidden away somewhere. Successful Piscean managers will have a strong-willed, matronly (or avuncular) secretary with a knack for fixing office machinery. Doomed Pisceans will have an ex-fashion model (female or male!) who cannot type. Say something nice about the paintings on the wall. It is more than likely the Piscean painted them.

The Company Car

A VW Beetle or a Beverley Hills-style limousine with chauffeur, boomerang TV aerial, in-built video and well-stocked bar. Pisceans are not too bothered about the company car as long as it moves and it does not need any looking after. They are not, generally speaking, the most technically-minded managers. Pisceans are not the best drivers in the world, with a tendency to daydream behind the wheel.

The material benefits of a company car are not a major priority in the lives of Piscean managers. Piscean representatives sent out on a debt-collecting mission may end up handing over their own salary and the keys to the company car anyway, just to help the fellow out during a difficult time. 'No, please. I insist. Take the car keys. I can always take a bus.'

The Business Lunch

If you are attending a sales conference dinner and a quiet voice apologizes for being a vegetarian and whispers shyly that 'A piece of bread and some water would be fine, really ...', you can bet it belongs to a Pisces. Non-vegetarian Pisceans are experts when it comes to seafood, and probably know an out-of-the-way, cheap-and-sleazy Portuguese restaurant in the seedy quarter of town.

There is, however, another side to Pisceans which means they feel secure in the anonymity of a large, established restaurant chain. You might end up in a Burger King or a Pizza Hut in order to avoid any service or presentation that borders on personal space. Pisceans become easily 'psyched by vibes': take some Pisceans to a place where there is a lot of noise and an aggressive and charged atmosphere, or just too many people, and they are likely to cringe in fear for the entire duration and get writer's cramp when it comes to actually signing the contract.

The Piscean Business Venture

Anything that presents an alternative reality is fine by Pisceans: they enjoy video shops, computer games, films, spy novels... . Transforming everyday trivia into sought-after treasures is an archetypally Piscean trait. Pisceans see in junk, rubbish and discarded artefacts, potential that others miss. With imagination and inspiration (two strong Piscean qualities), the Piscean brand of merchandizing can take a country by storm. Pisceans are adaptable souls and can readily apply themselves to almost anything, but favour large corporations and organizations, particularly related to media, film and art, whereby they can allow their identities to merge into something large and grand.

The ambitious Piscean favours enterprises on a global scale – they can feel at home just about anywhere, and do not disdain periods of isolation. Which is just as well – the Piscean big-timer usually ends up in the slammer taking an embezzlement rap. Not because they are criminal, but because they are misunderstood. Piscean stock-trader, Nick Leeson, with the best of intentions for his colleagues and his employers, bankrupted an entire bank.

Steve Jobs

Perhaps Steve Jobs sees himself as the complete Piscean personality; according to his biography, *Steve Jobs: The Journey is The Reward*, by Jeffrey S Young (1988) 'On February 24, 1955 in San Francisco... the Moon, Sun and rising star were all in Pisces.' Astronomically, however, this would be an impossible combination; the Sun and Moon in Pisces would indicate an earlier time of birth. Here we have settled for an Aquarius Ascendant, which is the closest possibility to the birth time provided.

Nonetheless, Steve Jobs' story – the man who founded Apple and revolutionized the computer industry – comprises much of the traditional Piscean mythology. Here is the fairy tale saga of the adopted child, a wayward and daydreaming young boy, a young man with a vision, interludes with drugs, mysticism and a journey to the East, and finally, success through following the dream, rather than hard-headed business acumen.

Asc	15 52 Aqr	
MC	03 17 Sag	
Sun	05 11 Psc	1
Moon	29 56 Psc	1
Mercury	14 23 Aqr R	12
Venus	20 32 Cap	12
Mars	28 41 Ari	2
Jupiter	20 32 Cnc R	6
Saturn	21 09 Sco	9
Uranus	24 09 Cnc R	6
Neptune	28 03 Lib R	8
Pluto	25 20 Leo R	7

Steve Jobs 22 Feb 1955 06:00 San Francisco CA (Source: ADB)

In 1976, at the age of 20, he and his friend Steve Wozniac made a circuit board in their garage in the region near San Francisco now known as Silicon Valley. They called it The Apple, and Steve Jobs set off to market it to the world. By 1980, when he was only 24, Job's Apple corporation was worth $10 million, and a year later, $100 million.

As the empire grew, however, Steve, according to associates and colleagues, became a despot, a visionary lost in dreams and unable to accept the harsh reality of declining sales. He resigned from Apple in 1985, more or less fired by the man he had coerced into running the company, John Sculley.

Jobs had approached Sculley in 1983, then CEO for Pepsi Cola, with the immortal words: 'Do you want to sell sugar water for the rest of your life or do you want to come with me and change the world?' Ten years later an ousted Steve Jobs concluded he had hired the wrong man. For Jobs the vision was more important than the business.

'Steve Jobs' grandiose plans of what Macintosh were going to be was just so far out of whack with the truth of what the product was doing,' said one colleague, and although everyone in the young Apple team had at some stage incurred the wrath of Steve Jobs, the inspiration and the vision left with him. A more subdued Steve Jobs returned to run the company on Sculley's departure in 1993.

Meanwhile Steve Jobs entered another world of fabricating dreams and fantasies; as head of Pixar, in partnership with the Disney corporation, he produced some of the most successful animated films of recent times: *Toy Story* (1995), *A Bug's Life* (1998), *Toy Story 2* (1999) and *Monsters Inc.* (2001).

Steve Jobs' natal chart is dominated by the elements of Air and Water – there is very little Earth. The visions and ideals lack the grounding of common sense management; Jobs displays the temperament and convictions of the passionate artist, ill-at-ease in the world of balance sheets and sales figures.

Reflecting on Apple's early attempts to market the Macintosh to companies, Steve Jobs admits: 'We had no concept of how to sell to corporate America because none of us had come from there. It was like another planet to us…

With Aquarius Ascendant and Mercury in Aquarius, Jobs' chart favours the inventive and innovative thinking associated with the formative years of the home computer. But the strong Sun–Moon combination in Pisces and the First House embodies the image of the Piscean dreamer. 'The problem with Microsoft,' he said in 1995, 'is they have no taste. They don't bring culture into their product.' Macintosh users, he argues, love the product: 'You don't hear people loving products very often… there was something really wonderful there.'

It takes a Piscean to bring concepts of love and passion into the world of computer technology.

Ivar Kreuger

Pisces, the gentle peace-loving day-dreamer, is not a Sun-sign generally associated with ruthless business and world domination. Yet at least two figures on the stage of world finance conjure up just such an image: the Swedish 'Match King', Ivar Kreuger, and the 'Dirty Digger', Rupert Murdoch.

In the 1920s Ivar Kreuger provided three-quarters of the world's whole supply of matches in what was then the greatest global marketing monopoly. After some years' travel as an engineer in his youth, he returned to Sweden in 1907 to start a construction company which won contracts throughout Europe. He invested in banking, and even in the film industry, financing a young Greta Gustafsson's first advertising film before she became Hollywood's Garbo.

In 1915 he began building up a match business and by 1917 controlled the Swedish match industry by virtue of access to phosphorus and potash denied his competitors. He expanded into Europe, Turkey, the Balkans, and Central and

South America, establishing companies, some of which were genuine, some bogus, laundering and manipulating funds over a multi-structured layer of corporate subterfuge.

Kreuger's enterprises expanded during the 1920s to create an unprecedented global business empire, and when the great crash came from Wall Street in 1929, he insisted that his group of companies was unaffected. He continued planning and announcing extravagant business ventures. In 1930, to dispel rumours of insolvency, he deliberately overpaid his taxes by $150,000.

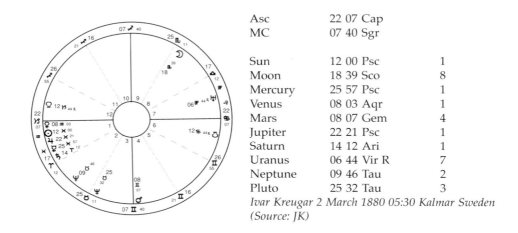

Asc	22 07 Cap	
MC	07 40 Sgr	
Sun	12 00 Psc	1
Moon	18 39 Sco	8
Mercury	25 57 Psc	1
Venus	08 03 Aqr	1
Mars	08 07 Gem	4
Jupiter	22 21 Psc	1
Saturn	14 12 Ari	1
Uranus	06 44 Vir R	7
Neptune	09 46 Tau	2
Pluto	25 32 Tau	3

Ivar Kreugar 2 March 1880 05:30 Kalmar Sweden (Source: JK)

He made an elaborate pretence of intimate involvement with world leaders, later putting together fake deals and forging notes, even including one from the Italian government for $143 million. To impress guests he would conduct imaginary telephone conversations with world premiers.

On 12 March 1932, 10 days after his fifty-second birthday, while in residence at his Paris flat, he wrote a note which read, 'I'm going mad. I can't take any more.' He then shot himself. To calm the market, accountants initially announced that, far from insolvent, Kreuger was in the black to the tune of about $200 million. After his death, however, Kreuger's financial empire soon crumbled, and debts were discovered in the multi-millions.

Pisces is the sign of the dreamer, and dreamers may be either visionaries or else great pretenders lost in their own fantasies. The personality of Ivar Kreuger represents both sides of the nebulous Piscean character – a man who fulfilled a vision of a global empire, but who was eventually no longer able to separate fantasy from reality. Neptune, which rules Pisces, is in the Second House. The message here is that money is not just hard work – a matter to be taken seriously – it is also tied to the Neptunian realm of fantasy and dreams. Neptune is concerned with illusion, escape, ecstasy; it can be linked with alcohol, drugs, music, poetry and religious visions. The Dionysian figure that danced for Kreuger had his hands filled with limitless wealth.

In addition, the Sun, Mercury, Venus and Jupiter are all placed in the First House – the House of self-image, which for Ivar Kreuger was of the great benefactor, and creator and dispenser of boundless riches. The chart is structured around the Pisces Sun and Capricorn Ascendant; Capricorn affords discipline and control, both of oneself and one's circumstances, to achieve one's aims.

Rupert Murdoch

The charts of Rupert Murdoch and Ivar Kreuger show a Capricorn Ascendant, but whereas Kreuger's Moon is in Scorpio (emotionally intense, secretive, even destructive), Rupert Murdoch's Moon is in Sagittarius, an indication of expansiveness, emotional directness, extravagance and a love of travel (many people who make their home abroad have Moon in Sagittarius). In addition, Sun, Uranus and Mercury, all in the Fourth House, emphasize the importance of 'the family business'.

Uranus in the Fourth indicates a disruptive and eccentric home environment – a restlessness which often results in breaking away from the family, and settling far from one's roots and the place of one's birth. Rupert Murdoch's case is extreme: he relinquished his Australian citizenship for that of the US in order to secure an American television franchise.

A Capricorn Ascendant is common in men of power – as well as Murdoch and Kreuger, examples include Aristotle Onassis and J P Getty. This indicates austerity, severity, caution, parsimony, persistence to the point of ruthlessness, and an ability to build on past success and to progress steadfastly.

Murdoch's family owned a company called Cruden Investment (Australia), which in turn owned major portions of News Corporation, News Limited, Newscorp Investments, and Ansett Transport Industries, with additional owning or controlling interests in over 50 Australian subsidiaries – TV stations and newspapers.

In the United States, Murdoch's involvements include News America, which owns newspapers across the country including the *New York Post*, *Boston Herald* and *Chicago Sun-Times*. More recent acquisitions include Twentieth Century-Fox, MGM and, almost, Warner Communications. So awe-inspiring is the name of Rupert Murdoch in the business world that his attempted buy-in to Warner during the early 1980s increased stock value as shareholders attempted to freeze him out. Within 12 months Murdoch sold his shares for a profit of $40 million.

In Britain Murdoch's British News International includes *The News of the World*, *The Sun*, *The Times* and *The Sunday Times*; also Sky Channel satellite TV. Murdoch's infiltration into Fleet Street during the 1970s and 1980s resulted in verbal onslaughts and pitched battles, as newspaper staff, printers and transport workers protested against Murdoch's move from Fleet Street, the time-honoured central London press quarter, to new modernized and computerized plants (with greatly reduced staff) in Wapping, a couple of miles further east. Despite strikes and protests, Murdoch remained adamant, and appeared unruffled. 'It's simple,' he said, 'either you work my way, or I close down the newspapers.'

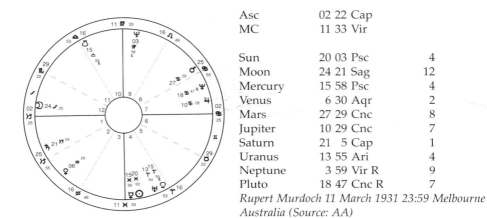

Asc	02 22 Cap	
MC	11 33 Vir	
Sun	20 03 Psc	4
Moon	24 21 Sag	12
Mercury	15 58 Psc	4
Venus	6 30 Aqr	2
Mars	27 29 Cnc	8
Jupiter	10 29 Cnc	7
Saturn	21 5 Cap	1
Uranus	13 55 Ari	4
Neptune	3 59 Vir R	9
Pluto	18 47 Cnc R	7

Rupert Murdoch 11 March 1931 23:59 Melbourne Australia (Source: AA)

During the late 1980s, when Sky Channel was by many accounts losing millions of pounds every week (and when Murdoch companies were offering employees free satellite dishes and still could not move them), Murdoch, rather than consolidate, expanded ruthlessly into the publishing business. He rationalized two of the major publishing houses on each side of the Atlantic. Harper and Row and Collins became HarperCollins, and to this conglomeration was added roughly a publisher a month: Thorsons, Patrick Stevens, Unwin Hyman, Gollancz, and others.

In a given set of circumstances, in one and the same day, you could read a newspaper, watch television, buy a book, rent a video, see a film, and buy lunch in a health-food takeaway, and find that in every instance your money had gone into the pocket of a small, lean-faced man with a dark suit and a severe gaze, and a horoscope that bears some resemblance to that of former international business entrepreneur Ivar Kreuger.

Murdoch reached 70 years of age in 2001, and his media empire remains a family-run business. Murdoch never entered politics himself, although his manipulations of the political arena, namely attempting to steer the Australian electorate away from Labour government towards the conservative Liberal party, have since been well-documented.

Another Piscean media baron made a more overt entry into the political arena; Sergei Berlusconi, one of Europe's most controversial politicians, accused of attempting to run Italian politics like a dictator. In 2002, he resigned his post as Foreign Minister, while retaining the post of Prime Minister.

David Puttnam

Film is a relatively recent interest for Rupert Murdoch, but for the British film producer David Puttnam moving pictures have been a life-long passion. As a young man, he claims, his world view was shaped solely by the cinema: 'That magic atmosphere where people are at their most vulnerable to impressions and to ideas – in darkness...'

In the 1970s and 1980s David Puttnam gained a reputation as the brightest creative light in the British film industry since Alexander Korda (see Virgo). After a string of UK successes he took over as Head of Production at Columbia Pictures, Hollywood. His mission was to save Hollywood from itself. He was sacked in 1987, leaving behind a trail of financial disasters and terminated contracts.

In a biography of David Puttnam entitled *Enigma – The Story so Far* (1989), the author Andrew Yule writes that the three most successful films with which Puttnam was involved in the initial negotiating stages during his Hollywood sojourn were *Moonstruck* (starring Cher), and sequels to *Karate Kid* and *Ghostbusters*. These were all commercial successes produced by other studios, and all three were films which Puttnam failed to secure for Columbia.

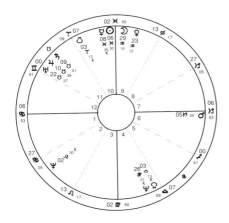

Asc	06 53 Cnc	
MC	02 50 Psc	
Sun	06 30 Psc	10
Moon	29 19 Aqr	9
Mercury	08 35 Psc R	10
Venus	23 12 Aqr	9
Mars	05 09 Cap	6
Jupiter	10 39 Tau	11
Saturn	09 51 Tau	11
Uranus	22 27 Tau	11
Neptune	26 51 Vir R	4
Pluto	02 30 Leo R	2

David Puttnam 25 Feb 1941 12:00 London (Source: AA)

In the UK he had produced *Midnight Express, Chariots of Fire, The Killing Fields,* and *The Mission* – films which heralded a rebirth of the ailing British film industry. These were critical and financial successes in Great Britain and abroad, especially in the United States, where success is measured in bucks only. Thematically all the films concerned struggles within men and between men. Puttnam said, 'I try to make films about morally accountable individuals trying to hold true to their beliefs against the mindless violence of ideological genocide or religious fanaticism.'

Once in Hollywood, and subject to the constraints of commerce, Puttnam produced commercial catastrophe after financial disaster, and the 'struggle between men' films with which he was involved included *Ishtar*, *Stars and Bars*, and *Memphis Belle* (US air force pilots stationed in Britain during World War II), all of which sank without trace at the box-office. In addition to these was a curious melodrama entitled *Zelly and Me*, starring David Lynch and Isabella Rossellini, which grossed one of the most meagre totals in recent Hollywood commercial cinema – $55,000.

Columbia, a subsidiary of Coca-Cola, is one of what Puttnam calls 'the global baronies': the media empires and multinational corporations which are 'the great patrons of today'. On returning from Hollywood in the late 1980s he said he sought patrons 'prepared to share my dreams and help me realize them'.

Embittered by his experiences in the United States, he offers a vision of 'Europe as custodian of a cultural heritage and the last bastion of artistic liberation'. Puttnam sees 'the problem for the artist... as how he can find the means to respond to a world that constantly seems to overtake his imagination in its horrors and deceits.' For this reason he says, 'I prefer naivety to cynicism . . . the naive have hope.' He describes film as 'an art form of uniting, in peace, that family of man of which we are all part'.

Puttnam's views come across as sweeping idealisms. The industry, particularly the US industry, perceives Puttnam as a 'loser'. It is a role which frequently falls to Pisceans. One need look no further than these pages, where names like Steve Jobs, Ivar Kreuger and Mikhail Gorbachev invite similar judgements.

But Puttnam, like many Piscean types, cannot see *himself* in that role, for the label of 'loser' is only relevant within what he would describe as the erroneous criteria of an industry that promotes money and commercial success over other values – culture, search for meaning and the capacity to enlighten. The question for David Puttnam is whether the European film industry retains these values he prizes, or whether the 'European artist' sells out for bucks too.

Rudolf Steiner

Rudolf Steiner, the founder of the spiritual movement called anthroposophy, died in 1925, yet his work is still relevant today, with his influence evident in many different arenas, including education, architecture, ecology, medicine, banking and economics, and even in the *Star Wars* films of George Lucas. According to Lucas the concept of the 'force' and the depiction of evil in the films have their inspiration in Steiner's teachings.

'Economic life is striving to structure itself according to its own nature, independent of political institutionalization and mentality. It can only do this through associations of consumers, distributors and producers, which are established according to purely economic criteria. Actual conditions would determine the scope of these associations. Practical necessity would indicate how interassociational relations should develop,' wrote Steiner in *Toward Social Renewal* in the 1920s.

In their book *The Future 500* (the 1988 sequel to *Creating Excellence,* 1984), Hickinan and Silva refer to eight major 'dimensions' which summarize the attributes of the companies which will survive into the next century. These relate to Steiner's views on social and economic change – whose ultimate aim is individual fulfilment – and are:

* the globalization of enterprise
* government business alliances
* collaboration amongst enterprises
* investor–company relations (and not manipulations)
* ethical and social leadership
* new organizational forms
* integrated subcultures
* individual fulfilment

Steiner's views of an interrelated global network were ahead of his time – the German National Socialist movement of the 1920s and 1930s considered Steiner and his movement as their primary adversary, forcing his followers to flee to Switzerland. Steiner's anthroposophical centre in Basle was burnt down by his opponents in 1922.

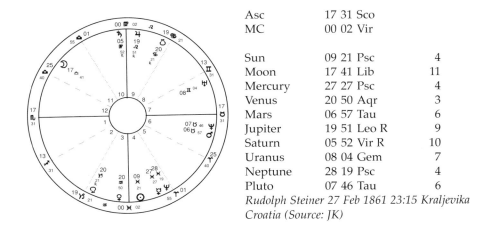

Asc	17 31 Sco	
MC	00 02 Vir	
Sun	09 21 Psc	4
Moon	17 41 Lib	11
Mercury	27 27 Psc	4
Venus	20 50 Aqr	3
Mars	06 57 Tau	6
Jupiter	19 51 Leo R	9
Saturn	05 52 Vir R	10
Uranus	08 04 Gem	7
Neptune	28 19 Psc	4
Pluto	07 46 Tau	6

Rudolph Steiner 27 Feb 1861 23:15 Kraljevika Croatia (Source: JK)

Today's management theories bear comparison to Steiner's analyses of inter-cultural political and economic development. Steiner defined the role of multinationals as the 'globalization of enterprise', that cross-cultural alliances between government and business would erode political boundaries while common economic and commercial interests would serve to unite nations.

Steiner envisaged a three-fold society – an interworking of the three spheres of culture, law and economics (feeling, thinking and will) – mutually related within the total single organism.

The centre of Steiner's 'new way of seeing', which he called anthroposophy – the study of man – was set up in Basle and included sections devoted to fine arts, literature, the performing arts, medicine, astronomy, mathematics, science and education. He founded the first Waldorf School in Stuttgart in 1919, and the first Waldorf School in the UK opened in Streatham, London, in 1932.

Today Waldorf schools throughout the world adhere to Steiner's teachings, which are finding a place in business, economics and banking. The practice of biodynamic agriculture, which is finding increasing support, is also based on the work of Rudolf Steiner.

Like the two fishes of Pisces, Steiner saw that he had a double task: to free science from materialism, and to reveal humanity's 'source of being'. In his memoirs, *The Course of My Life* (written at the request of others), Steiner recollects how, as a young child, he learned that he was understood when he spoke of some matters, but not understood when he spoke of others. He had his own particular world, which those around him could not enter, although he could enter theirs.

By the age of eight he had distinguished between 'a world seen' and 'a world not seen'. He was later described as 'a scientist of the invisible'. He foresaw that his task was to bridge the abyss in modern life between our inner and outer dimensions.

A scholar of science, mathematics and philosophy, he extended his studies to metaphysics, including reincarnation theories derived from Goethe's studies of metamorphosis. A biographer writes: '[Steiner] was the conscious bearer of an inner world of reality of which humanity had dire need, but he could find no entry to the minds of even his closest friends. They could only conclude that, capable as he was and practical, he was nevertheless caught up in some kind of dream.'

In 1897 he moved to Berlin and worked as an editor for a cultural journal; from 1902 to 1912 he was General Secretary of the German section of the Theosophical Society. He left when the society proclaimed the young Krishnamurti (Taurus) as the reincarnation of Christ (which Krishnamurti repudiated).

Steiner's interpretation of the past bears resemblance to the 'in-trance' utterances of Edgar Cayce, the 'Sleeping Prophet', outlining in detail an Atlantean civilization and the ancient epochs of Egypt, India and Persia which depart radically from the accepted view of classical history.

As well as Sun in Pisces, Steiner's chart shows a tight Neptune–Mercury conjunction indicating communication as 'mystical' – the expression of feelings and ideas relating to an alternative view of reality. This conjunction is in the Fourth House – relating to the family – in Steiner's case; he expressed his vision in terms of a 'universal family'. The Scorpio Ascendant intensifies both Steiner's vision and his sense of purpose, and Moon in Libra suggests an intuitive feel for harmony, art and aesthetic balance.

The Piscean vision of a world without boundaries of nationality, class or creed, expressed through the Sun, Mercury and Neptune in Pisces, remained Steiner's life-long dream.

Mikhail Gorbachev

Steiner's role as leader of an international enterprise bears comparison with Mikhail Gorbachev's role as a 'managing director' of what was once the world's largest conglomerate, with a personnel of 280 million people. The Soviet Union was a business venture based on the economics of Karl Marx (Taurus) and Gorbachev finally lost 'the company' in a takeover bid. Gorbachev's chart (the time is uncertain) shows a Libran Ascendant and a Leo Moon. Certainly Gorbachev's role has been that of the Libran mediator, and his six years in power were a cautious balancing act between the forces of change and reform, and those of the conservative 'old guard' intent on maintaining Party control and the status quo.

Piscean leaders tend to depart from the political arena under a shadow – leaders who have meant well, but who have not had a strong enough grip on reality. Even 60 years after the event, the image of British Prime Minister Neville Chamberlain returning from Munich in 1938 and waving a scrap of paper promising 'peace in our time' after his 'chat with Chancellor Hitler' is an icon of the idealist defeated by real events.

Mikhail Gorbachev as the final leader of a political experiment which dominated the twentieth century is as symbolic as the astrological signs with which the Soviet Union has been identified. Gorbachev might have chosen, with the backing of the KGB and Party militants, to retain power regardless of the cost. Indeed, Chinese leaders, with Deng Xiaopeng at the top, decided just that when they ordered troops to open fire on the student demonstrators in Beijing in June 1989. Gorbachev chose simply to 'let go'. The man who delivered his farewell speech from the Kremlin on Christmas Day 1991 seemed unexpectedly tranquil, even at peace with himself, considering that, with his political demise, his own cherished ideals of reformed Communism had ended.

The Soviet Union was conceived and brought into existence by Lenin (Aries); based on the material dialecticism of Karl Marx (Taurus); structured and controlled by Stalin (Capricorn); steered by his lackeys (with the possible exception of Krushchev, Aries, who attempted reform within, but was finally crushed by the Stalinist machine of bureaucracy); and finally laid to rest by a Piscean. An encapsulated history of the Soviet Union from the first sign of the zodiac to the last. (Another theory holds that Soviet leaders without hair are bona fide – Lenin, Krushchev, Gorbachev – and Soviet leaders with hair and bushy eyebrows are villains – Stalin, Brezhnev, Tjernenko.)

Mikhail Gorbachev, a farmer's son, studied law at Moscow University from 1950–55. He became a Party member in 1953, which was the year he married Raisa (Capricorn), and also the year in which Stalin died. He worked as a lawyer in

Stavropol until 1962, when his political career began in earnest. He gained membership of the Central Committee in 1971.

In 1978 Gorbachev moved to Moscow to accept the post of Central Committee Secretary responsible for Soviet agricultural administration. When Brezhnev died in 1982, Gorbachev was considered for the job of Party Secretary, but was rejected as being too young. The former head of the KGB, Yuri Andropov, got the post. With Andropov's health failing he encouraged Gorbachev to tackle the problems of the Brezhnev legacy: stagnation, internal corruption and an unworkable budget.

It is unsure, even today, why Tjernenko and not Gorbachev took over when Andropov died in 1984, but in March 1985, following Tjernenko's death, Gorbachev became Party General Secretary. In October 1988 he was elected Soviet Chairman, and he became President in March 1990.

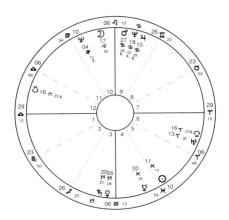

Asc	29 12 Lib	
MC	06 13 Leo	
Sun	11 14 Psc	5
Moon	17 50 Leo	10
Mercury	00 06 Psc	4
Venus	26 28 Cap	3
Mars	27 38 Cnc R	9
Jupiter	10 28 Cnc R	9
Saturn	20 20 Cap	3
Uranus	13 26 Ari	6
Neptune	04 13 Vir R	10
Pluto	18 52 Cnc R	9

Mikhail Gorbachev 2 March 1931 22:08 Privolnoje Stavropole Russia (Source: AA)

He enriched the world's vocabulary with 'glasnost' and 'perestroika', continually waging a silent and undeclared war with the KGB and the Party's 'old guard'. His career, like the two fishes of Pisces, pulled in different directions: one side towards reform and 'openness' and a new Soviet Union; the other towards the strengthening and consolidation of the Party position, holding on to Party values, Communist idealism, and continual appeasement of 'old guard' and KGB conservatism.

While 'glasnost' (openness) was visible through relaxed censorship and freedom of speech, 'perestroika' (restructuring) was soon to become an empty phrase. The shops were still empty, the queues still endless, and the only noticeable changes were in the underworld, where crime organized itself to an unprecedented level of efficiency.

At the point at which the Soviet parliament waited for Gorbachev to introduce economic reforms he hesitated, hoping for a less stringent solution – compromising in the face of adversity. Even before Gorbachev was awarded the Nobel Peace Prize for initiating the disarmament programme, Soviet government members predicted his demise.

It was Gorbachev himself who appointed the head of the KGB, Kriutchov, and his militant cronies to their high positions, in order to gain support from the conservatives, but this power base enabled them to initiate a coup the following year. Gorbachev's attempt at compromise alienated him from the reformers, and he lost the support he had gained from Russian President Yeltsin.

In the six years that Gorbachev was head of state, his image abroad (three planets in the Ninth House) was that of a man talking peace, signing disarmament agreements, and discussing aid programmes with world leaders, while at the same time Soviet soldiers were shooting Baltic States civilians demonstrating for independence. Red Army units assembled at strategic military points throughout the Union. Gorbachev, when pressed, had no answers. He was not sure what was going on, or if he was, he was not saying.

The enigma of the Soviet Union became the enigma of Gorbachev. Who was in control? Which side was he on? After all, Gorbachev, for all his reforms, had always spoken from the platform of Marxism and the official Party line.

After the 1991 attempted coup, Gorbachev returned to the Kremlin, victorious yet defeated. Soviet officials and citizens spoke openly of him as 'a tragic figure'. One political commentator described him as 'the Hamlet of our times... a tragic figure worthy of a star role directed in Cinemascope by our own time's Shakespeare.'

When Gorbachev initiated reforms and 'cancelled' the Cold War in 1985, his actions triggered off responses throughout the Eastern Bloc, culminating in the reunification of Germany, and the end of Communism in the Eastern European states and of their ties to central Soviet power.

Has Gorbachev 'lost the Soviet Union' but 'saved the world'? Is Gorbachev 'the man from Russia' Edgar Cayce predicted 50 years ago as the man who would bring peace to the world?

In the 1930s, the 'Sleeping Prophet' predicted a new age that would begin in 1998 (the year Neptune entered Aquarius and a few years after Pluto entered Sagittarius, and Uranus entered Aquarius). 'Changes are coming, this may be sure – an evolution, or revolution in the ideas of religious thought. The basis of it for the world will eventually come out of Russia; not Communism. No. But that which is the basis of the same, as the Christ taught – His kind of Communism.'

During another 'reading', Cayce claimed: 'On Russia's religious development will come the greater hope of the world... freedom in that each man will live for his fellow man!'

Other prominent Pisceans: Lord Baden-Powell, Alexander Graham Bell, Cyrano de Bergerac, Bernardo Bertolucci, Anthony Burgess, Johnny Cash, Neville Chamberlain, Frédéric Chopin, Lawrence Durrell, Wyatt Earp, Adolf Eichmann, Albert Einstein, Bobby Fisher, Kenneth Grahame, George Harrison, Rex Harrison, Victor Hugo, Edward Kennedy, Jack Kerouac, David Livingstone, Michelangelo, Ralph Nader, Florence Nightingale, Waslaw Nijinsky, David Niven, Rudolph Nureyev, Micky Spillane, John Steinbeck, Elizabeth Taylor, George Washington, Harold Wilson.

MANAGING THE COMPANY:
Corporate Alchemy

In the past the focus of management has been placed on tasks and the transaction. Today management skills focus on people and interaction. Corporate alchemy is a guide to understanding how different personality types interact with each other. In this section we look at the four elements of astrology and see how different combinations work in leadership, negotiations and business skills.

The Manager as Alchemist

The best of all rulers is but a shadowy presence to his subjects.
Next comes the ruler they love and praise;
Next comes the one they fear;
Next comes one with whom they take liberties.
When there is not enough faith, there is lack of good faith.
Hesitant, he does not utter words lightly.
When his task is accomplished and his work done
The people all say, 'It happened to us naturally.'

Tao teh ching XVIII

Today we think of alchemy as a medieval preoccupation concerned with transforming lead into gold, or finding the secret of eternal youth. In fact alchemy has existed since at least 500 BC, and was then, as now, based on the principle of 'transformation'. Alchemy has been defined as the seemingly miraculous change of a thing into something better. The alchemist is the one who performs the 'miraculous change' – what company can afford to be without one?

Every company has potential alchemists, as does every department within a company. They are the managers. Unfortunately few managers realize the alchemical powers at their disposal; fewer still are aware of the 'elements' with which they can perform 'miraculous deeds'.

As you read through the Sun-descriptions you probably noticed that the signs within each element share similar qualities. The Fire signs are impulsive and dominating; the Earth signs are practical and cautious; Air signs are organizing and analytical, while Water is service-orientated and artistic.

These elements embody four basic personality types. We all have some quality of Air and Water and Earth and Fire. But one element will be strong in a personality, and another element weak. The manager who comes in every Monday with a new grand vision of where the company is headed, and how many new accounts will be opened up – but then finds that the photocopying machine does not work because he forgot to ring for the repair man the week before – is a manager strong in Fire, weak in Earth. A fine sense of direction and possibilities, but hopeless when it comes to the practical details that keep the business running.

The dominant element in a personality can be seen in the horoscope. In most cases the Sun-sign is the dominant element, but not always. A Capricorn Sun with Leo Ascendant, Sagittarius Moon and five planets in Aries may well come over as more of a 'Fire type', though their 'inner nature' is still largely determined by the Sun-sign.

Management books nowadays emphasize the importance of interaction with people. Products and profits are one thing, but any business is a 'people' business. Managers who can manage books and ledger sheets but cannot manage people, are poor managers.

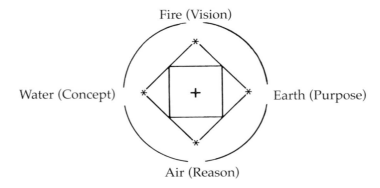

The four elements

Creative managers realize the resources at their disposal and use them to the mutual advantage of themselves, the company and the individuals involved. But how do managers assess their resources? How do they get the best from work colleagues and subordinates, while at the same time providing them with the chance to achieve individual fulfilment?

According to alchemists, matter is made up of the four elements. What we are concerned with here is the symbolic meaning of these elements. At the same time, we can note the symbolic meaning of the alchemist's obsession with transforming lead into gold. The alchemists gave planetary associations to each metal. Mercury is quicksilver, the Moon is silver; Saturn is lead, and the Sun is gold. As we have seen from our study of the planets, Saturn corresponds to restrictions, and the Sun corresponds to creative energy.

Alchemy can therefore be interpreted as transforming restrictions into creative energy – Saturnine 'lead' into solar 'gold'. By overcoming our obstacles we can create and 'actualize' our creative vision. The alchemist transforms base matter into the metaphoric gold of achievement. That is why it is to the advantage of every manager to understand the basics of alchemy and the inner meanings of the four elements.

The Elements of the Personality

The qualities of the elements can be summarized as:

FIRE (Aries, Leo, Sagittarius)   Leadership
EARTH (Taurus, Virgo, Capricorn) Consolidation
AIR (Gemini, Libra, Aquarius)   Organization
WATER (Cancer, Scorpio, Pisces)   Conceptualization

Let's look first at the qualities defined by each element.

The Element of Fire – Vision

> *The best soldier is not soldierly*
> *The best fighter is not ferocious*
> *The best conqueror does not take part in war*
> *The best employer of men keeps himself below them*
> *This is called the virtue of not-contending*
> *This is called the ability of using men*
> *This is called the supremacy of consorting with heaven.*

Tao teh ching LXVIII

As the element suggests, Fire signs are impulsive, seeking new activities, taking initiative and assuming command. Fire is fuelled by power – it activates energy in others while re-energizing itself.

Fire may represent the 'divine spark' but for the church of the Middle Ages, Fire was also the dominant element of hell; for those wary of change, action and the unexpected, the astrological Fire signs may indeed represent hell on Earth.

Fire signs take to the role of leader with gusto – they enjoy telling people what to do, and their confidence and natural aptitude usually allows them free rein.

The fiery 'gods', Mars, Sun and Jupiter, are masculine warrior gods, demanding change in the face of stagnation, resistance rather than acquiescence, a contest of strength rather than a battle of wit, and the manifestation of the will of the individual rather than subjugation for collective harmony.

The symbols of Fire signs are the symbols of 'wild' beasts – the ram, the lion and the centaur. The ram challenges by charging head first in a contest of brute strength. From the two opponents there emerges a winner and a loser. Rams do not negotiate, arbitrate or mediate. They charge.

The lion of Leo, by comparison, commands attention by roaring the loudest. Lions fight when they are hungry and when they are forced to. Leo battles only when all other means of maintaining power fail. The lion relies on the status of royalty, and the command of respect instilled by the position of leader. If this status is threatened, the lion will fight, but not before then.

195

The Sagittarian centaur is half-beast, half-man. The centaur aspires to the stars – his bow and arrow are aimed toward the heavens rather than at any Earth-bound adversary – yet he is bound to the Earth by his animal body. In Greek mythology the centaur was renowned for wisdom and knowledge. According to legend, the centaur Chiron, known for his healing skills, was unintentionally wounded by Hercules, whose arrow pierced his leg. Chiron, being immortal and facing the prospect of enduring the pain for eternity, exchanged his immortality for the mortality of Prometheus. For this act of sacrifice Zeus, or Jupiter, placed the centaur among the stars, as the constellation of Sagittarius. It was Prometheus who stole fire from the gods to give to humans.

Fire signs are visionaries, looking to the future, and looking to others to work out details and practicalities. 'You see things as they are and ask why; I dream of things that are not and ask why not,' wrote dramatist George Bernard Shaw (Leo).

Fire signs are the champions of causes, with a buoyant optimism, an innate trust in life, which carries them through the most arduous of tasks and situations. Fire likes challenge: Fire enjoys the game, the sport, fighting and winning, taking a risk and counting on the pay-off. And if that gamble fails, there is always the next one. Fire does not dwell on the past, nor reflect too much on the present. Fire 'seizes the day' with the intent of creating a future.

Fire is the element of energy – impulsive, seeking new activities, new challenges, and new conquests, acting on initiative and 'taking over' when the occasion calls for it. The 'shadow' side of Fire reveals itself when leadership becomes tyranny. Fire signs will attempt to convince their opponents and themselves of their benevolence, generosity, concern and good intentions. Then they'll demand not just loyalty but blind obedience.

The Element of Earth – Purpose

Tao is supreme, heaven is supreme
Earth is supreme and man is also supreme
There are in the universe four things supreme
   and man is one of them.
Man follows the laws of earth
Earth follows the laws of heaven
Heaven follows the laws of Tao
Tao follows the laws of its intrinsic nature.

Tao teh ching XXV

Whereas Fire sees possibilities, Earth sees practicalities. Where Fire rises to a challenge, Earth deals with the task at hand. Earth is concerned with reality, not dreams. Earth is the element of the pragmatist – cautious, consolidating, constructive – realizing what is possible rather than fantasizing about what *may* be possible.

Jung's definition, Sensation, refers to the sensory perceptions, and the Sensation type relies on the physical senses, placing value in what can be seen, what can be heard and what can be touched. The Sensation type is not concerned with the 'irrational'. Sensation preserves, stabilizes and relates to matter: to objects, and information perceived as factual.

For those with aspirations, projects and visions, being 'brought down to Earth' is an unpleasant experience. However, being brought down to Earth is a fundamental law of nature – as Capricorn Isaac Newton observed. What goes up must come down. Earth signs consolidate. They take an idea, discard the implausible, capitalize on the plausible. If there is gain to be had – money, security, physical or spiritual well-being – Earth signs will proceed.

The Earth 'gods', Venus, Mercury and Saturn, combine the qualities of harmony and sensual gratification (Taurus), analysis and discernment (Virgo), and the discipline of limitation and structure (Capricorn). These are qualities necessary to discriminate between the possible and the not-possible, to set about the task in hand and realize it. Earth signs do not create opportunities, but they seize the ones that are available and build on them.

Earth signs are the signs of nature, and their astrological imagery relates to the seasons: the Taurus bull of spring, the beast of burden, ploughs the soil; the late summer Virgo maiden, the 'human' sign of the Earth element, gathers the harvest; the Capricorn half-goat of winter endures the hardships during the period of the soil's replenishment. Whereas the Fire-sign imagery relates to the wilderness, and untamed nature, the imagery of the Earth signs is concerned with cultivation, work and domesticity.

Earth signs are concerned with building and producing. Aspirations are fine providing you have got a roof over your head and food to eat. Earth relates to satisfying appetites; physically, intellectually and spiritually. In Taurus this is concerned with fulfilling the basic needs of the body – survival and building a secure environment; in Virgo, satisfying the appetite of the intellect; and in Capricorn, fulfilling aspirations and achieving one's goals.

Earth signs identify with matter and the physical form of the body. Earth is the element that produces food, sustains existence, nurtures life. From the Earth all things grow and to it all things return. It is a conservative element: Earth conserves, making sure we put enough away today to ensure at least some security in the uncertainty of tomorrow.

Earth relates to the present, and, to safeguard the stability and continuation of the present, resists change. As a defence against change Earth signs impose rigid structures or maintain already existing ones. Earth signs value traditional social forms – whether it is the family, or an organization. The imposition of structure is part of Earth's striving for permanence.

The Earth signs are the bearers of responsibilities. They take on the tasks and burdens others avoid. The 'shadow' side of Earth emerges when assuming responsibilities leads to taking control. Earth signs' preoccupation with security resists change and opposition. They will preserve the present even at the risk of denying the future.

The Element of Air – Reason

Some lead while others follow
Some breathe gently and some breathe hard
Some are strong and some are weak
Therefore the sage avoids excess, extravagance and arrogance.

Tao teh ching XXIX

Air is the element of unification. Air sustains life, and unites life; people, plants and animals all breathe the same air. Air is the element of reason and harmonizing. Air may be as fresh and stimulating as a spring breeze (Gemini), as tranquil as an early autumn day (Libra), or as tempestuous as a winter's storm (Aquarius). Air is restless, adaptable, changing.

The Air signs are the signs of reason and intellect. Air values the intellect because reason perceives 'truth'. It is the most human of elements, and values the most human of faculties – the capacity to reason. Consequently, Air places less value on the senses, or on feelings, or on intuition. Where Earth says: 'This is real – I can touch it', Air says, 'This is so – I can deduce it.'

Jung refers to the Thinking type, who evaluates, assesses and compares. What is logical and rational, and can be objectified by the mind, is retained – the irrational and the illogical are rejected. The Thinking type relates to ideas and ideals. Just as Intuition and Sensation comprise a polarity, Jung regarded Thinking and Feeling as two opposites. Thinking relates to surface values – what can be observed; Feeling relates to concealed values – what can be felt.

The 'gods' of Air are Mercury (corresponding to Hermes, the messenger of the gods), adaptable, changeable, restless, intellectually discerning, always pursuing ideas; Venus, the harmonizer, seeing reason, neutralizing aggression, seeking peaceful resolution, embodying 'sense' both in its physical meaning (Taurus) and in relation to thought (Libra); and Uranus, the god of disruption, revolution, initiating new ideas to effect change. In Mercury change relates to the individual; in Uranus it concerns sweeping changes, affecting society, humanity and the collective.

The symbols of the Air signs are human symbols (Virgo is the only non-Air sign with a human face): the twins of Gemini, the water-carrier of Aquarius, and the scales-bearing maiden of Libra. Sometimes Libra is represented as the only inanimate symbol of the zodiac, a pair of scales alone (*libra* is Latin for balance), but more often the sign is represented by a woman holding the scales, as in the figure of Justice adorning law courts – scales in one hand, a sword in the other, and a blindfold across her eyes.

Air is the element of consciousness, questioning the whys and wherefores of all that surrounds it, as well as its own existence and purpose. Unlike the other elements, Air is self-reflective, seeking knowledge through information that can be analyzed, assessed and catalogued.

Consequently, Air is a socializing element, interacting with others by communicating, arguing and exchanging views. Air requires Fire, Earth and

Water, for all their lack of 'reason', as a measure of its capacity to judge objectively, unhindered by emotions, physical needs or impulsive irrational action. 'I think therefore I am,' declared the philosopher Descartes, as though only the mind is capable of 'awareness'. For the element of Air, it is just so – the mind is the measure of our identity.

Air is the grand processor – the other elements depend on Air for sustenance. The plant life of the Earth processes air; fire needs air to burn; and the cycle of water, from vapour to precipitation, transpires through air. At the same time Air takes these elements and processes them – Air assesses the physical needs of form (Earth), the visions of Fire, and the emotions of Water, questioning and analysing, retaining and discarding. What is useful in the pursuit of knowledge, Air will keep, disposing of what is left.

Air is not anxious to take on the burden of leadership, but when Fire consumes itself, or burns itself out with its own power, and when Earth, so fearful of change, lumbers to a standstill, Air takes the only reasonable course of action.

There is, however, a 'shadow' side to Air's 'reasonableness'. Too much reasoning and not enough feeling can lead to organizational imbalance. The Air element is drawn to systems and regulations that can be necessary to maintain structure and order. The risk is that the system can become more important than the people it was created to serve.

For Air, the logic of a system – whether it is a timetable, a work routine or office plan – may become more important than people's feelings. Air can be so taken with the 'perfect system' that the logic of people's emotions may escape them. At worst, Air can discard human compassion simply because an idea or a system must be upheld regardless of the impracticalities it may involve. The idea that nothing will ever be perfect is a tough lesson for Air. But human feelings – as irrational as they may be – are driven by an inherent logic. Those small imperfections that can drive Air crazy, are the imperfections that stimulate learning, development and growth.

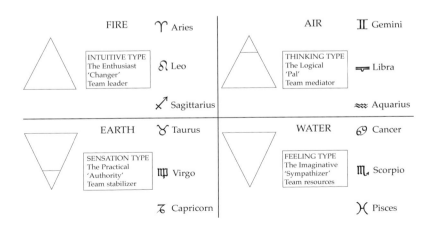

Signs and elements – Personalities

The Element of Water – Concept

The highest goodness is like water.
Water is beneficent to all things but does not contend.
It stays in places which others despise.
Therefore it is near Tao.

Tao teh ching VIII

Images of water evoke feelings, whether it comes as rain, tears, ocean waves or a flowing river. Water is the element that seeks its own level, always returning to its spherical form – as the seas encircling the planet, or as a drop of rain, or as dew forming in the early hours of the morning. The process of water is cyclical – evaporating from the sea, transforming to cloud, precipitating as rain, and returning to the sea.

Water is an element seeking to return to its original state. It may be liquid as water, vapour as steam, or solid as ice. More than 70 per cent of the Earth's surface consists of water, more than 70 per cent of the human body consists of water.

Water signifies depth of feeling, the imaginative and mystical side of the human personality, and the instinctive and unknown facets of character. Jung defined such personalities as Feeling types.

Writing in the 1930s, Jung described feeling as 'undeniably a more obvious characteristic of feminine psychology than thinking,' and that 'the most pronounced Feeling types are to be found among women'. The Feeling type is receptive, sensitive, imaginative, relating to experiences through emotions rather than intellect.

The 'gods' of Water rule over the unknown and the hidden. The Moon (ruling Cancer) governs the ocean tides, menstrual cycles, and the subtle energies affecting moods, sensitivity, and even lunacy. Pluto (ruling Scorpio, together with Mars) is the lord of the underworld, which some see as hell (as in Christian theology), and others as a hidden kingdom rich with treasures (in accordance with Greek and Roman mythology). For Scorpio, it may be claimed that 'the path to heaven lies through hell'. Neptune (ruling Pisces, along with Jupiter) is the god of the oceans, and oversees the realm beneath the water's surface. It is at the same time a world of seduction and escape, and a world of mysticism and secrecy.

The Water-sign symbols of the zodiac consist of the crab, the scorpion and the fishes. These are primitive, cold-blooded life forms that live by instinct alone, and which have survived unchanged since the dawn of time.

Life began in water, which sustains the most primitive and instinctive of life forms. Water is the most primeval of elements. Fire is untamed and bestial, and represents power through aggression; Earth is bestial and domesticated, representing power through endurance; and Air is humane, self-reflective and rational, representing power through reason. Water represents the primitive power of instinct.

In his book *Siddhartha* (originally published 1923), Hermann Hesse (Cancer) portrays the 'great teacher' as a river: he describes how the water continually flows, is always new, yet is always there. He asks himself how it is possible to conceive something that is always the same, and yet every moment is different.

The element of Water has this nebulous quality, that is drawn to the irrational and the unexplained, that submerges into the depths of the unknown. Consequently, Water signs are well known for their delicate grip on reality, and for lacking the ability or interest to contend with the issues that relate to the material world.

Ask a Water sign: 'But why choose that particular one?' 'I don't know,' answers Water, 'it just feels right.' Water signs do not deduce or reason well – they express themselves out of an inner feeling, an instinctive sense of what is right. But Water is also the element of illusion and fantasy. It may just be that Water signs are fooling themselves and everyone else. Water is the element of the poet – it is up to the reader to discern the wisdom from the fantasy.

When it comes to power and leadership, Water signs, as with everything else they become concerned with, favour a subtle approach. They are driven to power by instinct and a sense of destiny.

Fire strives to dominate through force; Earth through purpose, stability, and the promise of security; Air through reason, organization and structure. Water makes no overt effort to dominate, or assume control. Water allows events to take their own course. Water allows creativity and individual freedom, but the 'shadow' side of the Water element resents structure and organization. Yet it is just these attributes which allow Water's 'concepts' to find a place in the real world rather than remain in the realm of fantasy and aspirations. There is a side to Water that is unconcerned with the danger of 'anarchy' – disorder, after all, is the price for individual freedom. Water may feel that from chaos, a new order shall emerge. But for everyone else it may seem only like chaos.

The Elements of the Personality

The idea of four personality types has been around a long time. In 500 BC the Greek philosopher Empedocles said that all matter was made up of four elements: Fire, Earth, Air and Water. A century later Hippocrates designated these four elements to the human body: Yellow Bile, Black Bile, Blood and Phlegm. Claudius Galen, a Greek physician of the second century AD, redefined these four 'humours' as 'temperaments', based on the varying degrees of bodily fluids affecting character. Cholerics were easily aroused to anger; melancholics were subject to mood swings; sanguine personalities were optimistic, and phlegmatic described stolid and unexcitable character types.

Carl Jung, in the 1930s, cited Galen as one of western psychology's founders, and went on to develop a typology which continues to influence studies in behavioural sciences, management and human resources to the present day. All of today's management and recruiting systems based on four types, began with the four elements – the foundation of natal astrology!

The personality types described by Jung are Intuitive, Sensation, Thinking, and Feeling. These types correspond to the elements in astrology and alchemy:

FIRE (Aries, Leo, Sagittarius)   Intuitive type
EARTH (Taurus, Virgo, Capricorn)   Sensation type
AIR (Gemini, Libra, Aquarius)   Thinking type
WATER (Cancer, Scorpio, Pisces)   Feeling type

According to Jung, the Intuitive type is an envisioning personality that creates the widest range of possibilities. The Intuitive type is interested in potentials, projects and new ideas. Sensation refers to the sensory perceptions; the Sensation type relies on the physical senses, placing value in what can be seen and heard and touched. The Sensation type is not concerned with the irrational. Sensation preserves, stabilizes and relates to matter – to objects, and information perceived as factual. Jung regarded Intuition and Sensation as two polarities – Intuition creates, Sensation preserves.

A Thinking type evaluates, assesses and compares. What is logical and rational, and can be objectified by the mind, is retained - the irrational and the illogical is rejected. The Thinking type relates to ideas and ideals. The Feeling type on the other hand relates to emotions. The Feeling type responds instinctively to situations rather than mental analysis; is receptive, sensitive, imaginative, relating to experiences through emotions rather than intellect.

Intuition and Sensation make up one polarity, Thinking and Feeling another. Thinking relates to surface values – what can be analyzed; Feeling relates to concealed values – what can be felt. Jung maintained that every individual has each of the four 'functions' within them – just as all the elements are present in each person's chart – but that one is usually dominant, or 'superior', and the 'opposite' function (in the Intuition/Sensation, Thinking/Feeling polarities will be 'inferior' or poorly developed.

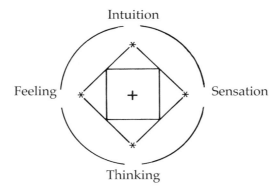

Psychological types

In the 1980s many companies – firstly in the USA, then elsewhere – began using the Myers-Briggs Type Indicator, as an approach to evaluating personality in business, management, recruiting and teambuilding. The personality evaluation test devised by Isabel Myers-Briggs indicates one of sixteen personality types based on Jung's descriptions. A candidate is defined as Extrovert or Introvert; Sensation or Intuition; Thinking or Feeling; Perceiving or Judging. So Extrovert Sensing Feeling Perceiving types (ESFP) 'love people, excitement, fun. They are spontaneous, impulsive and love to entertain…'

Since Myers-Briggs many similar evaluation techniques have emerged: the Keirsey Temperament Sorter, DISC Breakthrough Networking (Dauntless – Indefatigable – Supportive – Careful), and others, but all fundamentally variations of Jungian typology. In 1994 neurologist Jerome Kagan suggested that Galen's original theory of humours has a scientific basis, and that temperament is 'a part of the genetic lottery' (*Galen's Prophecy*, 1994). For example, timidity (according to Kagan) is due to an overactive neurochemistry that enables a neural circuit centred on the amygdala to be easily aroused. Kagan lists four types based on his theory: bold, timid, upbeat and melancholy. Two and a half thousand years after Empedocles, the four elements continue to fascinate and illuminate.

Just as Jung's typology and its many spin-offs have found practical applications in business and management, so too can the astrological elements. After all, why drink from the well, when you can drink from the source?

So how can we best apply our understanding of the four elements to individual business styles? How can the elements of natal astrology help us evaluate the people we work with, or the people we want to work with? How can we use the elements to assess our strengths and weaknesses in negotiating, recruiting, or just dealing with people on an everyday basis? Let us begin with this question: how would you define your own style? Are you a Fiery Enthusiast, an Earthy Pragmatist, an Airy Analyst or an Imaginative Water-type? What about your colleague? Your boss? A Sun-sign may be our predominant element, but the natal chart will give us a much more precise indication.

In business and management the predominant styles of the elements show that:

- Fire motivates.
  But can be too dominating, over-optimistic.
  Needs to be more practical.

- Earth gets things done.
  But can be too serious, too pessimistic.
  Needs to see possibilities, not problems.

- Air stimulates.
  But might be too theoretical, too abstract.
  Needs to apply ideas rather than just devise them.
  Needs more empathy, more feeling.

- Water inspires.
  But can be too vague, too sensitive.
  Needs to be more realistic, more rational.

Fire Types – Enthusiasts

impulsive • eager • expansive • idiosyncratic

Fire prefers actions over words, is quick to get involved in new projects, strong initiative – good at starting new projects, not so good at seeing them through. Where others see problems Fire sees possibilities. Always new ideas, new plans, new enterprises. They function best in roles of influence, persuasion and status, motivated to take on leadership by power and prestige. There is an extravagant side to the Enthusiast – lack of money should not hinder creativity!

Motivation

'I want to be first.'

Good Points

Fire wants to be noticed, wants to be followed, loves an audience or a crowd of spectators to cheer encouragement. Fire can be a guide and inspiration to others, an innovator, the individual who takes risks that others would not consider.

Fire's action-orientated style is expressed in different ways by the different Fire signs: Aries are the individualists who choose their own way; Leos enjoy more the central role in social situations; while Sagittarius' action is manifested outwardly – in educational or ideological pursuits.

Watch Out For

Being first means being fast. Fire is always in a hurry, in a rush, lacks patience and method, ends up making a mess of things, leaving the chaos of unfinished projects for other people to clean up. An egoist, inconsiderate to others.

Presentation Style

Persuasion is the delivery style of the Enthusiast. Persuasion inspires the audience, arouses their interest, uses eloquent speech and a rousing style to convince the listener. This is the rhetoric of the politician, of the salesman, of the actor. It is one-way communication. The Enthusiast is a good active talker; not so good as an active listener.

Negotiation Style

Fiercely competitive, Fire treats the negotiation as a contest – a game. Fire is out to win at the expense of the other side; a win – lose scenario. There is competition in any negotiation and Fire plays it out to the full.

A Competitive style needs a positive attitude and good humour. Otherwise the competition can become too aggressive. With a win–lose scenario the prestige in 'winning' is intensified and the objectives of the negotiation become obscured by the contest. To defuse an all too intense competitive negotiation, remind each other of mutual benefits, objectives for both sides, play out 'what if...' alternatives, or do as other competitors – take 'time out'.

Fire Strategy

Winning style; keywords include enthusiasm, act like a winner, self- confidence, persuasive, belief in a cause, sense of adventure, performance, the 'game'.

Risk Zone

Aggression: getting angry, standing up for your case, indignation, threats. Risk of communication breakdown, which can also lead to deadlock.

Fire is undermined by Water's personal style. The Competitive style is strong on showmanship, a performance. The Personal approach prevents Fire from performing, because being personal requires a candid, direct exchange of two personalities. This approach defuses the potentially hostile atmosphere, whereas a rational, analytical (Air) approach might only exacerbate the conflict.

For Aries, aggression can surface in one-to-one business situations – the negotiation can develop into a personal duel which Aries 'must win'; Leos have a cooler attitude in one-to-one situations, but can become fierce when defending their group; while Sagittarius – philosophers that they are – inadvertently create aggressive situations by being too open, too blunt and too direct.

Earth Types – Pragmatists

realistic • problem-solving • practical

Earth is a down-to-earth realist with little patience for schemes and projects that have not been thought through. Earth is practical, a problem-solver, who, once having taken on a task, gets on with it until it is done. Compared to Fire, Earth seems pessimistic by nature, yet it is often the Pragmatist – although slow to rouse to a new enterprise, who is the driving force to its completion.

Motivation

'I want to be strong.'

Good Points

Takes on responsibilities that others shy away from, hard-working, patient, persevering, refuses to give up. Like Sisyphus, the Pragmatist endures and perseveres, finding reward in the task itself.

Watch Out For

Intolerance of weakness in oneself is projected on to others – intolerance, prejudice, unreasonableness. Can get burdened down with too many tasks, too many responsibilities out of fear of being seen to be weak.

Presentation Style

Earth instructs. Delivers the facts, uses statistics, appeals to common sense. It is the rhetoric of the engineer, the technician, the production supervisor, the accountant, the traditional leader. It is one-way communication – the listener takes notes. The Pragmatist talks and listens, but has difficulty showing enthusiasm.

Negotiation Style

The Organizational style represents the organization, the company, corporate policy. Whereas Fire's competitive approach speaks in 'I' form, the Earth negotiator uses 'we', and promotes the company view, company objectives, official company policy. This ensures a formal 'by the book' approach to negotiations which does not become too competitive, nor too personal. Business is business. The style is pragmatic, thorough, understanding and aims to fulfil obligations on behalf of the company or organization.

Consequently Organizational style negotiations require patience – they can be exhausting, wearing down the opposition with facts and figures. The risk of deadlock becomes apparent when both sides negotiate for the Company – if the two Company bottom lines do not match, what happens next? The Company dictates the terms. In such cases some personal input (Water – Personal style), or 'what if...' alternatives (Air–Cooperative Style), or dog-eat-dog competitive aggression (Fire–Competitive Style) is necessary to break the impasse.

Earth Strategy

Facts; keywords include statistics, reason, information, rational, pragmatic, one-way communication

Risk Zone

Bottom line – can't move, rigid, budget limits, down-to-earth, impasse, final offer (forces other side to make concessions). Risk that other side walks away, but this can also break deadlock.

Earth responds well to Air's cooperative style. By presenting 'what if...' scenarios, the company-driven negotiator has the means of breaking a deadlock without having to commit to a compromise. The objective here is to keep the channels of communication open. By presenting exclusively the company policy the organizational style risks a deadlock – cooperative style opens up possibilities without forcing an issue.

Air Types – Analysts

intellectual • rational • logical • idealistic

Air is logical, communicative and enjoys the social interaction a workplace has to offer; discussing plans and strategies, working out systems, how best to set up some new enterprise. Air is rational and reasonable, so avoids conflicts and emotional situations. The problem with being so reasonable is how to cope with the rest of the world that is less reasonable. Air appreciates knowledge for its own sake and collects facts, theories and information for their own sake, attracted to ideas and abstracts. The Analyst is an organizer who works best in a team in order to formulate strategies and systems.

Motivation

'I want to be best.'

Good Points

Rational, logical, applying the faculties of reason and common sense. Air is motivated by wanting to be best, the most clever, the most qualified, the most knowledgeable.

Watch Out For

Losing touch with feelings is to lose touch with humanity. Systems, knowledge for its own sake, the scientific experiment, take precedence over the people they were intended to benefit.

Presentation Style

Logic is the rhetoric of Air , with observations are based on reason, and theories developed from knowledge and expertise. It is the rhetoric of the researcher, the strategist, the planner. Air needs feedback – open questions and audience response. Whereas Instruction demands attention and Persuasion grabs attention, Logic requests. Thus it is two-way communication - the listener participates. Air talks actively and listens actively, but may have difficulty dealing with feelings.

Negotiation Style

Cooperative, looking for mutual benefits – there is always a better deal for both sides. The Peacemaker doesn't want a conflict, just a good deal and ongoing positive business relations. No trouble. Air hypothesizes: what if we? could you then...? what about...? A lot of 'what if' questions and alternative scenarios to allow the other side to consider the possibilities without having to commit to a proposition. This works well when the other side comes back with further 'what if...' alternatives, and the two sides work their way cooperatively and amicably towards a proposition that best suits both sides. Air's style of negotiating is sociable, maintains a positive atmosphere, emphasizes team work and mutual benefits.

It is also a style so concerned with fair play and cooperation that both sides might lose sight of their objectives and end up with a compromise neither side feels happy with. Air prefers to stick to a system or to principles or a theory or legal technicalities rather than understanding the real needs of those involved. When the Cooperative style works, it is a highly effective negotiating style; when it doesn't the negotiators need to consider being more competitive – what's in the best interests of the company – or introducing a personal element rather than stick to the negotiating rule-book.

Air Strategy

The natural communication skills of the Air signs makes them skilful business strategists. Air's techniques include the 'minimax' top-price–bottom-price bazaar technique, working towards a compromise between high and low; two-way communication.

Air provides 'what if...' scenarios, maintains a positive atmosphere, keeps communication going without commitment – is explorative, seeking compromise, solution and mutual benefits.

Risk Zone

Too cooperative – the risk with too much peace is that nothing happens. The Peacemaker might lose sight of objectives or be so busy cooperating that instead of mutual benefits, the benefits become one-sided – in favour of the opposition. If this happens, some competitive spirit redefines the issues and compels the negotiators to focus on the objectives.

Water Types – Imaginatives

resourceful • original • artistic • sensitive

Water seeks meanings and responds to situations and problems with instincts and hunches. This is the creative individual in search of deeper meanings and values with an innate feel for concept. Water's creativity makes them unpredictable – the Imaginative has difficulty being tied down to routines and schedules, and functions better with intensive periods of concentrated work, followed by periods of lethargy. Water has a strong sense of empathy which works well in managerial positions, although this individual has difficulty maintaining credibility in roles of authority. Water's need for approval can prevent them from making necessary but unpopular decisions.

Motivation

'I want to be appreciated.'

Good Points

Deep empathy and understanding of what other people want – an ability to tap into the needs of the collective. Strong sense of humanity and drive to help others, to please others. Water provides the creative gifts of art and poetry to enable others to get in touch with their feelings.

Watch Out For

Feelings are good for empathy with others, but not always so good for building up self-esteem. Water types may experience periods of feeling unappreciated, thus seeking approval to overcome a sense of low self-worth. They feel they must try and please others to over-compensate and achieve recognition. Even success can be a burden for the heavily characterized Water type. Success can be accompanied by feelings of guilt, over-indulgence and fears of living up to a reputation. A positive way to win over emotional Water types is to give constructive feedback (never criticism), and level-headed praise for concrete achievements.

Presentation Style

Emotional – an individual and personal presentation style which appeals to the listener through feelings. It is the rhetorical style of the Imaginative to create images with words, to move an audience by evoking an emotional response of love, hate, joy, or sadness. This kind of presentation functions when an audience responds; with a non-responsive audience the presentation falls flat.

Negotiation Style

Personal – a negotiation is founded on human interaction, a relationship between two people or two teams of people. In most instances negotiators stick to their professional roles, whether Competitive, Cooperative or Organization's representative. When positive personal values are introduced to the negotiation they can inspire confidence, credibility, reliability, goodwill. The personal touch means strong empathy, and values beyond the bottom line of an agreement. It is far easier to negotiate prices, contracts, conditions when you strike a personal chord with the business partner.

This is something you can never plan for – in personal chemistry, like compound chemistry, some elements mix and others don't. You can hope for it, and work towards it, and when it happens appreciate a situation that becomes more than just business, but the beginning of a friendship. The Personal style is individual, does not stick to rules, and demands the kind of intimacy that enables your needs to be understood while understanding and appreciating the needs of the other side.

Being personal has its risks, however. When you don't stick to the rules a lot of feelings can surface, not always positive. In every negotiation the personal factors are there, but our professional role-playing rarely allows these hidden feelings to surface. These are feelings which affect attitude about the job, the company, future prospects: bad feelings – negative attitude; good feelings - positive attitude.

There is always the risk that having developed a good personal relationship, it can turn sour over business problems. Can the two sides revert back to their professional roles or are business relations permanently damaged? In this case it can be helpful to consider the other styles: be analytical, rational – understand the events over which you can exert influence and adjust to the ones you can't; consider the interests and priorities of the company/organization on whose behalf you are negotiating; introduce an element of competitive spirit. A good contest is a sure way of evaluating your own priorities.

Water Strategy

Personal appeal; keywords include revealing personality, emotions, feelings, true sentiments, honesty, trust, being reliable, all cards on table, personal feelings, warmth, friendship, cutting through the facade of sales talk and company policy, introducing the unexpected, the unpredictable.

Risk Zone

Personal issues – being personal is being friendly, but there are also risks. Personal input in negotiations can have positive effects – the risk is that if negotiations become too personalized, the issue of business becomes obscured by sentiments and impulsive agreements that both sides may regret later in the cold fiscal light of day. Water types can look to the practical and organizational style of Earth to redress an imbalance. In business situations the Water type needs to set up guidelines to allow both sides to focus on the needs and commitments of their respective organizations, as well as the space to develop personal relationships.

An Overview of Individual Business Styles According to Astrological Element

FIRE (Enthusiast)

	+	—
Style	makes things happen	leaves things unfinished
Presentations	convincing	superficial, misleading
Negotiations	goal-orientated	hostility
	win = maximum benefits	loss = no benefits

EARTH (Pragmatist)

	+	—
Style	solves problems	doesn't like new ideas
Presentation	down to earth, factual	dull, uninspiring
Negotiations	thorough	inflexible, impersonal

AIR (Analyst)

	+	—
Style	well organized / use systems	systems, not people
Presentations	well structured, clear, logical	theoretical, complicated
Negotiations	mutual benefits, fair play	aimless, compromising

WATER (Imaginative)

	+	—
Style	creative input, good ideas	lacks initiative, confidence
Presentations	individual, personal, genuine	sentimental, irrelevant
Negotiations	empathy, understanding	too personal, no business

The Company We Keep

A company too has a 'personality' – there are 'Fiery' companies, 'Earthy' ones, 'Airy' companies and 'Watery' companies. They are defined both by their mode of operation and by the nature of their enterprise.

Fire companies are hierarchical, bold, risk-taking, innovative and expansive. They create their own markets, and are the initiative of a strong and driving personality. Examples include F W Woolworth, Ford, Amstrad, Sinclair Electronics.

Earth companies build on or move into an established market, are solid, stable, purposeful, bureaucratic, avoid danger and run the risk of becoming 'dinosaur' corporations. IBM is one such example; government or state-financed companies could be others.

Air companies are systems-orientated, changing and adapting to the needs of the market; they use strategy and plan to accommodate all possible market developments. The Chrysler Corporation under Iacocca is one example.

Water companies fulfil a need in the market, play by hunch, are service-orientated, and use specialist knowledge or expertise. The Water company-style focuses on creating and maintaining networks and personal relations.

A model devised by the Ashridge Teamworking Services (which appeared in Devine's *The Photofit Manager* (1990), credited to Briner and Tyrell) describes in detail the following 'archetypal' organizational environments:

Power Organization

- clear direction and set priorities
- hierarchical
- teams and individuals are divided – survival of the fittest
- non-negotiable leadership
- leadership 'personality cult'
- deals with individuals, not groups
- closely guarded information – internally and externally
- what the leader says, goes!

Bureaucracy Organization

- decisions by committee
- use of precedent
- clear job responsibilities
- slow response to changes
- leader as part of system
- direction through appropriate channels
- formal procedures
- clearly defined boundaries

Teamworking Organization

- adaptable organizational structure
- meetings both formal and informal to resolve problems
- few hierarchical boundaries between people
- work is varied
- leaders adapt to changing corporate vision
- leaders are accessible

Expert Organization

- authority based on professional expertise
- low-profile management – it just happens
- a hierarchy based on professional competence
- keep within the particular field of expertise
- keep within parameters of assigned task

International consultant Fons Trompenaars defines corporate cultures in more Jungian terms: Intuitive, Practical, Logical and Inspirational (*Riding the Waves of Culture*, 1993), and with similar basic descriptions. The parallels between these organizational structures and the qualities as defined by the four elements are:

FIRE   Entrepreneurial – power organization (intuitive)
EARTH   Traditional – bureaucratic organization (practical)
AIR   Teamworking organization (logical)
WATER· Specialist – expert organization (inspirational)

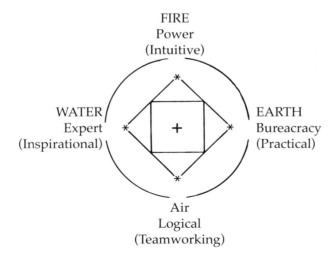

Organizational structure

Company Cultures

There are as many company cultures as there are companies. Defining a company culture is a 'type' approach (like evaluating personalities) to focusing on the core values of a particular organization.

The entrepreneurial company (Fire) may be weak on history, but strong on possibilities. Its culture embraces risk taking as a matter of policy. It is called future investment.

The traditional company (Earth) on the other hand is based on past achievements, and responses to present situations are based on precedent. The Earth company has a strong sense of company identity but is slow to adapt to changes. Slow and steady wins the race.

The teamworking company (Air) is firmly established in the here-and-now. It deals with and adapts to present issues – flexibility enables the company to adapt quickly to the needs of the market.

The specialist company (Water) may be a one-person operation, a consultancy firm, or a small business relying on their own knowledge base, expertise and a network of clients. The expertise and specialization are commodities of the future; innovation, speculation and foresight. The practicalities of the present can be an Achilles heel with this kind of personalized organization.

Company culture does not stand still – it is an ongoing process of development or decline. Often the large, conservative, traditional company was once a small specialist concern that developed an entrepreneurial corporate culture with growth and expansion. As a traditional company it may need to develop a new corporate culture – elements of teamworking, or a new input of entrepreneurial initiative – to prevent it from becoming a dinosaur company lumbering its way towards extinction.

Awareness and flexibility are the keywords. Small specialist companies that are stuck in the past, unable to innovate and provide the market with the kind of replenishment that specialist corporate culture represents, will perish as surely as the teamworking organization that fails to define or redefine goals and objectives.

The ATS describe an additional structure, which they call a networking organization, which approximates to an alchemical balance. They include their own organization as an example. Characteristics include:

- self-determination, shared values
- simple administrative central control
- rotating leadership according to activity
- shared leadership tasks
- everyone is an owner

The 'new age' management that is currently popular favours decentralized organizations over centralized. 'New age' is a curious term which crops up in a lot of contemporary management literature – particularly in the plethora of 'Excellence' books – though few define what 'new age' means. Every generation creates its own 'new age' – in management, as in everything else. As each astrological age lasts more than 2000 years, it may be more helpful to look in detail at the more rapid changes in the business world.

Tom Peters in *Thriving on Chaos* (1988) refers to the 'age of uncertainty'. He describes the contrast of 'a past age' with 'a new age' as follows:

Past Age	New Age
Pyramids	Alliances
Centralized	Decentralized
Top down	Bottom up
The boss	Self-management
Management	Autonomous worker action
Manuals and procedures	Visions and values

Yet there is always a 'past age' just as there is always a 'new age'. In management we need to look at the past, the future and the 'now age', the 2000s. If the 1980s was the age of the 'star', the company visionary and leadership by decree, then the 1990s emphasized coaching, dialogue and interpersonal skills.

And the 21st century? Futurologist Rolf Jensen describes the corporate values of the 2000s in *The Dream Society* (1999); it is not the company with the best product that will succeed, he concludes, but the company with the best story.

1980s	1990s	2000s
The Vision	The Team	The Story
IQ	EQ (emotional quotient)	Insight
Business skills	Social skills	Psychological skills
Directives	Suggestions	Interaction
CEO as 'star'	CEO as coach	CEO as story teller
Mission statement	Values	Narrative
Support	Mutual benefits	Inspiration

If the 1980s emphasized company values and mission statements, then the 1990s – with so many established corporations threatened by the changes brought by new technology – focused on 'core values' and ways to profile a distinctive corporate image. Levis or Wranglers? Nokia or Ericsson? Honda or Rover? What difference does it make if the same product is made in the same factory, but just branded with a different name? The difference, as we discover in the 2000s, lies in the story: which brand inspires us? Which story do we want to be a part of?

Stories require story-tellers, and story-tellers need insight. Managers of the 1980s needed credibility, MBAs and degrees; managers of the 1990s had to have EQ (emotional quotient), social skills, be good listeners and be able to delegate. In the 2000s managers need insight, and the tools of insight are story-telling skills, myths, psychology and, yes, astrology.

An Overview of Corporate Cultures According to Astrological Element

FIRE – Entrepreneur

	+	–
Style: Top Down	strong leadership, goal-orientated	high risk
Leadership: Directing	visionary, decisive	dominating, oppressive

EARTH – Traditional

	+	–
Style: Hierarchical	security, experience, credibility	conservative, bureaucratic
Leadership: Coaching	purposeful, responsible, secure	resists change, dogmatic

AIR – Teamworking

	+	–
Style: Team-orientated	consensus, mutual benefits	weak leadership, no goals
Leadership: Supportive	flexible, strategic, listening	indecisive, aimless

WATER – Specialist

	+	–
Style: Network	flexibility, expertise, personal	unstable, unrealistic
Leadership: Delegating	individual responsibility, concepts	insecurity, no leadership

The Elements of Management

When *The One-Minute Manager* was published in the late 1970s, it marked the beginning of a new and creative approach to management. The authors, Kenneth Blanchard and Spencer Johnson, outlined a model describing four styles of leadership. These they called: Directing, Coaching, Supporting and Delegating.

Leadership Styles

Successful management, they argued, depended upon top management's ability to adapt to any given situation. A manager is not classified as one of these four types, but rather needs to identify four basic approaches to leadership, and apply the most appropriate style.

Directing management is dominating, issuing instructions and supervising how tasks are carried out. Coaching leadership is also dominating, continuing to direct and supervise, but explaining decisions and open to suggestions. Supporting management allows middle management to take initiatives in making decisions, and shares responsibility in the decision-making process. Delegating leadership means the leader gives responsibility for making decisions and solving problems over to subordinates without interference.

'A fast changing world needs all kinds of leaders', says Kenneth Blanchard. 'It's no longer possible to predict what kind of leader we need tomorrow... management will be required to adapt quickly to the demands of employees and the rapidly changing needs and demands of the outside world.'

Corporate survival, he summarizes, depends on leadership's flexibility, the ability to make quick decisions, adaptability to market requirements (particularly in quality and service), a strong financial base and the individual employees having more say in the running of the company.

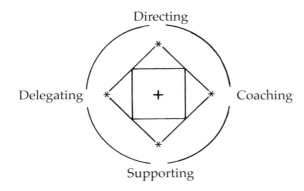

Leadership styles

The four leadership styles bear comparison to the four elements. Directing leadership corresponds to Fire, and its demands for complete authority; Coaching corresponds to Earth, and a leadership that supports initiatives from middle management but within well-structured guidelines; Supporting corresponds to Air, and Air's flexibility and need to communicate, but to retain decision-making in accordance with a well-researched strategy; Delegating corresponds to Water, which relies on expertise within each department. 'They know what they're doing – they're the specialists – let them make the decisions.'

However, just as Kenneth Blanchard describes leadership 'styles' which management can apply depending on the situation, the elements correspond in the same way to 'archetypes'. Leadership is rarely all 'Fire' or all 'Air' (some employees may argue the point); elements define identifiable modes in which leadership is expressed. In identifying the mode which applies most to a company, the question remains as to whether it is the most appropriate. Alchemy is concerned with the *combination* of elements which will produce the best results – or what the alchemists described as the 'miraculous change'.

Fire Signs – Directing Leadership

Aries	the entrepreneurial manager
Leo	the encouraging manager
Sagittarius	the expansive manager

Earth Signs – Coaching Leadership

Taurus	the consolidating manager
Virgo	the 'systems' manager
Capricorn	the organizing manager

Air Signs – Supportive Leadership

Gemini	the communicating manager
Libra	the mediating manager
Aquarius	the group-orientated manager

Water Signs – Delegating Leadership

Cancer	the nurturing manager
Scorpio	the protective manager
Pisces	the sympathetic manager

Team Roles

Just as the characteristics of the four elements can be applied to the style of leadership, so can they be applied to team roles. Meredith Belbin at the Henley Management College was concerned with shaping a team adept at creative problem-solving. After researching both successful and unsuccessful teams in a wide range of enterprises, he found eight different roles.

The Chairman

Coordinates the efforts of the team, and balances the team in accordance with members' strengths and weaknesses, ensuring that everyone has their say. A listener and a summarizer, who makes decisions on behalf of the group.

The Shaper

A dominating leadership role that inspires action and demands results. 'Shapes' and directs the team's efforts.

The Organizer

Belbin labels the Organizer as the 'company worker'. Disciplined and systematic, transforms abstract concepts into realizable working procedures.

The Completer

Ensures that the goods are delivered. Checks details, is thorough, conscientious and makes sure that deadlines are met.

The Monitor-Evaluator

A critical, rather creative role, involving the analysis and structuring of concepts and proposals.

The Resource Investigator

An 'ideas' person who interacts with other members, collating and analysing the ideas of colleagues. More a developer than an innovator. Highly sociable, constantly in conferences and meetings.

The Teamworker

Sensitive to the needs and concerns of team colleagues, aware of the group's emotional undercurrents. A service-orientated role that ensures the team's efficiency by taking care of people.

The Plant – the Original Thinker

The creative element of a team. Belbin uses the term 'plant' because when 'planted' in a team such people enhance creative output with original and innovative ideas, though to all appearances they are quiet, withdrawn personalities.

Once more, if we examine these 'team roles' we discern similarities in some roles, and a correspondence between their functions and the qualities as outlined in the Corporate Alchemy paradigm:

- The Chairman and Shaper are leadership roles and correspond to introvert and extrovert Fire.
- The Organizer and Completer are 'actualizer' roles and correspond to introvert and extrovert Earth.
- The Monitor-Evaluator and Resource Investigator are 'mediating' roles, corresponding to introvert and extrovert Air.
- The 'Plant' and the Teamworker are service and creative roles, corresponding to introvert and extrovert Water.

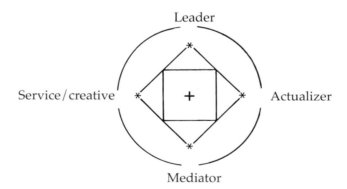

Structure within the organization

Belbin emphasizes there are no hard and fast rules for shaping the perfect team. There may be anything from two to ten team members, and several may fulfil similar roles. However, in accordance with the principles of Corporate Alchemy, identifying team roles enables a manager to assess strengths and weaknesses within a team. Belbin's research demonstrated that teams with highly talented individuals might be effective without a 'team-worker' or 'plant' individual to instil a sense of team solidarity. For the manager, the essential skill lies in appreciating and valuing the different strengths of team members. The enlightened manager – the 'corporate alchemist' – is aware of their limitations, and understands that a diversity of inputs can only enhance a team's efficiency.

Setting Up the Team

Regardless of the company's size, a working unit within a department usually consists of three to five people – and four people on average. Even within a large sales department, for example, daily interaction will be divided up into smaller units of about four people; say a manager, an assistant, a secretary and an administrator. The titles and job descriptions may vary, but any individual's daily work routine within an office generally involves three colleagues. A few hours in a company building is enough to provide a feeling for which departmental units function well, function adequately, or do not function at all.

We hear the word 'chemistry' often applied to the way people interact, but before chemistry came alchemy. Getting the right people together within a departmental unit, and providing them with the motivation needed to extract the optimum from each member, is an alchemical skill that most managers disregard, relying on chance or intuition. What they are involved in is the alchemy of personalities. Astrology provides the chance to refine an intuitive process into a science of exactitude, to the advantage of the manager and colleagues within the departmental unit.

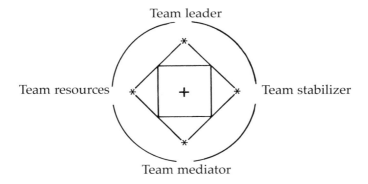

The elements of a team

Just as we have defined four different kinds of corporate structure, management and personality types, we can likewise consider four types of 'team'.

A Fire Team (Aries, Leo, Sagittarius):

Takes initiatives, begins new enterprises, sees possibilities and grabs them. Aggressive, enthusiastic, but not always well organized – campaigns may suffer through poor planning and an inability to deal with practical details. The Fire team takes risks, and, as 'risk' implies, may win or may lose. The Fire team enjoys the gamble – and has sufficient confidence to believe that if this one does not pay off then the next one will. This is the competitive and high-spirited team that plays to win. As the 'game' is more important than profit, this is a team that innovates and follows an 'all-or-nothing' philosophy. This is the team that makes a killing, or sends the company to the bankruptcy courts. Genius costs.

An Earth Team (Taurus, Virgo, Capricorn)

Methodical, steadfast, reliable and with a strong sense of purpose, the Earth team values profits, sets its sights on a realizable goal, and works steadily towards achieving it. A Fire team might consider Earth as the 'tortoise', but the tortoise did beat the hare. 'Slow and steady wins the race,' says Earth. This is a team that sees a problem and deals with it head-on, and perseveres through adversity to accomplish what it carefully set out to accomplish. The Earth team does not take risks, exercises caution and makes progress through hard work without the short-cuts. The Earth team favours steady gains rather than a big win. This is the team that works by the book, investing profits prudently along the way. It is also the team that might miss the boat by being too cautious, or turn into a 'dinosaur' by being too inflexible when it achieves success.

An Air Team (Gemini, Libra, Aquarius)

This is the team that consists of business school graduates that have studied the latest business strategies and techniques, and who have read all the reports on why Japanese companies are so successful: strategists, planners and organizers. This is the team that originated the 'working breakfast', where fresh-faced young executives in Kenzo suits talk shop in the coffee bar from 7:30 am to office opening time. And they will still be talking shop in the winebar that evening. Clever, dynamic, and, above all, contemporary – this is the team that is up-to-date and beyond – well-read and well-researched, with all the options and possibilities worked out in advance. If the situation changes, the team can change with it. This is also the team that might talk its way out of ever doing anything. All strategy and no product will not pay for the croissants and orange juice.

A Water Team (Cancer, Scorpio, Pisces)

This is a low-profile team that will not become involved in enterprises that are speculative or superficial. This is the 'art for art's sake and money for art's sake' team, that values its integrity and its talent. The Water team specializes and provides expert service in its chosen field of enterprise. The emphasis is on creativity and the danger here, as with any artistic enterprise, is that it is easier and more prestigious to be the failed artist – the creative genius the establishment refuses to take seriously – than to succeed quietly. It is an attitude that wins friends who are already unemployed, and loses contracts. This is probably the team that invented Trivial Pursuit after being sacked from the advertising agency for refusing to demean itself with chocolate bars.

The Alchemically Balanced Team

Monty Python's Flying Circus was first broadcast on the BBC on 5 October 1969, and ran for four series, ending in November 1974. The Monty Python members had previously been involved in the Cambridge Footlights, and a number of radio and television programmes.

The success of the Monty Python enterprise led to a number of spin-offs – four Monty Python feature films, as well as tapes, records and books – and established each member sufficiently to proceed with an independent career.

The members are:

FIRE   Eric Idle (Sun in Aries, Moon in Capricorn and Leo Ascendant)
EARTH   Michael Palin, (Sun, Moon in Taurus, Leo Ascendant) and Graham Chapman (Sun, Ascendant in Capricorn, Moon in Taurus)
AIR   Terry Jones (Sun, Ascendant in Aquarius, Moon in Leo)
WATER   John Cleese (Sun, Venus, Mercury in Scorpio, Moon in Aries, Virgo Ascendant)

According to John Cleese, the writing partnership between him and Graham Chapman (Water/Earth; the creative input from Cleese – Water – made 'substance', formed by Chapman – Earth) was quite distinguishable from the sketches of Terry Jones and Michael Palin.

The signature of Michael Palin's (Taurus) input was opening a sketch with a scene of arcadian idyll – a field, a brook, a park – which swiftly moves into absurdity. The Cleese/Chapman combination produced sketches of people verbally and physically abusing each other. Terry Jones and Michael Palin's sketches began with lyrical openings and contained a more defined narrative form.

Eric Idle (Fire) contributed independent material, as one might expect of an Aries Sun-sign. Terry Jones went on to direct the Python feature films, acting as the organizer and 'systematizer' of the group. According to both Jones and Cleese, the 'dynamic' of the team was primarily between Scorpio Cleese and Aquarian Jones. They argued.

Terry Gilliam (Sun on the Scorpio/Sagittarius cusp; between 29.50 Scorpio and 00.10 Sagittarius), the animator, had a peripheral role in the Python team, producing animated sequences independent of the scripted sketches, and was more or less left to his own devices. Gilliam went on to become a successful film director in his own right.

When John Cleese left the team in 1973, the alchemical balance was sufficiently disrupted to bring the series swiftly to an end.

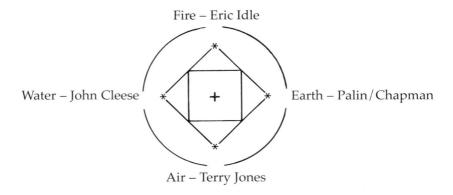

The elements of a team: Monty Python

Nearly 30 years after the end of the series, John Cleese speculates that its success is because the Python characters represent archetypes which anyone could identify regardless of cultural background:

Terry Jones (Aquarian) – the eccentric (usually cross-dressed)
John Cleese (Scorpio) – cruel, heartless, manic
Graham Chapman (Capricorn) – the authority figure
Michael Palin (Taurus) – safe, repressed, colourless and middle class
Eric Idle (Aries) – 'the cheeky chappie', or endlessly optimistic

In other words, by aligning their projected characters on to their astrological types – by being true to their inner selves, rather than just performing fabricated characters – the team succeeded in creating both credibility and the alchemical balance that would endure across time and culture.

Ideally every company is looking for the ultimate alchemical combination – the right balance of team members that will ensure a positive work environment, a strong creative spirit and an economic foundation to ensure continuity.

Theoretically, the alchemically balanced team should consist of a Fire-sign leader, an Air-sign administrator, a Water-sign designer and an Earth-sign 'worker'. The four-person team of the Swedish office of Mondadori, an Italian printing and publishing agency, provided just this combination. It was established mainly by the branch's founder and company head, Bitte Hall, who is an Arian.

FIRE   Bitte – founder and managing director (Sun in Aries, Sagittarius Ascendant, Moon in Libra)
EARTH   Rose Marie – production assistant (Sun in Taurus, Virgo Ascendant, Moon in Pisces)
AIR   Maria – office manager, co-ordinator (Sun in Libra, Cancer Ascendant, Moon in Leo)
WATER   Ulla – designer (Sun in Scorpio, Ascendant and Moon, Libra)

The elements of each person correlate with their 'archetypal' functions: Fire as leader, Air as mediator, Water as the creative input – the source of concepts (in this case production design) – and Earth as 'actualizer'.

In addition, the elements are balanced by a Cardinal polarity and a Fixed polarity. Bitte and Maria make up the Aries–Libra polarity (Cardinal positive signs), and are involved in the managing of the team and coordination with head office – sales, strategy, direction, and the outer face of the company.

Ulla and Rose Marie make up the Scorpio–Taurus polarity (Fixed negative signs), involved with design and production – the creative and internal workings of the company.

This team worked together for one year under harmonious conditions, and according to the company's founder, functioned efficiently and profitably. But in 1991 the Mondadori head office, having undergone a change of management, closed down most of their overseas agencies, including the Swedish office.

Focused Team-making

These two examples illustrate alchemically balanced team combinations. This is unusual as in most teams one element will be strong, and another weak. The dominance of one element or the lack of another is not necessarily a bad thing – a four-person team with three Air signs and one Earth sign will simply have different qualities than, say, a four-person team with two Fire signs and two Water signs.

To assess your own team, or another team (or division, or department), consider the charts or Sun-signs of team members. If the team consists of two Geminis, a Taurus and an Aries, then it will be 'strong Air/weak Water'. If it is a team of two Air signs, two Earth signs, and an Aries manager who makes all the decisions, then chances are it is 'strong Fire/weak Water.'

There are no hard and fast rules here – consider first the 'elemental' strengths and weaknesses of your associates, then see what picture emerges in describing the elemental strengths and weaknesses of the team as a whole.

So you realize you work in a team that is 'strong Fire/weak Earth'... what next? Sack a Sagittarian colleague and hire a Taurus? This would be a drastic measure with no guarantee for success. Awareness of the situation, and a willingness to work on weak points, may well be enough. If the team's 'weakness' lies in dealing with practical day-to-day problems like fixing photocopying machines, having enough money in petty cash to pay the courier, and remembering to buy tea-bags and toilet rolls, then it is a matter of learning to contend with those tasks in the same way that the team copes when it launches into a new sales campaign – thus bringing about 'alchemical' transformation from within.

In some situations, the imbalance may be too great to overcome without a change of personnel, particularly if there is one individual who seems unable to adapt or pull their weight. Alternatively, other than sack someone, outside help may be sought to provide the 'missing element'. A US consultancy firm (Executive Mystic Inc) describes an advertising agency they worked with that were 'all

Geminis and Leos and no Earth', which was 'excellent for a group's creativity, but hinted at a lack of order and financial prowess'. They quickly went out of business. Another firm, with a predominance of Fire, Water and Earth, but not a single Air sign, were advised to enlist the help of an outside Libran writer and designer to help them out with their brochures and press material. The alchemical balance worked out well for the company – the new member provided the necessary analytical input.

These are the likely profiles of the various possible team types:

Strong Fire/Weak Earth

Headstrong, bold, innovative, with new ideas and strong sense of enterprise. Difficulties getting ideas off the ground – inhibited by practical considerations, such as money and resources. A tendency to assume that the practical details will take care of themselves, and then give up when they do not.

Strong Fire/Weak Air

Innovative, enterprising, impulsive. Projects inhibited by poor organization and administration. An enterprise might get off the ground, then run into problems through lack of planning and strategy – or not having been thought through sufficiently.

Strong Fire/Weak Water

Ambitious, goal-orientated, enterprising. An initiative, however, may lack originality. It may be a project with structure, drive and financial backing, but team members may lose their sense of direction, unable to find a deeper meaning to their work.

Strong Earth/Weak Fire

A team that confronts problems head-on, understanding what can be accomplished with the resources available. However, a deep-rooted conservatism prevents taking risks or innovating. A solid, stable team – yet too much stability may lead to stagnation.

Strong Earth/Weak Air

A sense of purpose and stability – a team that takes on enterprises which are feasible and profitable. But a lack of administration, planning and strategy may lead to difficulties in adapting to the unexpected or contending with sudden changes of circumstances. A team strong on the process side of an enterprise, but weak on strategy and self-analysis.

Strong Earth/Weak Water

Stable, steadfast and reliable, motivated by profits and self-preservation. Weak on originality, it approaches problems 'by the book', maintaining a traditional view of a team's role. When things go wrong the boss can always take the blame.

Strong Air/Weak Fire

Organized, adaptable and full of ideas. This is a communicating team that likes to discuss, confer and negotiate. Strong in administration but weak in 'direction', it lacks the necessary drive and vision to fulfil all the plans and possibilities that have been outlined in the twice-weekly meetings.

Strong Air/Weak Earth

Communicative, outgoing, sociable – a team with many ideas and strong in strategy. However, there is a tendency to become bogged down in impractical schemes that look good on paper but are too implausible to work. Projects are well reasoned, consistent and logically conceived, but too abstract and idealistic.

Strong Air/Weak Water

A well-organized team with enthusiasm and idealism, planning thoroughly before undertaking a new enterprise. It is a team that collects ideas, rather than originating new ones.

Strong Water/Weak Fire

Original and imaginative with an instinctive sense of what can work. However, this team may lack confidence and direction to push its ideas – bad self-promoters. Inhibited by lack of team-confidence, and may get overtaken by pushy people with inferior work.

Strong Water/Weak Earth

Imaginative, original, with a genuine flair for coming up with the right solution to a given situation. Inspired, sincere, well-meaning, yet finds difficulty in coming to terms with the practical details of reality.

Strong Water/Weak Air

Inspired, creative, a strong sense of drama, but a lack of organization, and enterprises that sound good but have not been thought through. Excellent schemes may miss out through lack of strategy and planning, or a project that makes everyone enthusiastic may be impractical, or fail to live up to requirements.

Recruiting

For most managers, recruiting is the 'fun' part of the job where they can build up a team, personalized by their own selections. Most people claim to know a good candidate when they meet one – who needs a system for recruiting?

All too often a bad decision means that a team, or company department, is stuck with a co-worker who inhibits effectiveness. Choosing the wrong candidate costs money, obstructs production, and may even create irreconcilable rifts in a previously well-functioning and well-coordinated team. Yet what do most managers rely on when it comes to recruiting? The firmly-held belief that they know what they are doing. And a resolute conviction that they are astute judges of character. This kind of methodology, applied to any other aspect of company decision-making, would be called, quite accurately, 'hit or miss'.

There may be no such thing as 'a right decision', but a combination of astrology, psychology and common sense can undoubtedly help in making a better decision.

Managers think they can recruit – but often they choose personalities to match their own, rather than personalities to complement their own. What is the most common fault managers make in recruiting? It is assessing a candidate on subjective criteria. An employee is selected on the basis of the manager's personal views and preferences, rather than on the basis of who would be most suitable for the well-being of the team.

For example:

Fire signs are easily-inspired personalities and a candidate who generates enthusiasm and envisages boundless possibilities is often the candidate managers will favour. Fire leaders may soon find, however, that the kind of employee or team member they really need is someone who can take care of practical details and 'actualize' the Fire leaders' inspired visions. But it is just these pragmatists and 'ordered' people that Fire signs often regard as inhibitive and restrictive. Since it is a side of their own personality that they reject, they may reject the methodical but 'uninspiring' candidate, when it is exactly that kind of discipline that the Fire-led team needs to fulfil its objectives.

Earth signs favour solid, reliable personalities – people who are not going to rock the boat. Earth leaders value methodical, hard-working candidates with practical experience. They are traditional and keep a look-out for the right school tie, or a good university, or a suitable former company or place of employment. Earth leaders are suspicious of overtly creative types or sensitive, moody individuals – they are blunt and down-to-earth and expect their approach to be reciprocated in kind. Earth managers seek a candidate to fulfil a purposeful role and have no time for speculative or risky arrangements like: 'We'll give it a month and see what happens.'

It is quite possible, of course, that Earth leaders need a person who *will* rock the boat, who will instigate change, have creative ideas, and who will innovate instead of conforming. Perhaps this is the candidate who will initiate a new computer system or modernize office routines that the Earth managers have neglected. Earth signs look at trees: maybe they need someone to tell them about the forest.

Air signs depend on information and facts and value a candidate's intellectual abilities. Air managers put faith in the file before them, and are reluctant to trust their instincts. They may employ someone who appears to have all the right prerequisites and capabilities only to discover they have hired a troublemaker. Air signs like sociable and reasonable people – people they can communicate with, exchange ideas with, and from whom they will receive intellectual stimulation. Air leaders value academic qualifications and merits, also versatility, and the candidate who is team-motivated. They are wary of strong 'individuals' who appear unpredictable. Yet Air signs may need just that kind of individualism to avoid being bogged down with systems and strategy, without a concept to work with. Like Fire signs, perhaps, they need an 'actualizer' – someone who can take an idea or a scheme and make it work.

Water signs rely on an instinctive feel about a person – they favour sensitive people, and those with whom they can strike up a rapport. The Water manager's interviews might not be so much about the position or the nature of the work, but about the candidate's background, personal likes and dislikes. Water signs are not too bothered about academic qualifications and pieces of paper – if the candidate seems right for the job, then that is enough. But maybe what Water leaders really need is the qualified technician, or the organizer, so that when they say, 'It'll work out – just let it happen,' an organizer can say, 'It won't just happen unless we can plan it.' Water signs might be comfortable with a little creative freedom, while in the executive suite they are talking about 'the chaos in *that* department'. System, structure and organization may not appeal to their sense of the poetic, but help in creating order may at least secure Water leaders' positions in the company.

To summarize: managers tend to want to recruit the people they feel most comfortable with, and this usually means those who resemble themselves. Yet we need opposites. We may be reluctant to face the 'shadow' side of our own personality – yet only through confronting that side can we develop, and realize our own inner 'alchemy'. Fire needs Earth in order to actualize ideas; Earth needs Fire in order to take risks and prevent stagnation; Air needs Water in order to assess values and meanings; and Water needs Air to organize and rationalize feelings.

Managers rejecting the qualified candidate are just possibly rejecting a part of their own personality.

MANAGING ASTROLOGY:
The Astrological Basics

Astrology is a rich and complex study, with many branches and directions. Financial astrology is the study of transits and planetary cycles and their effects on economic fluctuations; mundane astrology studies the chart of a company or a country at the moment of inception. Our focus is on natal astrology; how planetary cycles affect the personality at the moment of birth. Astrologers working in management have made significant contributions in team building, recruiting skills and interpersonal relations. As in other areas of astrology, our starting point is the horoscope.

The Horoscope: a Personal Guide

'Horoscope' means an observation of the hour. A natal chart calculated by an astrologer is a measure of a specific moment of time. Astrology is based on the concept that each moment of time has its own intrinsic quality. A horoscope is not a measure of the human personality, but of the moment in which the individual is born. A natal chart is calculated from the moment of the first breath. The quality of that moment describes characteristics that can be interpreted as personality traits in the newly-born individual.

The horoscope, or natal chart, consists of 10 planets (the Sun and Moon are counted as planets), each at a particular point in one of the 12 signs, plus the Ascending sign (the sign that is on the horizon at the moment of birth), and Midheaven (the sign directly overhead). As the Sun takes a year to move through the 12 signs, we can know our Sun-sign by our birthday, without drawing up a chart. The Sun is the most important single influence in the chart, and can be regarded as describing a peson's 'essence', but many astrologers are critical of 'Sun-sign' astrology because it disregards the complexities of the overall chart.

However, most of us have come to astrology through a study of Sun-signs and, providing we realize these indicate 'types' rather than providing a total assessment of an individual's character, Sun-signs serve as a useful shorthand for describing the different kinds of personality. The person born in the middle of April, who seems more typical of the description of a Taurean than an Arian, may have their Ascendant, Moon or other planets in Taurus.

The basics of astrology can be summarized as signs, planets, Houses and aspects.

Symbol	Sign	Ruling Planet	Glyph	Element	Quality
♈	ARIES	MARS	♂	FIRE	CARDINAL
♉	TAURUS	VENUS	♀	EARTH	FIXED
♊	GEMINI	MERCURY	☿	AIR	MUTABLE
♋	CANCER	MOON	☽	WATER	CARDINAL
♌	LEO	SUN	☉	FIRE	FIXED
♍	VIRGO	MERCURY	☿	EARTH	MUTABLE
♎	LIBRA	VENUS	♀	AIR	CARDINAL
♏	SCORPIO	MARS/PLUTO	♂♇	WATER	FIXED
♐	SAGITTARIUS	JUPITER	♃	FIRE	MUTABLE
♑	CAPRICORN	SATURN	♄	EARTH	CARDINAL
♒	AQUARIUS	URANUS	♅	AIR	FIXED
♓	PISCES	NEPTUNE	♆	WATER	MUTABLE

Astrological symbols – planets and signs

The positions of the Sun, Moon and planets in a natal chart indicate an individual's sources of energy and motivation. Our Sun-sign describes one of 12 personality types. Just as the Sun is clearly visible in the heavens, the Sun-sign personality is, in psychological terms, the most easy to identify. The Sun represents the creative spirit, the source of individual energy.

Other planets represent different sides of the personality: Mercury indicates the way in which we communicate with others, the capacity for analysis and assimilating information; the Moon embodies feeling, instincts, intuition – the way in which we relate to our immediate environment and the people around us, and how memories of past events influence our behaviour in the present. Venus and Mars embody the two sides of personal relations: attraction and interaction. Jupiter and Saturn describe personal values and ideologies – Jupiter is expansive, Saturn disciplinary; a strong Jupiter influence seeks freedom, ideas and abstracts, the strong Saturn is earth-bound, seeking structure and permanence. The outer planets – Uranus, Neptune and Pluto – take many years to complete a single cycle through the ecliptic, so their positions in a chart relate to generations rather than individuals. For example, anyone born between 1942 and 1957 has Neptune in the sign of Libra, a placing which describes a culture (or counter-culture) manifested in the late 1960s, and continuing through the 1970s, when this generation was in their twenties.

How Horoscopes Work

In order to see the full workings of a horoscope and its implications, we can examine the chart of a famous historical figure. The chart shown here is that of Napoleon Bonaparte. A similar chart could be calculated for the moment at which a company is founded, or a country established, or the moment at which a question is asked or when an event occurs. These different branches of astrology are all based on the interpretation of the horoscope.

Asc	11 56 Lib	
MC	14 01 Cnc	
Sun	22 41 Leo	11
Moon	27 51 Cap	4
Mercury	6 02 Leo	10
Venus	6 58 Cnc	9
Mars	12 00 Vir	11
Jupiter	15 01 Sco	2
Saturn	25 59 Cnc	10
Uranus	11 35 Tau	8
Neptune	8 41 Vir	11
Pluto	13 24 Cap R	3

Napoleon Bonaparte 15 Aug 1769 09:50
Ajaccio Corsica (Source: JK)

Each planet describes different parts of the personality. Planets in Houses suggest the way in which these planetary energies are realized through what the person does. To summarize: planets in signs represent who the person is; planets in Houses represent what the person does. The Ascendant is also concerned with what a person does, with an individual's direction in life; it shows the point in the zodiac that is rising on the easten horizon at the moment of a person's birth. It shows where the individual is headed, and what may be on the horizon.

Bonaparte's Sun-sign is Leo, his rising sign – Ascendant – is Libra. Leo is the sign of the autocrat, of benevolence, of grand gestures and extravagant living. Libra is the sign of the mediator, the peacemaker, a connoisseur of fine things and harmonious living: a romantic.

The Moon refers to the more subtle aspects of human nature, a side hidden from public view. It incorporates a person's emotional responses, feelings and instincts – things often deeply rooted in childhood memories, or the long-forgotten past. Bonaparte's Moon is in Capricorn. This is the sign of caution and consolidation, of hard work and sense of purpose. It is an Earth sign, and favours pragmatism and common sense over dreams and abstractions. Those with a Capricorn Moon guard their feelings, wearing a mask of controlled austerity.

There is much of the strong Leo character in Napoleon: a leader who bestows upon himself the title of 'emperor' and, through conquest, creates an empire to go with the title. The Napoleon syndrome is synonymous with the madman locked away in an asylum, bent on world domination. Napoleon, in true Leo style, instigated pageantry, pomp and colourful military ritual on an unprecedented scale. Napoleon was more a visionary than a pragmatist, with dreams of a world-embracing empire and himself as the crowned leader, ruling with grandeur and munificence. When Napoleon finally met his Waterloo it was a Taurus military leader, the Duke of Wellington, who brought about his downfall.

Napoleon, like many other leaders instilled with a strong sense of destiny, was a fatalist par excellence. He used astrology and tarot, and even devised his own system of numerology, constantly reassuring himself that the 'heavens' collaborated with him and condoned his many conquests. During his Egyptian campaigns Napoleon spent a night in seclusion in the King's Chamber of the Great Pyramid of Giza. At sunrise, the story goes, he emerged ashen white and trembling, wide-eyed and speechless. Many years later, shortly before his death in exile on the island of St Helena, Bonaparte revealed what had shaken him so thoroughly during that fateful night. 'I saw my own future,' he said.

As a military commander Napoleon bears comparison to General Schwarzkopf (Leo, with Leo rising). Napoleon was authoritative towards the troops, but never aloof: a patriarchal figure with a magnanimous bearing that ensured loyalty from the soldiers and the adulation of the people of France. It was this support that enabled him to seize power in 1799 and appoint himself first consul, then Master of France. He was 30 years old. The constitution he created gave him unlimited power, but disastrous campaigns in Russia (1812), Leipzig (1814) and finally Waterloo (1815) forced him to abdicate and he lived in exile until his death in 1821, aged 51.

However, as Napoleon's chart suggests, his was a complex personality; Leo, Libra and Capricorn (Sun, Ascendant and Moon) describe singularly contradictory characteristics; Mars in Virgo, Venus in Cancer, similarly discrepant, and so on throughout the chart. History emphasizes the Sun-sign side of Napoleon's career, while for Napoleon, his romantic campaigns (Libra Ascendant) were as significant as his military ones.

Libra concerns partnerships and marriage, and a Libra Ascendant suggests resolving one's own identity through partnership or a relationship. The Libra Ascendant seeks completion, wholeness and inner harmony through 'marriage', either literally, or through union with another identity – a person, a company, a country, a cause, even a manufactured image of oneself. Libra is ruled by Venus; in addition to partnership, Libran issues relate to harmony, and good taste, the creation and shaping of an environment that is pleasing to the senses, and to the restoration of fairness and order in the face of injustice and inhumanity.

Napoleon's search for a wife began in 1795: he proposed to Eugénie Désirée Clay, who later became Queen of Sweden; then, fearing rejection (or impotence, it has been claimed), he withdrew the proposal. Still in his mid-twenties, he proposed first to Mademoiselle de Montansier, aged 60, then Madame Permon, aged 40. Though his proposals were serious, they were not regarded as such by the two women, and Napoleon continued his search elsewhere. He married courtesan Joséphine Tascher de la Pagerie in 1796, in a simple civil ceremony. He lied to her about his age, saying he was 28 when he was 26; she lied about her age, claiming 28, when in fact she was 32. Napoleon insisted on a new wedding just prior to his coronation in 1804; this time it was administered by the Holy Church, in pomp and splendour.

Joséphine's dalliances during his military campaigns prompted his comment: 'Far-sighted nature had placed the wherewithal to pay her bills beneath her navel,' though the general, too, had his share of extra-marital liaisons. He divorced Joséphine – the marriage was childless and Napoleon needed heirs to further his dynasty – in 1809, and out of political expediency married the 18-year-old Marie-Louise of Austria. His celebrated romantic involvement at this time was with Marie Waleska, who, according to Napoleon, was the true love of his life.

Napoleon's Moon was in Capricorn – the Moon relates to past memories, childhood (particularly the mother-child relationship), feelings, instincts, and the side of the personality kept hidden from public view. Capricorn is a sign that takes obligations and duties seriously, with an innate respect for social order. It is an Earth-sign that transforms ideas and abstracts into physical reality and a productive sign wary of quick results, placing value on work and endeavour.

Historians describe the young Napoleon as a solitary and introspective child who was given to violent tantrums in order to get his own way. Napoleon's father was a meek figure, lacking in authority, and Napoleon's mother Letizia (who died in 1836) ruled the household both morally and physically. Napoleon was placed in the Ecole Militaire in Brienne at the age of nine, and by all accounts endured the life of an orphan in an institution, forbidden any family contact. He became, according to a fellow pupil, 'gloomy, savage, almost always shut up in himself'.

He graduated from the military school, aged 16, in the year his father died, and returned to a family in financial crisis. The next few years, and until his military career began in earnest, were a time of hardship and resignation.

This is by no means the complete picture of a horoscope cast for the time at which the newly-born Napoleon Bonaparte drew his first breath. Far from it. There are eight more planets, nearly all of them in different signs, and in several of 12 different Houses. They all have their own story to tell. So, too, do the planetary Aspects – conjunctions, oppositions, squares and trines – indicating how planetary energies work with each other or against each other. This is not a reading of a chart, simply an illustration of how the diversity of the personality has correlations in the horoscope.

The Signs

Any successful enterprise begins with an idea, which is then actualized, and this leads to its assimilation. A story, for example, consists of a presentation, a conflict and a resolution. A day consists of sunrise, midday and sunset; in fact anything and everything has a beginning, a middle and an end. The zodiac has three phases and within the zodiac, signs also have three 'qualities'.

The Qualities of Signs

Cardinal Signs: Aries–Libra, Cancer–Capricorn

The Cardinal signs indicate enterprise, initiative, and the seizing of an opportunity. Each Cardinal sign represents the start of a new phase. The Cardinal quality is rich with ideas and aspirations; it is competitive and produces the enthusiasm for beginning new projects. Cardinal signs activate change.

Fixed Signs: Taurus–Scorpio, Leo–Aquarius

The Fixed signs are resolute, productive and stable. They are strong-willed signs, thorough, and they concentrate on one thing at a time. The Fixed quality concerns the actualizing of ideas and abstractions. It is a quality that is unyielding, persistent, with a propensity to dig in its heels and refuse to budge.

Mutable Signs: Gemini–Sagittarius, Virgo–Pisces

The Mutable signs indicate assimilation and represent dualities: the twins, the two sides of human nature, in Gemini; half-man, half-beast in Sagittarius; the harvest-bearing maiden representing intellect matched against form in the sign of Virgo; and two fishes pulling against each other – matter against spirit – in Pisces. The Mutable signs are versatile, adaptable, restless, often with spiritual yearnings.

The Three Phases

The zodiac is a cycle that envelops from one phase to another. In Nature the yearly cycle has four seasons; the cycle of personality has three phases. The individual phase begins with Aries, the first sign of the zodiac, and ends with Pisces, which represents collective and spiritual qualities, as well as the dissolution of ego.

Individual Signs: Aries, Taurus, Gemini, Cancer

The first four signs of the zodiac represent the self as an independent individual. These signs have a strong sense of identity and developed ego. 'Self-centred' has negative connotations, but the 'centring' of the 'self' is about asserting oneself, seeing the world from the perspective of the individual – 'I' and not 'we'; the personal.

Social Signs: Leo, Virgo, Libra, Scorpio

The perspective of the social signs is that of interaction, socializing and identification of the 'self' through another. Social signs are concerned with relating and interrelating, often within the family unit and situations where the individual is seen as a unit within a social group; the private – the world of 'you and me'.

Universal Signs: Sagittarius, Capricorn, Aquarius, Pisces

The universal signs provide a broad view, a universal perspective: the perspective of 'we' the collective, the individual as part of humanity. The individual sees the 'self' in the context of the whole.

Sun-signs

The Sun-sign indicates a person's 'source of creativity'. As the planets in the solar system are illuminated by the Sun in the centre, so the planets in the chart, the more subtle sides of the personality, are illuminated by the Sun-sign. Signs are described fully under 'The Astrological Elements', but the attributes of the Sun-signs are summarized below.

Aries (Cardinal Fire)

Enterprising, resourceful, champion of the underdog. Energetic, aggressive, wary of authority figures. Better at giving orders than taking them.
What motivates Aries: fighting, competing, winning.

Taurus (Fixed Earth)

Reliable, loyal, thorough, steadfast, productive.
What motivates Taurus: owning things, money, security, purpose.

Gemini (Mutable Air)
Versatile, quick, restless, communicative.
What motivates Gemini: wheeling and dealing, communicating.

♊

Cancer (Cardinal Water)
Creative, imaginative, sensitive, possessive.
What motivates Cancer: nurturing, mothering, looking after people, taking care
of situations.

♋

Leo (Fixed Fire)
Theatrical, authoritative, playful, dominating.
What motivates Leo: performing, ruling, commanding.

♌

Virgo (Mutable Earth)
Sees work as service, will work for little reward. Concerned with precision,
especially in modes of expression. Obsessed with detail.
What motivates Virgo: obligations, duty, learning, analysing, perfecting.

♍

Libra (Cardinal Air)
Diplomatic, strong sense of justice and fair play. Strategic, able to see two sides of
a situation with clarity and objectivity.
What motivates Libra: negotiating, harmonizing, mediating, clinching the deal.

♎

Scorpio (Fixed Water)
Perceptive, resilient, penetrating, thorough. A task or situation is tackled
exhaustively, or not at all. Abhors superficiality.
What motivates Scorpio: work, exploring, investigating, resolving.

♏

Sagittarius (Mutable Fire)
The grand visionary. Bad on detail. Entrepreneurial: sees business as a cosmic game.
What motivates Sagittarius: travel, ideology, conversion.

♐

Capricorn (Cardinal Earth)
Persistent, determined, resourceful, constructive. The task is paced out ensuring
its completion.
What motivates Capricorn: esteem, status, respect, control.

♑

Aquarius (Fixed Air)
Idealist, scientist, scholar. Intellectually alert, humanitarian.
What motivates Aquarius: experimenting, understanding what makes other
people tick.

♒

Pisces (Mutable Water)
Devoted, self-sacrificing, imaginative. Poet, mystic and dreamer.
What motivates Pisces: sacrifice, belief in a cause, devotion.

♓

The Houses

When astrologers interpret a chart, they look at planets in signs for personality traits, and planets in houses for actions and attitudes. The Sun-sign describes character, the Ascending sign direction – an individual's chosen path. The Ascendant marks the First House cusp, the Midheaven the Tenth House cusp.

Fire Houses (First, Fifth, Ninth) 'anything's possible'
Earth Houses (Second, Sixth, Tenth) 'get real'
Air Houses (Third, Seventh, Eleventh) 'analyze this'
Water Houses (Fourth, Eighth, Twelfth) 'feel, but don't show'

First House: about image, identity
Fifth House: about creativity, family, achievements
Ninth House: about journeys, ideas

Second House: about possessions, money
Sixth House: about obligations, physical well-being
Tenth House: about career, social status

Third House: about communicating, meeting people
Seventh House: about relating and partnerships
Eleventh House: about the community, friendships

Fourth House: feelings about background, childhood
Eighth House: feelings about life, death, sexuality
Twelfth House: indefinable feelings – fears and inspirations

Planets in Houses are like gods, entering different spheres of human enterprise: manipulating, aiding and hindering. Saturn, for example, is an austere recluse who demands discipline in order to achieve tangible goals. The Second House concerns wealth, material well-being and attributes associated with the sign of Taurus. Saturn in the Second House may demand of its subjects periodic denial of financial security, and even loss of possessions. In return, the subject may fulfil Second-House aspirations in later years, having understood a deeper meaning to material values; the restraints of Saturn are often tempered with maturity.

1st (Aries)	Self-image	Projected image	7th (Libra)
2nd Taurus)	Material values	Spiritual values	8th (Scorpio)
3rd (Gemini)	Communicating	Travelling	9th (Sagittarius)
4th (Cancer)	Family	Career	10th (Capricorn)
5th (Leo)	Self-expression	Collective expression	11th (Aquarius)
6th (Virgo)	Duty	Sacrifice	12th (Pisces)

Sign-House Polarities

First House – Image

The sign on the cusp of the First House is the Ascendant (Rising Sign). Thus, the First House relates to appearance, the outer personality, and a person's image as it is perceived by others. Planets in the First House indicate that the person will have a strong sense of identity, will be noticed, and often find themselves in the public eye.

Queen Elizabeth II, with three planets in the First House, insisted on the first-ever television coverage of a royal event: the 1953 coronation. She instigated the 'walkabout' where members of the royal family meet the public face to face, and transformed the public image of the monarchy by bringing the royal family into the public eye, mainly through television.

A particular planet in the First House suggests a personality's kind of image. Uranus – planet of invention, eccentricity and originality – is Clive Sinclair's First House planet (together with Moon), which characterizes the image of the inventive thinker.

The First House Saturn in the chart of Rupert Murdoch suggests an image of austerity and control.

Bill Clinton has Venus (relationships), Mars (drive and energy, in particular sexual energy), Jupiter (optimism and good humour), and Neptune (ideals, visions and illusions, which also provides an image of vulnerability and naivety) all in the First House.

Second House – Money

Money is a measure of material worth, and Second-House issues relate to material values. This can apply as much to ideas as to acquisitions; the philosophy of many Taurean/Second-House thinkers relates to tangibles and actualities, avoiding the abstract and the theoretical.

A chart is not going to tell us whether or not someone is destined to become rich; it can describe a relationship to money rather than quantify wealth in a person's life. The experience of money suggested by a Saturn placing in the Second House is that of hard work. Money is a source of discipline and restraint. Saturn in the Second House will not indicate if there is much money in the person's life or no money at all: it will simply define an attitude. Money, whether you have it or not, equals hard work.

This placing occurs in the chart of Prince Charles, whose working hours are consumed in the raising of money for communities, charities, and unemployed youth, and in the chart of former General Electric CEO, Jack Welch. In each case, money is an issue to be taken seriously, which is Saturn's decree.

Hugh Hefner has four planets in the Second, Queen Elizabeth, three planets. Rupert Murdoch has a Second House Venus and Oprah Winfrey has Mercury, Sun and Venus all in the Second House: money comes easily, but it is more than money that motivates empire building.

Third House – Self-Expression

The Third House concerns communication, the way in which we express ourselves to others. Strong Third-House individuals are often writers, journalists, broadcasters, and so on. Uranus in the Third represents originality in self-expression; Jupiter in the Third, ideology in expression; Mars, purpose and aggression in self-expression, and so on through the planets.

Ronald Reagan has Sun and Venus in the Third; he began as a radio broadcaster and sports commentator, then became an actor and finally a politician. Richard Branson has Neptune conjunct Mars in the Third – a combination of Neptune's dreams and visions with Mars' detemination. Vladimir Putin, whose oratory style is considered by many to be intimidating, has Mars in the Third, whereas George Bush's more informal style is represented by Moon conjunct Jupiter in the Third.

Fourth House – Home and Family

The Fourth-House relates to family issues. A Moon in the Fourth suggests strong family ties, while Uranus in the Fourth indicates breaking with family conventions, and even moving far from home.

Prince Charles, with four planets, including the Sun, in the Fourth House, suggests someone who is tied up with the 'family business'. Rupert Murdoch, who took over his father's business, has three planets in the Fourth, including the Sun and Uranus: he gave up Australian citizenship for American, for the sake of the company. Indira Gandhi, who carried on the family dynasty of political leadership in India, has both Sun and Mercury in the Fourth.

Prominent Fourth-House natives often inherit the obligations of the family and carry on the family business, or retain a strong sense of identity through the family, home and the mother. They rarely stray far from their place of birth. The concerns of the family are private concerns; they represent the domestic scene found behind closed doors and drawn curtains. Bill Gates, with four planets in the Fourth House, brought an entire industry to his home town of Seattle.

All the 'Water' houses concern personal issues, and unseen influences: things that are hidden away, unspoken dreams, and secret aspirations.

Fifth House – Creativity and Procreation

The Fifth House, Leo, concerns creativity and productivity. This also relates closely to family issues: the urge to procreate may be through a family, or through being productive and creative with ideas, enterprises, and so on. Fourth-House family matters usually relate to the past and are often hidden away. The family as represented by the Fifth-House concerns the immediate future: possibilities and public exposure. As one would expect in the Leo house, the family is in the public eye with 'mother' showing off her 'children' to the rest of the world.

For J P Getty, Neptune and Pluto in the Fifth House concerned family dreams and aspirations (Neptune) and dramatic and unforeseen changes (Pluto) which were very much in the public eye. Getty planned a family dynasty to carry on the philanthropic works financed by his accumulated fortune. Two of his children died, one by suicide; a third became a drug addict, and the fourth sold the company off for a song.

Sixth House – Service

The Sixth House relates to service, work and health. It is the House of self-analysis, examining one's obligations, the tasks to be carried out and the effects they are likely to have on one's well-being.

Howard Hughes, who spent half of his adult life devoted to work in film, aviation and industry, and the other half in self-imposed confinement, masked and gloved and ensuring he made no physical contact with anyone for fear of germs, had a Saturn–Mars conjunction in the Sixth House. Saturn in any House often indicates fears, or at least restrictions: limitations to be overcome.

Otherwise it is interesting to note that the Sixth House – which relates to serving others – is so under-represented in the charts of business and political leaders. The Sixth House is the House of Virgo, which is similarly under-represented in astrological management, yet strongly represented in vocations such as nursing and social work. Mother Theresa, for example, was born under the sign of Virgo.

Seventh House – Partnership

If Saturn in the Sixth relates to health fears, in the Seventh it suggests fear of marriage and commitment. The First House relates to the projection of self, while the Seventh House concerns identifying the self through another, through partnership, relationship, marriage, a company image, a family image, a national image or an image attached to a cause.

Mahatma Gandhi (Pluto and Jupiter conjunct in the Seventh) spent a lifetime attempting to deny himself physical relationships, identifying himself with the cause of non-violent revolution, and with his country. Adolf Hitler, with three planets including the Sun in the Seventh, identified himself with Germany and the Third Reich; Charlie Chaplin, with Neptune, Mars and Venus in the Seventh House, had a life dominated by paternity suits, marriages, and complicated relationships which jeopardized his career (Mars and Venus), while at the same time his own identity was deeply submerged into his fantasy 'little tramp' character (Neptune). Prince William has Sun and Moon in the Seventh House, which, combined with four planets in the Sagittarian Ninth House, suggests romantic involvements with foreigners. Britney Spears, it should be noted, is not only American, but also a Sagittarian.

Eighth House – Values

Where the Second House is concerned with material values, the Eighth House is concerned with the significance of things, with finding deeper meanings and spiritual values. As with the Fourth and Twelfth Houses, Eighth-House issues are hidden away, and are concerned especially with sexuality and death.

John Kennedy's chart included the Sun, Mercury, Mars and Jupiter in the Eighth. Hindu astrologers claim that Mars in the Eighth indicates a violent death, Moon in the Eighth indicates longevity. John De Lorean, with Venus in the Eighth, spent most of his life chasing money and cars (Venus concerns attractions, desires things that provide comfort), then, in the face of financial ruin, abandoned the material world for Christianity.

Ninth House – The Journey

The Sagittarius House relates to broadening the horizons, through either travel or ideological pursuits. It is a House of expansion, and a prominent Ninth House indicates someone who sees a broader picture, and is more concerned with global issues than domestic issues. The expansive side of the Ninth House hates restrictions and impediments of any kind; a strong Ninth House could indicate carelessness or extravagance concerning money, material things, even personal and physical considerations.

Mikhail Gorbachev has Mars (ambition, career), Jupiter (ideology, journeys) and Pluto (transformation) all in the Ninth; he never achieved the popularity in his own country that he achieved abroad, and domestic issues were at times secondary in his preoccupation with global disarmament and an end to the Cold War. He travelled more than any other Soviet leader (with the possible exception of Lenin), and his expansive Ninth-House ideologies transformed not only the Soviet Union, but world history.

As noted, Prince William has four planets in the Ninth House and, apart from his many travels, has expressed strong interest in global environmental issues. Another European monarch, Karl XII of Sweden, with six planets in the Ninth House, having been crowned at the age of 26 (in 1704), scarcely set foot in his own country again, leading successful campaigns against Denmark, Poland and Russia, and taking his army as far south as Turkey. He died in Norway, once more leading his army, aged 36.

Tenth House – Career

The Tenth House is related to Capricorn and the Midheaven, the highest point in the sky at the moment of birth. It indicates aspirations, ambitions, the status desired. The Tenth House concerns an individual's outward, worldly success. It is the House of public office and social ambition.

Richard Nixon, with Moon, Neptune, and Pluto in the Tenth, endured each setback in his life-long political career with tenacity: defeated by Kennedy, he persevered until he finally attained the presidential office. His personal aspirations (Moon) were thwarted by darker elements at work beneath the facade of power (Neptune and Pluto). He attempted to maintain this facade (Neptune: fantasies, inability to accept reality) and finally brought down upon the presidential office an ignominy of unprecedented magnitude (Pluto: change, transformation through suffering).

John Kennedy, Nixon's one-time opponent, had both Neptune and Saturn in the Tenth. Forty years after his assassination one can still wonder whether his failure to accept certain realities of public office (Neptune) invoked the austere hand of Saturn (discipline, restrictions) to end his political career.

The stronger the Tenth House, the stronger ambition is expressed, and the battle against adversity and hardship is that much more prominent a life-theme. Ted Turner has both Moon and Mars in the Tenth House.

Eleventh House – Ideals

The Eleventh House is the House of Aquarius and relates to ideals, abstracts, the collective, groups and associations. Strong Eleventh-House personalities tend to be unconventional, original and to identify with an organization or an ideal rather than with individuality. Eleventh-House issues concern systems, social awareness and social transformation.

Jan Carlzon, with five planets in the Eleventh House, transformed SAS – Scandinavian Airline Systems – from a bureaucratic and hierarchical organization into a system of integrated units: teams which could function independently within the organization's structure, eliminating time-wasting red tape.

Oprah Winfrey, a Sun Aquarian, has Mars and Moon in the Eleventh House, and her commitment to social and collective issues reaches television audiences around the globe.

Former British Prime Minister Margaret Thatcher has Sun, Mercury and Mars in the Eleventh, and her immovable stance on systematizing aspects of British society contributed largely to her political ideology, and her political demise.

Twelfth House – Matters Undisclosed

The Sun-in-the-Twelfth-House natives are those whose birthday everyone forgets: the people who are ignored in the post office queue, the inconspicuous figures no one notices. If they are not working as plainclothes police or for an undercover terrorist organization, they may find a career as a performer, or they may well be manipulating business empires behind anonymous facades – they may be the Great Gatsby, a Tony Blair (five planets in the Twelfth) or a Vladimir Putin (four planets in the Twelfth).

Where First-House issues relate to an individual's sense of image, the Twelfth House is concerned with loss of individual identity. Many media personalities, particularly in film and television, have prominent Twelfth House placings.

In the chart of Madonna Ciccione, Sun, Mercury, Uranus and Pluto are all in the Twelfth: she is a 'media star' who has 'sacrificed' her own image for the sake of the collective. Madonna is no longer Madonna the individual, but Madonna the collective archetype who represents a contemporary image of the 'feminine'. Madonna does not own her identity, nor even the privacy of her love affairs – they belong to everyone. Actress Marilyn Monroe is another example of a prominent Twelfth House media personality.

Many Twelfth House personalities offer up their individuality to a large group or institution, working in hospitals, government offices or large multi-national corporations.

The Twelfth House is also a House of undoing, of 'matters undisclosed' that could lead to prominence or notoriety. Twelfth-House natives frequently see themselves as victims of conspiracies. Orson Welles, with Jupiter, Mars and Venus in the Twelfth, claimed his career was sabotaged by the hidden and unknown forces of RKO studios and the Hearst media empire. These 'forces' can be just as much aspects of one's self which the conscious mind keeps hidden away, responsible for our own undoing..

W R Hearst himself, who controlled a formidable media empire, had Sun, Mercury and Pluto in the Twelfth. Rupert Murdoch has the Moon in the Twelfth, as do many prominent media people and personalities involved in global networks and multi-national corporations.

The Planets

Our sense of identity, who we are and what we do, is represented by the Sun. The Moon concerns more subtle energies: our feelings, instincts and moods. Each planet has its own energy, defining aspects of our personality; each planet brings a particular quality into the chart. The first seven planets are the planets visible to the naked eye. In a natal chart they are the planets representing personal affairs, aspects of our personalities, even the stages of life from birth to death. These seven planets manifest energies we can recognize and implement.

The three outer planets, Uranus, Neptune and Pluto, are invisible to the naked eye, and are not recognizable in our conscious state; these planets represent energies and events over which we have no apparent control. These are the slow-moving planets that affect generations, rather than individuals; they affect our lives in subtle ways but with far-reaching consequences. The next Uranian phase, as the planet transits Pisces from 2003 to 2010, represents a shift from the technical and turbulent revolutionary aspects of Uranus in Aquarius, to the more Piscean values of spirituality and religion. Leading up to the year 2011, when Neptune enters its own sign of Pisces, this Uranus transit can be seen as forging new spiritual systems as science develops into the religion of our age.

The Ascendant and Midheaven, though not planets, are also described here, since they also represent powerful energies that affect our personality.

Sun

The Sun is the source of power and will. It represents our creative energy, the expression of the self through actions. It is also the source of our identity and individuality: it indicates the quality of our achievements. The Roman astrologer Tacitus described the Sun as 'the chorus master of the planets'.

Ascendant

The Ascendant is the point in the zodiac that is rising on the eastern horizon at the moment of an individual's birth. The cycle is completed over 24 hours, so the Ascendant moves through each sign in about two hours, and cannot be calculated without an accurate birth time. As the Ascendant denotes the First House cusp, House positions also depend on knowing the birth time.

The Ascendant indicates in which direction we broaden our horizons: our path of action in life. For example, a Sun in Aries chart describes a personality with a strong sense of individuality, but with an Aquarius Ascendant that individuality might well be directed towards serving a large group or an organization where the individual will work on behalf of the collective.

Midheaven

Medium Coeli (MC) means 'in the middle of the sky' and indicates the highest point in the sky at the moment of birth. It represents our aspirations: that which we may never attain, but which we strive for, consciously or otherwise. These aspirations usually come later in life, or at least that is when we become aware of them. Many people with an Aries Ascendant, depending on the latitude of birth, will have a Capricorn Midheaven. The youthful and burning, even reckless, energy with which such people tackle issues in their formative years tends to be disciplined in later years, and these people become 'achievers'. Many Capricorn Ascendant personalities, again depending on the latitude, will have Libra at the Midheaven, and their aspirations regarding commitment to marriage or partnerships often mature with age.

Moon

The Sun and the Moon are the two luminaries: two discs that illuminate the sky. The lunar light is far more subtle and affects only the hours of darkness. Our Sun-sign is a reflection of the personality on open display for all the world to see, while the Moon-sign illuminates the 'dark' areas of the subconscious, the personality beneath the surface. The Moon affects tides, the flow of blood (many surgeons avoid operations during a full Moon) and the menstrual cycle – a biological rhythm which affects all our births. It represents the instinctive side of the personality, that which is concerned with memory, our receptiveness to situations, places and other people. These feelings and sympathies may not be logical or rational, or even definable; they govern our responses, our impressions and our need for new experiences. The Moon is associated with nurturing – often with the mother figure – and with formative memories that later create childhood associations and our sense of the past.

Mercury

The analytical and discerning qualities of the intellect are represented by Mercury. It rules Gemini and Virgo and is concerned with the gathering of information and knowledge – the accumulation of experiences to be assessed and evaluated. Mercury discriminates and communicates; it defines, names and quantifies. Mercurial qualities include adaptability, versatility, a critical and argumentative mind, inconsistency, and an aptitude for learning and knowledge. Mercury expresses itself through facts, not feelings. It is the fastest moving planet in the solar system and the mercurial individual is fast-thinking and quick to pick up new ideas.

Venus

The influence of Venus is a harmonizing, tempering force with kindness, anger with reason and conflict with compromise. Where we find Venus in a chart, there we find what attracts us, what pleases us. Venus relates to the pursuit of pleasure, so an over-emphasized Venus may lead to self-indulgence, the pursuit of pleasure for its own sake, laziness and indolence.

Venus, the goddess of beauty (Aphrodite in Greek mythology), rules both Libra and Taurus, and is a mellowing influence, seeking to make smooth the rough. It creates harmony from disorder, and maintains a just balance between two opposing elements, whether they are partners in a marriage, opposing sides in a legal contest, or conflicting armies at war.

Mars

In personal relations, Venus represents those we are attracted to, but it is Mars that initiates the connection. Where Venus desires, Mars takes action. Sometimes these two energy sources are compatible, sometimes not. Venus seeks love, and Mars wants physical satisfaction. Similarly, in business affairs, Venus plans, schemes, aspires and hopes, but it is Mars that leaps in and initiates a project, or through too much energy, sabotages it.

Mars, the god of war, is the ruling planet for both Aries and Scorpio. There are characteristics of the 'warrior' in both signs, but the energy of Mars is a healing energy as well as the source of power, dragging Aries into action, conflict and impulsive deeds. Mars is 'leap first, then look.' Given a choice of two courses of action, Mars chooses the hard way over the easy, regards the hard way as a challenge. Mars likes change, because it offers possibilities. Harmony means stagnation, which must be disrupted.

Mars does not dwell on the past, considering only the possibilities for the future. Tact and diplomacy Mars leaves to others: Mars prefers tackling problems head-on. Mars seeks new conquests, new challenges and is easily bored. Mars is a fierce adversary to a rival, a champion of the weak, but merciless to the indifferent.

Jupiter

The largest planet in the solar system, Jupiter symbolizes expansion, optimism, benevolence and broad-mindedness. The Jovian personality is impulsive yet tolerant, boastful yet good-humoured, conceited yet wise. Jupiter seeks to broaden experiences through journeys, through religion, through new ideologies or ways of thinking. This is the energy of free development that abhors restraints or limitations. The total freedom an uninhibited Jupiter might bring about leads to a plethora of possibilities – perhaps so many opportunities that the individual faces only chaos.

Saturn

Where Jupiter sees opportunities, Saturn sees only the responsibilities and the work that such opportunities bring. The expansiveness of Jupiter is balanced by the limitations and discipline imposed by Saturn. Where Jupiter dreams of things that might come about, Saturn sees things as they are. Saturn consolidates, concentrates and actualizes.

Some see Saturn as a manifestation of Chronos, or time: given time, hard work will bring its rewards; given time, the gravest problems can be resolved, the most difficult trials endured. For others, Saturn is synonymous with Satan, the devil who brings with him hardship, difficulties and crises. But where Jupiter, with all good will and benevolence, aspires to development, real development only comes by overcoming difficulties and resolving the crises which confront us.

Uranus

Uranus is a 'higher octave' of Mercury, relating to the mind and to original, eccentric and even revolutionary thinking. Uranus brings change, sometimes violently, always disruptively. The effects of a Uranus transit through Capricorn, which began in 1988, can be seen in the disruption and breakdown of established conservative structures (Capricorn). The totalitarian structures in the Soviet, former Yugoslavia, Eastern Europe, etc, have collapsed, giving way to new political structure. The conservatism of European independent states is breaking down to create a new interdependent expanding European Union.

A Uranus cycle lasts 84 years, seven years in each sign. In 1995 Uranus moved into its own sign of Aquarius; during the following years we saw the introduction and application of the Internet, leading to a new era in technological development and international communications. On the positive side, this new Uranian technology united the farthest reaches of the globe; on the negative side it provided networks for subversive and terrorist organizations, and forms of social revolution that are only becoming apparent in the new millennium.

Neptune

Neptune rules Pisces and is considered a 'higher octave' of Venus. Whereas Uranus is concerned with mental 'revolution', Neptune indicates spiritual revolution. When the generation born 1942–56, as Neptune traversed Libra (the sign of 'peace and love'), reached the age of 'dissent', the Beatles/Woodstock generation developed a counter-culture in which only spiritual values were important.

Neptune seeks mystical, religious experiences; it is prominent in the charts of mystics, religious leaders, poets and film-makers; also alcoholics and drug addicts. Cinema, religion and drugs are means to transcend the ego, by directing the spirit to a higher cause, or destroying individuality.

Neptune rules the oceans: one is mesmerized and lured by the forces of Neptune, and the 'poet' in us may ride the waves or the addict in us may drown, both lured by the promise of ecstacy. Like the ocean, Neptune recognizes no boundaries (the erratic orbit of Neptune sometimes extends beyond the orbit of Pluto); it is the planet of the visionary.

A Neptune transit began through Capricorn in 1984 and remained in conjunction with Uranus until the mid-1990s. Consequently, the social and political upheavals of Uranus were combined with Neptunian visions of social order and internationalism

Pluto

Pluto is the last planet in the solar system (although astrologers and astronomers are considering the implications of a small planetoid beyond Pluto's orbit, discovered in 2000) and traditionally the Pluto orbit has been the boundary for other planetary influences. In mythology Pluto ruled the underworld; his was the final authority, a power bringing about transformation on an unprecedented scale, or mass destruction.

Pluto was discovered in 1930. In 1939 Pluto entered Leo, a transit correlating with global conflict and mass destruction. During this period, lasting until 1958, society and world politics were transformed totally.

From 1984 to 1995 Pluto was in Scorpio, its own sign. Pluto is the planet of transformation, denoting unforeseen changes over which the individual is seemingly powerless. Scorpio issues involve the search for deeper meaning, often in connection with sex and death. In 1984 came the first reports of a sexually transmitted disease for which no cure could be found. The effect AIDS has had on the transformation of society is multi-fold. A new morality has emerged, sexual issues are expressed with unprecedented candour, the limitations of medical science are clear and the vulnerability of human life is evident. Plutonium has also been an issue during this period. The nuclear power plant meltdown in Chernobyl, Ukraine, occurred just as Pluto entered Scorpio.

Pluto has a cycle of 284 years, but, due to its erratic orbit, stays in some signs longer than others. Pluto entered Sagittarius in 1995. Sagittarius issues relate to ideologies, foreign countries, expansion and global affairs. Since the mid-1990s the world has experienced social upheavals through the expansion of ideologies. The development of the Internet has created a global community, national boundaries are disappearing in Europe and the former Soviet Union. Conflicts are less about national borders and territories, and more about confrontations between ideologies and beliefs.

The Aspects

Aspects are formed when two or more planets join together in a horoscope, or form a geometrical angle, so that the effects of both interact. Astrologers recognize aspects as existing if they are accurate to between 5 and 10 degrees, with 8 degrees as a prevalent compromise; the greater the accuracy, the more powerful the effect of the aspect.

In earlier times astrologers referred to aspects as 'benefic' or 'malefic', good or bad. These days we think in terms of 'hard' and 'soft', or 'easy' and 'difficult'. For example, a Venus–Jupiter aspect is 'easy', indicating good fortune, comfort, and achieving desires. But comfortable living and getting what we want could be a recipe for self-indulgence and lethargy. Similarly, a Mars–Saturn aspect might be 'hard' (extremely 'malefic' in the old days), indicating aggression, conflict, limitations and discipline. But perhaps this is just the aspect required to make the Venus–Jupiter native get up out of the armchair and achieve great deeds.

Conjunctions

These can represent a hard or soft aspect, depending on the planets. Two planets together combine energies. Conjunctions between Mars and Saturn are considered difficult; conjunctions between the Sun and Venus or Jupiter are considered easy.

Oppositions and Squares

These are formed by 180 or 90 degree aspects, which are considered difficult and indicate a dynamic interaction between two or more planets. They are two energies at cross-purposes denoting tension and obstacles. Some oppositions can complement each other; oppositions are regarded as less difficult than squares.

A full Moon signifies an opposition between the Sun and Moon, and, depending on an individual's chart, can indicate tension between what a person wants to do (Sun) and they feel about it (Moon).

Trines and Sextiles

These are 120 and 60 degree aspects, and are considered harmonious. Trines usually join up signs of the same element. The Sun in Leo trine Jupiter in Sagittarius, for example, unites two Fire signs. Trines often indicate getting benefits without any effort, which has both positive and negative sides.

Sextiles indicate opportunities.

Some Final Words... Becoming Who We Are

Never mind if the people are not intimidated by your authority
A Mightier Authority will deal with them in the end . . .
The Sage knows himself but does not show himself
Knows his own power but does not display it

Tao teh ching LXXII

We began with the question as to whether we can seriously consider astrology as a means to successful management. We looked at Sun-signs and in-depth astrological profiles of leaders in business and politics, finding that astrology is a far more complex approach to understanding personalities than newspaper horoscopes would have us believe. We looked at the elements not only as the foundation of astrological charts, but as the basis of personality typing, from antiquity to twentieth century psychology and twenty-first century applications in recruiting, team-building and management skills.

In our study of personality types we looked at changing management styles over the past 30 years. If we are to understand future management trends, we should analyze what has happened in the past. We examined the leadership style of the 1980s; the decade of the visionary, the entrepreneur, the decision-maker, the 'star'. The 1980s was the age of Reagan and Thatcher, the rise of Murdoch and Maxwell, the company transformers, Jan Carlzon at SAS, Richard Branson at Virgin, Lee Iaccoca at Ford.

It was a time in which corporate and political leaders were reacting to a 'past age' generation of management-by-authority. Leadership had been taken to mean that employers and company directors told subordinates what to do. Instructions were carried down a hierarchy akin to military ranking order. Such a system supports stability but stifles creativity. The respect for rank is based more on tradition and trepidation than on genuine respect for managerial capability. Management thinking had been entrenched in a Cold War mentality and a military style of authority two decades removed from a world war.

In the 1990s management saw the rise of the coach, person-orientated leadership, the age of EQ (emotional quotient), and workshops and seminars on communication skills. In some respects this was a reaction to the concept of the leader as visionary. The corporate 'stars' of the 1980s, Iacocca, Branson, Carlzon, advocating 'flat-management' and tearing down pyramids, created a hierarchy of idols. Hollywood glamour came to the world of business – 'management by charisma'. So the 1990s was the age of MBWA; 'management by walking around' became the buzz-phrase.

The new leadership style meant leaders became team-players, adopting a new person-to-person style. From the new 'military coach' style of General Norman Schwarzkopf in the early nineties, to the 'sport coach' style of Sven-Göran Eriksson in the late nineties, this was a style that made a strong impact on managing companies and organizations.

What is next for the twenty-first century, and why astrology?

Management today is not just action, but interaction. Team-building is not just directing the team to the same goals, but ensuring that a team of different personalities works together harmoniously as a unit. Recruiting is no longer just finding candidates with qualifications, but personalities who are compatible with their prospective colleagues, and who can contribute to the team with their own unique qualities.

Natal astrology is not the only tool of psychological insight, but it is a highly sophisticated system, based on ancient traditions, and has much to offer those who are willing to study it.

Some critics say that astrology denies individual freewill and self-determination. Indeed, some branches of astrology are more fatalistic than others – yet few natal astrologers reject the idea of freewill. Much of contemporary astrology is in line with humanistic psychology, which subscribes to the view that human beings develop in accordance to their potential, if the necessary environmental factors allow it.

By overcoming various needs, the individual may realize what psychologist Abraham Maslow termed 'self-actualization'. Maslow described a 'hierarchy of needs'. When an individual has overcome the basic physiological needs of hunger, thirst and shelter, they aspire to 'security needs', and so proceed eventually to 'self-actualization'; fulfilling the potentials of the personality.

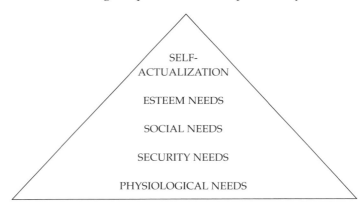

Maslow's 'hierarchy of needs'

So how do we evaluate those potentials? The natal chart is a good starting point. The horoscope outlines our individual potentials, our strengths and our weaknesses – it is a guide to becoming who we are. Astrology can help us to understand the components of our own complex individuality, and of the people with whom we interact, but our 'destiny' is as much up to ourselves as the influences that affect us. If life is a journey then the natal chart is a map – how we go about finding our way is, for better or worse, up to us.

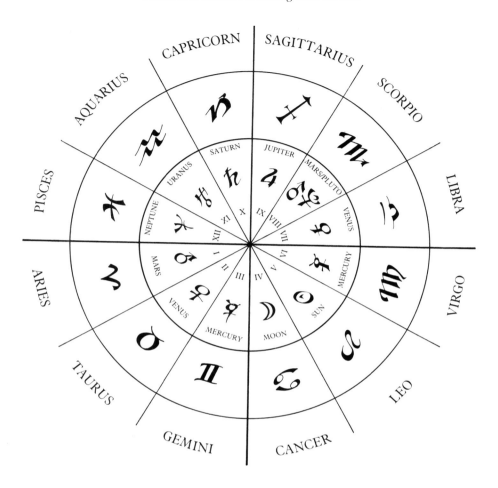

Signs, Houses and Planetary Rulers

Sources for Astrological Charts

ADB   Lois Roddens Astro Databank (www.astrodatabank.com)
AA   Astrological Association (UK) (www.astrologicalassociation.com)
JK   Jan Kampherbeek: *Cirkels 800 Horoskopen van Bekende Mensen*; Uitgeverij Schors Amsterdam, 1980
MP   Marc Penfield: *An Astrological Who's Who*; Arcane, Maine 1972
JMcE Joan McEvers: *12 Times 12*; ACS Publications, San Diego CA, 1983
DS   Debbi Kempton Smith: *Secrets from a Stargazer's Notebook*; Bantam, 1982
AE   From the files of Anders Ekström (Swedish astrologer)
RE   From the files of Roger Elliot (UK astrologer)
JA   From the files of the author: from biographies and official sources

Recommended Reading

Astrology

Cornelius, Geoffrey, Hyde, Maggie and Webster, Chris: *Astrology for Beginners;* Icon Press, 1995
Eysenck, Hans: *Astrology – Science or Superstition*; Maurice Temple Smith, 1982
Greene, Liz: *The Astrology of Fate*; Allen & Unwin, 1984
Hand, Robert: *Planets in Transit*; Whitford Press, 1976
Kampherbeek, Jan: *Cirkels 800 Horoskopen van Bekende Mensen*; Uitgeverij Schors Amsterdam, 1980
Kempton Smith, Debbi: *Secrets from a Stargazer's Notebook*; Bantam, 1982
McEvers, Joan: *12 Times 12*; ACS, 1984
Mann, A T: *Life Time Astrology*; Allen & Unwin, 1984
Mann, A T: *A New Vision of Astrology*; Simon & Schuster, 2002
Rodden, Lois: *Profiles of Women*; AFA, 1979
Ruperti, Alexander: *Cycles of Becoming*; CRCS, 1978
Sasportas, Howard: *The Twelve Houses*; Aquarian Press, 1988
West, John Anthony: *The Case for Astrology;* Arkana, 1986

Management

Andersson, Per: *Stenbeck*; Pan Stockholm, 2000
Belbin, Meredith: *Management Teams – Why They Succeed or Fail*; Heinemann, 1981
Birkenshaw, Julian and Crainer, Stuart: *Leadership the Sven-Göran Eriksson Way*; Capstone, 2002
Blanchard, Kenneth & Zigarmi, P and D: *Leadership and the One Minute Manager*; Fontana, 1979

Carlzon, Jan: *Riv Pyramiderna*; Bonniers, 1985

Coll, Steve: *The Taking of Getty Oil*; Macmillan, 1987

Cringley, Robert: *Accidental Empires*; HarperBusiness (1996)

Devine, Marion (ed): *The Photofit Manager*; Unwin Hyman, 1990

Edmunds, Francis: *From Thinking to Living – The Life and Work of Rudolf Steiner*; Element, 1990

Evans, Roger & Russel, Peter: *The Creative Manager*; Unwin Hyman, 1989

Heller, Robert: *The Making of Managers*; Penguin, 1990

Hickman, Craig & Silva, Michael: *Creating Excellence*; Allen & Unwin, 1986

Hickman, Craig & Silva, Michael: *The Future 500*; Unwin Hyman, 1988

Iacocca, Lee: *An Autobiography*; Bantam, 1984

Jensen, Rolf: *The Dream Society*; McGraw-Hill, 2000

Kennedy, Gavin: *Everything is Negotiable*; Arrow Books, 1989

Peters, Tom: *Thriving on Chaos – Handbook for a Management Revolution*; Macmillan, 1987

Robinson, Jeffrey: *The Risk Takers*; Allen & Unwin, 1985

Robinson, Jeffrey: *Minus Millionaires*; Allen & Unwin, 1987

Torekull, Bertil and Kamprad, Ingvar: *Historian om IKEA*; Wahlström and Widstrand, Stockholm, 1998

Trompenaars, Fons: *Riding the Waves of Cultural Diversity in Business*; Nicholas Brealey Publishing, 1994

General

Atkinson et al: *Introduction to Psychology [15th Edition]*; HBJ, 1996

Hjelle, L & Ziegler, Daniel: *Personality Theories*; McGraw Hill, 1981

Robinson, Lytle: *Edgar Cayce's Story of the Origin and Destiny of Man*; Berkeley, 1976

Rowan, John: *Discover Your Subpersonalities*; Routledge, 1993

Index of Natal Charts

Index